THE
LAVENDER
VOTE

✔ ✔ ✔

Lesbians, Gay Men, and
Bisexuals in American
Electoral Politics

MARK HERTZOG

NEW YORK UNIVERSITY PRESS
New York and London

NEW YORK UNIVERSITY PRESS
New York and London

© 1996 by Mark Wm. Hertzog

Library of Congress Cataloging-in-Publication Data
Hertzog, Mark, 1960-
The lavender vote : lesbians, gay men, and bisexuals in American
electoral politics / Mark Hertzog.
p.   cm.
Includes bibliographical references and index.
ISBN 0-8147-3529-0 (cl : alk. paper).—ISBN 0-8147-3530-4 (pbk.
: alk. paper)
1. Gays—United States—Political activity.   2. Bisexuals—United
States—Political activity.   I. Title.
HQ76.3.U5H49 1996
306.76'0973—dc20   96-4520
CIP

New York University Press books are printed on acid-free paper,
and their binding materials are chosen for strength and durability.

Manufactured in the United States of America

10 9 8 7 6 5 4 3 2 1

FOR CHRIS

CONTENTS

ACKNOWLEDGMENTS

You never know just how grateful you are until time comes to thank everyone who ought to be thanked on a project like this and you have too little space to do it. So I'll stick to the big "thank-yous" here and hope everyone else in my life knows how much their kind words, tips, and encouragement helped this along.

Dr. Steven Finkel at the University of Virginia comes first. It was Steve who made a scholar out of me, showing me the right questions to ask, the right way to ask them, and the best way (we have awfully few "right" ways in political science) to find and interpret the answers. He's also clued me in to many of the mysteries of the profession that otherwise would've escaped me. Now all of this is what any good adviser and mentor would do, but he also performed some professional magic that allowed me financially to go on to Ph.D. study, and has always encouraged *my* interests — even when, as with this study, they don't exactly coincide with his own — and made them his interests as well. My debt to Steve will never be repaid; all I can do is try to pass on to someone else what Steve has done for me.

Then there are the other members of my dissertation committee, which is where this study began. Dr. Paula McClain, now chair of the Woodrow Wilson Department of Government and Foreign Affairs at U.Va., served as my second reader and was an enormous help in getting this work theoretically grounded. Dean Bernard Mayes of the U.Va. College of Arts and Sciences endeavored to get me away from the trees of the data to see and talk about the forest — what this study means and why it matters. Dr. Kenneth Sherrill at Hunter College, City University of New York, served on my committee, corrected my errors, shared his enormous knowledge of LGB politics in New York, and helped me flesh out my ideas.

Two other people were instrumental. Dr. Robert Bailey, now at Rutgers-Camden, kindly acted as an unofficial fifth committee member, reading all my drafts, making welcome comments, encouraging me to hang in when things looked bleak, and taking me step-by-step through the Glick poll on which chapter 5 is based. Dr. Murray Edelman of Voter News Service put the LGB self-identification question in the national and state exit polls in the first place; without his leadership in including sexual identity in national political polling, this book would not exist. Bob, Murray, and Ken Sherrill taught me as much as I could learn about exit polling and strongly encouraged me to pursue this line of research.

My editor at NYU Press, Jennifer Hammer, patiently waited for this manuscript, finally got it months after first inquiring about it, and worked with her firm to make it come to print. I also thank the anonymous reviewer who gave a detailed and very constructive critique of the book, which improved it greatly.

Finally, when you live with a book for more than four years, there are times when you never want to see it again and wish it would go away. My partner, Chris, has saved me more than once from chucking in the towel, soothed my nerves, and assured me through a couple of rejection letters that at some point someone would find this work of value. I am blessed that someone has.

Should you find any howlers within, they are my own fault. I hope you find that the rest of the book makes up for them.

 O N E

Virgin Ground

On election night 1992, as Bill Clinton savored his victory, a minority of Americans long chastised and, until recent times, usually invisible savored a great victory as well. For the first time in their history, the American people had elected as their president a man who had openly and strongly campaigned for the support of homosexuals and bisexuals.

The new president's longtime friend David Mixner, a gay California business-man who had helped raise an estimated $2 million from the lesbian, gay, and bisexual community for Clinton (Gallagher 1992), proudly if erroneously claimed that one of every six Clinton voters was a lesbian or gay man—and thus provided the Democrats' five percentage point margin of victory.[1] Leaving aside the statistical stretch, Robert Bray, a spokesman for the National Gay and Lesbian Task Force, called the election "a rite of passage from the margins to the mainstream, from social pariah to political partner" (McAllister 1992).

In the quarter century since the Stonewall riots of June 1969 in New York City's Greenwich Village, which launched the national gay rights movement in earnest, the estimated 5 to 10 percent of the U.S. population that is gay[2] or lesbian, and the additional, uncertain percentage that can be called bisexual (Kinsey et al. 1948; Institute for Sex Research 1953; Fay et al. 1989; Janus and Janus 1993; Laumann et al. 1994)[3] has emerged from almost absolute invisibility to assume a significant place in the public consciousness, and to have its demands for legal and social equality considered seriously. The role of lesbian, gay, and bisexual voters also is becoming significant, especially in major coastal cities, and urban politicians increasingly are making direct appeals for these votes. Now, so has the president of the United States.

1

The pages that follow report the results of the first detailed examination of self-identified lesbians, gay men, and bisexuals as a factor in the electoral politics of the United States. This study assesses differences in demographics, attitudes, and voting behavior between self-identified bisexuals and homosexuals and the rest of the voting population, as well as those between gay and bisexual women and men, and the factors explaining those differences.

The greatest part of the hard number analysis is made possible by unprecedented data from 1990 and 1992 national and state general election exit polls. In these two elections, for the first time ever, lesbian and gay general election voters across the land (joined by bisexual voters in 1992) could identify themselves by their sexual orientation in national political surveys.[4]

This study will show that self-identified lesbians, bisexuals, and gay men in America (from here on often abbreviated "LGB" or "LGBs")[5] constitute a disinherited social minority that has begun to acquire some electoral power; that they think and act differently politically from the majority; that sexual self-identification by itself has a measurable, independent effect on certain political attitudes and, often, on how people vote; and that self-identification as gay, lesbian, or bisexual correlates directly with youth, and that therefore the percentage of self-identifiers is likely to grow as time goes on.

The Importance of the LGB Vote

At first it may seem that, despite the controversy "gay rights" issues engender, this group of voters would be too small to care about. Before and after this study, random-sample surveys asking respondents' sexual orientation found that only a small share of Americans, from 1 to 4 percent, would identify themselves as lesbian, gay, or bisexual (Harry 1990; Miller and Bukolt 1990; Edelman 1991; Edelman 1993; Janus and Janus 1993; Rensberger 1993; Laumann et al. 1994).

 Yet even so, in the 1992 presidential election, self-identified LGB voters were as numerous as Latino voters, and outnumbered Asian voters two to one. Further, a disproportionate share of LGB self-identifiers, in various prior studies (Bell and Weinberg 1978; Jay and Young 1979; Harry 1986) and in the exit polls we shall examine here, were under the age of forty-five; and it is likely, therefore, that as the generations change the share of "out-of-the-closet" LGB voters will grow substantially in the next quarter century.

Beyond the question of raw numbers, within the past few years it has become increasingly clear that, while political science has paid little heed to LGBs as a political force, the politicians and the popular media have put great stock in a "gay vote" and, in like manner, an "antigay vote" comprising mainly older voters and religious fundamentalists.[6] Given all this attention, there should be a natural interest in learning about LGB voters—who they are, how many they are, where they stand, and how they vote.

⌈In addition, LGB people increasingly are classed by politicians, the news media, and some courts of law as a discrete and insular minority (Arriola 1988), and the gay rights movement consciously has followed the models of the earlier movements for black civil rights and women's rights⌋ (Marotta 1981; Schiller and Rosenberg 1985; Adam 1987). Given especially the context of LGBs as an "invisible" minority, most members of which cannot be identified by others unless they so identify themselves, it is particularly interesting to learn whether the models previously developed to measure political activation and cohesion among feminists, organized labor, and racial minorities hold up when applied to what increasing are called "sexual minorities."

Much outstanding work has appeared on the gay rights movement that has arisen in America since World War II (e.g., Marotta 1981; D'Emilio 1983; Adam 1987; Timmons 1990; Marcus 1992), and the popular news media from time to time have given attention to LGB politics in certain cities, particularly New York, San Francisco, and the LGB enclave of West Hollywood, California. However, until 1993, no study of this group of voters had appeared in the published scholarly literature. The obvious questions that arise are, Why not? and Why are these people important anyway? The first question is answered better once we look at the second.

The years 1992 and 1993 proved to be banner years for attention, be it positive or negative, to LGB voters and their political aspirations.

Challenged from the right by commentator Pat Buchanan, and pressured by religious fundamentalists, President George Bush and the Republican Party took new and extraordinary steps to distance themselves from LGB people (Schmalz 1992a, 1992b). Representatives of LGB Republican organizations were forbidden to address the GOP platform committee (Schwartz 1992). An openly gay Bush campaign employee was demoted and later fired, he alleged, because of pressure on his superiors from the Religious Right (Brown 1992), and Moral Majority founder Jerry Falwell responded by saying flatly, "There is no room for homosexuals in the Republican Party" (*ABC News Nightline*, 22 July 1992).⌋The Republican platform opposed all federal, state, or local gay rights legislation and supported the ban on homosexuals in the armed forces. *LGB* President Bush, in published interviews, reiterated his support for the military ban and condemned parenthood by same-sex couples as "abnormal," while Vice President Dan Quayle averred that homosexuality was "a choice, and a bad

choice" (De Witt 1992) The GOP convention, in the midst of a long economic
recession, focused on "family values," which in the eyes of numerous commentators was a code phrase for attacking gay rights and single parents. Buchanan
and evangelist-politician Pat Robertson used the convention podium to launch
attacks on gays and lesbians in prime time (Schmalz 1992a). The Republicans
backpedaled on all this only when postconvention surveys revealed that a
significant percentage of middle-class heterosexual voters were turned off by
the appearance of "gay-bashing" in their campaign (Turque et al. 1992; Rosenthal 1992). In the meantime, the Log Cabin Federation, a national organization
of LGB Republicans, responded to all this by publicly refusing to endorse Bush
for reelection (Clines 1992).

At the same time, the Democrats were making an unusually strong appeal
to bisexuals, lesbians, and gay men. All five presidential primary candidates
vied for LGB voters, with the strongest appeal from former Massachusetts
senator Paul Tsongas, original Senate sponsor of the first federal gay civil rights
bill in 1979. Even the consciously moderate nominee, Bill Clinton—governor
of a conservative Southern state in which homosexual acts between consenting
adults in private still are criminal offenses—promised to repeal the military
ban, outlaw antigay discrimination in the federal workforce, appoint a cabinet-
level "czar" to coordinate action on AIDS research, treatment, and education,
and sign a federal gay rights law, provided religious organizations were ex-
empted and clear rules of judicial interpretation were adopted in the statute
(Clinton and Gore 1992). One hundred eight openly lesbian or gay delegates
and alternates attended the Democratic convention, and numerous pro-gay
rights signs and speakers were in evidence, including openly gay, HIV-positive
Clinton environmental adviser Bob Hattoy (Bull 1992). This can be compared
with the two openly gay alternates attending a Republican convention at which
numerous signs proclaimed "Family Rights Forever, 'Gay' Rights Never" (Pugh
1992).

Shortly after taking office, the new president found himself on the receiving
end of vociferous criticism from conservatives and military leaders over his
intention to lift the fifty-one-year ban on LGBs in the military. In January
1993, after a week in which the issue was the top news story in the nation,
Clinton agreed to delay lifting the ban for six months, during which final
discharges would be stayed but servicepeople facing such discharge would be
placed on "standby reserve" (unpaid administrative leave). After well-publi-
cized hearings by the Senate and House Armed Services Committees and a
long-planned march on Washington in April by hundreds of thousands of LGB

people and their supporters,[7] Clinton agreed to a policy forbidding LGB servicepeople to be open about their sexuality, which later in the year was written into the statute books by Congress.

At the state level, Colorado adopted an amendment to its state constitution in November 1992 repealing all gay rights legislation or regulations at the state and local levels and forbidding the passage of new ones. A similar, simultaneous measure in Oregon, which additionally declared homosexuality "abnormal, wrong, unnatural, and perverse" and lumped it together with bestiality, failed to pass but won the support of 43 percent of the state's voters; local versions of that initiative measure were adopted in several Oregon counties and municipalities the following year. Although the Colorado amendment was declared by a Denver court, and later by the Colorado Supreme Court, to violate the U.S. Constitution, and although the local-level Oregon initiatives were invalidated by a state statute overriding them, campaigns for antigay initiative measures were undertaken in at least eight states in 1993 and 1994. Voters in certain localities, most notably Cincinnati, Ohio, Lewiston, Maine, and Gainesville, Florida, repealed gay rights ordinances passed by their city or county councils.

Were this past activity not enough, a compelling reason to study LGB voters is that LGB-related issues are certain to play a considerable role in the 1996 presidential election.

First, emotionally charged litigation will force LGB rights onto the national agenda. The U.S. Supreme Court will rule during its 1995–96 term on the constitutionality of Colorado's antigay Amendment 2. (The previous term it ruled unanimously that LGB marchers may be excluded from municipal holiday parades sponsored by private groups.) Several conflicting federal district and circuit court rulings on gays in the military will have to be sifted through by the high court in short order. And, unless the state's constitution is amended in the meantime, Hawaii's Supreme Court may rule in the midst of the 1996 campaign that the state's ban on same-sex marriage violates the Hawaiian constitution (a preliminary ruling to that effect was handed down by the Hawaiian justices in 1994). At that point, the other forty-nine states will be faced with recognition of Hawaiian same-sex marriages under the U.S. Constitution's "full faith and credit" clause; this volatile question eventually will be resolved in the U.S. Supreme Court.

Second, religious conservatives again will try to place antigay initiatives on numerous state and local ballots in 1996, worded as broadly as permitted both by the need to gain majority support and by the eventual Supreme Court decision on Amendment 2. President Bush managed to ignore these initiatives in 1992, but the eventual Republican nominee will be pressured to take a stand on them in 1996. President Clinton already has come out against them.

Third, any Supreme Court rulings favorable to the LGB cause may lead social conservatives to demand their rescission through one or more federal constitutional amendments. A ruling requiring states to recognize Hawaii's same-sex marriages is the most likely to engender such a response (Rotello 1994).

Finally, President Clinton's record (discussed further in Chapter 7) of seeking to allow open LGBs into the military and appointing open lesbians and gay men to high government positions is certain to be attacked by, at the very least, the farthest right of the GOP candidates and spokespeople.

More than in any prior election in our history, then, candidates for president, Congress, and state governorships and legislative seats in 1996 will have their opinions on same-sex relations demanded of them.

Despite all this attention to LGB people and LGB issues from national political leaders, until Edelman's article on LGB voters in the Clinton election (1993) there was *no* published scholarly work on lesbian, gay, or bisexual voters as a factor in electoral politics. The first research papers presented on this group of voters only have appeared within the last half-dozen years (Bailey 1989; Sherrill et al. 1990; Edelman 1991; Hertzog 1992). It is necessary, therefore, that a baseline study be done to assess who these voters are, what attitudes they hold, and—most important for practical politicians—how numerous they are and how they vote.

Whatever the actual number of homosexual and bisexual voters in America may be, they likely would not be a significant factor in American politics worthy of mention were it not for the unique disabilities imposed on them by the heterosexual majority (Editors of the Harvard Law Review 1990; Sherrill 1991). These disabilities, and the visceral fear that underlies them (Sherrill 1991; Challandes 1992) may seem irrelevant at first blush to the scholar of politics. They explain, however, why this fertile field of research remains unfurrowed, and why someone must break the ground. Thus I think it appropriate to devote a few pages to this subject.

As discussed in chapter 2, no other group of persons in American society today, having been convicted of no crime, is subject to the number and severity of legally imposed disabilities as are persons of same-sex orientation (detailed in Editors of the Harvard Law Review 1990). They are forbidden to serve in the armed forces, reserves, National Guard, or even in the ROTC. They are forbidden to teach in most public school districts. They are forbidden in most places, by statute or policy, to adopt children or even to provide foster care. They are forbidden to protect their relationships through marriage. If fired from their jobs, evicted from their homes, expelled from their schools, denied credit, refused service in public businesses or restaurants or refused public lodging, solely on the ground of their actual or perceived affection for members of the same sex, in most of the United States they have no recourse in law or equity. They are legally assumed in most states to be unfit to keep custody of their own children, unless they prove their fitness, and one state, Missouri, concludes they are unfit automatically as a matter of law. Homosexuality is not permitted to be discussed in many public school systems, even in high school sex education courses, and objective written material about the subject is forbidden in numerous public school libraries.

These only cover the formal legal disabilities. The extralegal oppression is far greater (for overview, see Herek 1984; Adam 1987; Sherrill 1991; Blumenfeld 1992). The U.S. Department of Justice reported in 1993 that lesbians, gay men, and bisexuals—gay and bisexual men especially—often are subject to random violent attack, sometimes lethal. If they choose to report such attacks, they face the likelihood that their status will become known to unsympathetic employers, family members, and neighbors, subjecting them to additional punishments. If a case is brought to trial, a jury, or even a judge, often will mitigate the offense or the penalty because of the victim's sexuality alone. Most Christian churches condemn them, many expel them from membership, and nearly all forbid them to serve in the ordained ministry (*Alyson Almanac* 1990). Positive, or even neutral, news stories about LGB people remain rare in much of the country. Hundreds of daily newspapers and local television stations refuse to publish advertisements or announcements by support groups for gay people, or for their heterosexual family members and friends.[8] As young people they are ostracized, subject to being beaten, chased, and spat upon, and exposed to various forms of degradation, including sexual assault. Worst, perhaps, is that a significant percentage of parents of homosexual and bisexual children physically or verbally abuse them, seek to force them into religious or psychological counseling in order to "change" their orientation, or disown them, cutting off all emotional and financial support and sometimes forcing them onto the streets—simply because they are attracted to persons of the same sex as themselves.

This combination of laws and social practices have made the status and rights of LGB people a cutting issue in U.S. politics.[9] It also makes it likely that those persons who do self-identify as bisexual, gay, or lesbian would find such conditions intolerable, and would be expected to band together in order to change these conditions through unified action employing, among other means, the electoral process.

Relevance to the Study of Minority Politics

It may seem to the impartial observer that no group of persons could tolerate such oppression as described above, and that, if that group in fact constitutes a tenth of the population, it would rise up in righteous rebellion. That this has happened only to a very limited extent among American lesbians, gay men, and bisexuals, therefore, must seem curious indeed. This brings us to the second essential reason for the study: to look at this group in light of existing theories about minority group politics. These theories, which I shall test in the bulk of the study, will be set forth more thoroughly in chapter 2, but warrant brief introduction here.

Group identification and cohesion. Campbell et al. (1960) defined the terms in which later scholars have studied group voting behavior in America. In their schema, the foundation stone of distinctive group voting is "group identification." Particularly in the case of objectively working-class voters who identify with the middle class, mere objective status as a member of a deprived (or dominant) group is not sufficient to bring about cohesive political action for the group's benefit; members also must express a psychological sense of belonging to the group. In the case of LGBs, the absence of legal protection, the positive legal and extralegal sanctions against them described above, and—perhaps most important—the ability to hide their homosexuality or bisexuality at most times and to "pass" for heterosexual would appear to militate in favor of extremely low levels of group identification, and therefore a very small "lavender vote" in comparison to the estimated share of "lavender" voters.

Strength of identification and group consciousness. A secondary consideration will be whether self-identifiers are possessed of "group consciousness" (Verba and Nie 1972; Shingles 1981; Miller et al. 1981), meaning identification with the group *plus* a positive assessment of it, an understanding of its relative political power, a belief that the system rather than the individual or group members is responsible for unfavorable disparities, and (Shingles adds) a strong sense of personal political efficacy. Among the LGB population, the impediments to group identification are so great that group identification may possibly be treated as synonymous with group consciousness. If true, we should expect that those who do self-identify would tend to be much more politically liberal and partisan than those who do not, and that self-identifiers could be mobilized with relative ease for the common cause.

Organizational and activist influence. Research indicates that the ability of community organizations, such as black churches, to motivate and activate group members varies from group to group. Among working-class people, union membership contributes greatly to levels of group identification and consciousness. Similar levels of consciousness are found among self-identified feminists. In each case, however, the number of union members and feminists is small compared with the total number of working people and women, respectively.[10]

In the case of the LGB community, such community as exists has been built from scratch and must be discovered and explored independently by each person who comes out of the closet. In this context, we shall wish to determine the extent to which organizational activity, and especially LGB political organizations or media, influence group consciousness and cohesiveness. We should expect, as above, that self-identified LGBs would vote cohesively, and in line with the wishes expressed by activist groups.

Coalition building: The Adam hypothesis. Finally, the LGB example can be instructive in assessing the building of electoral coalitions with other "oppressed" groups, and with segments of the white heterosexual majority. Adam (1987) states categorically that the gay and lesbian movement is one with, and an essential component of, the "new social movements" of the left that have gained great influence in the Democratic Party in this country since the 1960s. One of my aims will be to test this hypothesis.

Constructing an LGB Voter Profile

The aim of this study is to take the available evidence and construct an initial profile of self-identified LGB voters, and of what may be an LGB voting bloc. To do this we will need to carry out the following tasks:

- Determine the approximate number of self-identified gay, lesbian, and bisexual voters, and present as complete and accurate a demographic, attitudinal, and voting behavior profile of these voters in the United States as the data allow;
- Compare LGB voters to non-LGB voters and determine significant differences, particularly the extent of bloc voting, if any;
- Formulate and test theories as to the causes of any significant differences;
- Assess the relative success of lesbian and gay organizations active in electoral politics, in a locality (Manhattan) in which such organizations are relatively quite strong, in influencing the voters they claim to represent.

These tasks imply a number of essential questions that must be answered if we are to construct an LGB voter profile.

1. How many LGB voters are there? As discussed in chapter 2, the very definition of "lesbian," "gay," or "bisexual" is a matter of considerable dispute. The only usable demarcation available to us is self-identification; clearly we cannot measure respondents who will not say they are gay or lesbian or bisexual on survey forms. I shall seek to determine whether a consistent percentage of self-identifiers can be established, and whether the rates of identification vary from place to place.

It is important to state, and to restate occasionally, that this study does not encompass the attitudes and voting behavior of all Americans with a same-sex orientation. It is possible that those who remain "in the closet" think and vote exactly like their heterosexual friends and neighbors, and even if not, it is at any rate impossible to say that those homosexual and bisexual Americans who will not identify themselves as such are in any way similar to those who do self-identify. Indeed, it is possible that those who self-identify will be those already more inclined to break with conventional norms in their political thinking. Looking at the LGB self-identifiers remains important because they constitute the immediate constituency of the LGB political leadership.

2. Who are LGB voters? I next consider whether these voters differ in their demographic characteristics from the rest of the population, and whether these demographic differences tell us anything about the likelihood of self-identification. Thus, special attention will be paid to self-identification by age and education level, two correlates of group consciousness, and by sex, as women have been found in the sex surveys noted previously to self-identify at about half the rate of men.

3. Do they think and vote differently from the rest of the public? From there I look at the distinctiveness of the LGB respondents in attitudes on issues, party affiliation, and voting behavior. Special attention will be paid to the rate and consistency of liberalism and whether liberal attitudes translate into votes for Democratic nominees.

4. What political divisions exist among self-identified LGB voters? It is unlikely that a minority group encompassing members of all racial, religious, and ethnic groups and both sexes will be monolithic in its attitudes and vote choice. Particular attention will be paid to finding the sources of partisan divisions within the community, and to determining the existence and extent of a "gender gap," divisions based on race, and distinctions within the group caused by identification with feminism.

5. *Is there a "sexuality gap" in American politics?* It may be that, after accounting for demographic differences between "gay" and "straight" voters, we will find no real difference in attitudes and voting behavior between the sexual orientations at all. If LGBs are disproportionately urban baby boomers, then, even if they are strongly liberal as a group, they may be no more liberal than their heterosexual neighbors; and the self-identifiers in the suburbs, who are fewer in number, may vote like their suburban neighbors.

If this is *not* true, however, there may in fact be an LGB *vote,* as opposed merely to LGB voters. If we do detect clear differences between LGB and non-LGB voters, what explains these variations? Are these factors similar to those found among other groups with high levels of internal cohesion and/or distinctive voting behavior? Further, is there a certain degree of difference that, it appears, we cannot explain for demographic reasons other than that of sexual self-identification?

6. *Does local leadership affect cohesion?* Finally, does the extent to which local LGB political organizations take part in a given election campaign influence the extent of distinctive voting? If so, we would expect that regions in which organizations are active and united around particular candidates would demonstrate higher levels of LGB voter cohesion, whereas those with weak or bickering organizations would show fragmented voting.

Surveys of LGBs

We return to the question raised earlier: why no one has studied LGB voters before. The singular difficulty in examining the LGB vote was the complete lack until 1988 of random-sample political surveys in which respondents were allowed to indicate their sexual orientation. That impediment is now gone.

The first surveys to include a lesbian and gay self-identification question were exit polls taken in certain Democratic presidential primaries in 1988 (Bailey 1989).[11] In the 1990 general election, for the first time, two large national samples and separate polls in twenty-one states were taken, again as exit polls, which included a self-identification question for gays and lesbians (Edelman 1991). Then, in 1992, the self-identification question was first posed to voters in a presidential election—and self-identified bisexuals were included for the first time (Edelman 1993).

Before the Exit Polls

Prior to the exit polls of 1988, 1990, and 1992, information on LGB political behavior was culled from anecdotal evidence and surveys that did not use random sampling.

Anecdotal evidence has long suggested that there exist in many cities gay enclaves or "ghettoes" large enough to encompass one or more voting precincts (Levine 1979; Weekes 1989). San Francisco drew a supervisorial district with a substantial lesbian and gay population in 1977 based on such evidence. By the mid-1980s, sufficient demographic indicators had been assembled to identify such precincts readily in San Francisco, Los Angeles, New York, Houston, Philadelphia, Boston, Washington, and perhaps other cities; based on this information, a portion of the city of Los Angeles was carved out in 1984 to become the city of West Hollywood, with a population estimated in the popular press to be at least 40 percent gay and lesbian. The new city promptly elected an openly homosexual majority to its city council and a lesbian as its first mayor. In 1991, New York state carved out an assembly district in lower Manhattan to protect the lesbian incumbent elected the preceding year by including predominantly LGB precincts, and New York City included many of these precincts in a new city council district expressly designed to elect an open lesbian or gay man.[12] The identification of such areas, and the extent of the LGB population, has been made somewhat easier since the U.S. Census Bureau released its 1990 data on household composition, reporting the number of self-identified unmarried couples of the same sex living within a given census tract.[13]

The anecdotal evidence has been supplemented by some surveys of LGB political attitudes and behavior. Jay and Young (1979) compiled a ground-breaking study of the demographics and attitudes of several thousand LGBs. This sample, however, cannot be used as a valid baseline. Not only was the sample self-selected, but the venues of exposure to the mail survey were largely limited to gay bars and bookstores, feminist and gay liberation organizations, and *Blueboy,* a popular gay men's pornographic magazine of the day. (Half of the more than five thousand male respondents answered the survey in the magazine.)

The unreliability of self-selected sampling with respect to political behavior was seen graphically in the presidential election of 1992. Overlooked Opinions, a Chicago market research firm that concentrates on LGB consumers, found that 90 percent of self-identified homosexuals planned to vote for Bill Clinton, and LGB activists touted this figure. The sample, however, was culled from lists of patrons of LGB bookstores and subscribers to LGB-oriented magazines and catalogs, necessarily involving considerable indirect self-selection. As discussed below, the election day exit poll conducted jointly for the four major broadcast news organizations found that a smaller, although still very substantial, percentage of self-identified LGBs supported Clinton.

In contrast to nonrandom sampling, probability sampling of the sexual-minority population was in its infancy. Fay et al. (1989) report the first such sex study employing a random sample, which included only men and used data from 1970. Janus and Janus reported the first quota sample study to incorporate both sexes only in 1993; and the first reliable, national random-sample sex survey in the United States was not published until 1994 (Laumann et al. 1994). Beyond the realm of sex research, only one random-sample study in which (male) respondents could identify themselves as gay or bisexual appeared in the published literature (Harry 1990).

The CBS and VRS Data Sets

A joint exit poll by CBS News and the *New York Times* of voters in the 1988 New York Democratic presidential primary included the first known use of a gay/lesbian self-identification question in the history of scientific political polling, and that survey has served as a model for subsequent polls asking the respondent's sexual orientation. The question was asked to assess the effectiveness of candidate Jesse Jackson's direct appeal for the votes of lesbians and gay men in a state with a relatively well-organized LGB political community. The New York survey revealed that 4 percent of Democratic primary voters checked the "gay or lesbian" box, and that a large majority of these, black, brown, and white alike, had voted for Jackson (Bailey 1989).[14]

CBS and the *Times,* therefore, asked the question in each subsequent Democratic primary survey for the rest of the campaign. The question was not asked, however, in the 1988 general election exit polls. Each network conducted its own separate poll, and none appeared to believe either that the question was particularly relevant in that year or that the response rate would justify asking the question.

In 1990, for the first time, the four networks collaborated in a single national exit poll, administered by Voter Research and Surveys, Inc. (VRS),[15] during the congressional midterm elections; and an additional version of the poll for CBS alone also was administered by VRS. In both versions of the national survey, the gay/lesbian self-identifier question was included. The same was true in twenty-one of the forty-two separate state-level exit polls conducted on behalf of the four networks by VRS.

The self-identification question, now amended to read "gay, lesbian or bisexual," was included in selected 1992 Democratic primary exit polls, and, for the first time, in the joint four-network exit polls on the general election. Since the 1992 election, VRS exit polls on the mayoral elections in Los Angeles and New York City in 1993 also have been conducted in which the LGB self-identifier question is asked. To date, however, no known random-sample national or state-level political survey, other than an exit poll, has included an LGB self-identifier question.

Other Data Sources

In addition to the VRS exit polls, the *San Francisco Examiner* in 1990 included a gay/lesbian self-identification question in its preelection survey of voters. This proved to be prescient, for in that election, two lesbians were among the six at-large members elected to the city's governing Board of Supervisors, an openly gay teacher won first place in the election for the city's school board, and a referendum measure granting benefits to unmarried "domestic partners," including lesbian and gay couples in long-term relationships, was adopted. (These electoral victories were labeled "the Lavender Sweep.")[16]

A couple of months earlier, a survey was taken that has an important role in our study. In September 1990, Democrats in a downtown Manhattan district nominated (and the district later elected) an open lesbian, Deborah Glick, to the New York State Assembly, making her the first open homosexual in a state legislative body in the mid-Atlantic region. Presuming that a large gay and lesbian population inhabited the district, researchers at Columbia University and CUNY's Hunter College, working with VRS staff, conducted an exit poll in randomly selected precincts in the district. This survey asked two forms of a self-identifier question, one of the VRS "grab bag" variety and a second specifically asking voters to identify their sexual orientation on a five-point modification of Kinsey's (1948) seven-point scale. As discussed in chapter 5, this "Glick poll" data base is particularly useful in that it also asks which of several endorsements, if any, were important in the voter's decision.

Reading the Results: A Caveat

The reader will find the data sets used here thoroughly described, and occasional cautions regarding them set forth, in chapters 3 through 6 and in the appendix; but I should advance one initial note of caution here. It will be noted periodically in the pages that follow that some of the samples or subsamples discussed in this study are rather small. This is particularly true of the state-level exit polls. Of the 21 states in which the self-identifier question was asked in the 1990 exit polls, in only three states was the self-identified gay and lesbian sample size in excess of 30 respondents—the minimum acceptable for analysis in political science and sociology.

My analysis of the state polls in chapter 4, save for a pair of simple descriptive tables at the beginning, has been confined to those three states. In addition, when dealing with relatively small subsamples in the national exit polls (self-identified LGB Republicans, for example), I generally state actual numbers of respondents when reporting data in the text, in addition to (or in lieu of) weighted percentages.

I trust that any conclusions I draw here from these smaller samples will be the subject of further study. Nonetheless, even the small samples, read conservatively, have yielded some valuable information helpful in drawing our picture of the LGB American voter.

Americans with same-sex orientations are reputed to cast anywhere from 1 to 10 percent of the nation's votes. At the same time, these voters also are subjected to severe legal and social disadvantages and have organized, in the past quarter century, a far-reaching movement to eradicate these disabilities and change society's hostile attitudes toward them. One important aspect has been to attempt to organize LGB voters into a cohesive and decisive voting bloc. The time has come to see whether, and to what extent, the movement to weld together a "lavender vote" has succeeded.

The hostile and fearful attitudes we have noted, together with the homosexual person's ability to "pass" for heterosexual, have retarded research on this potentially important topic, and until recently prevented the gathering of information on the demographics, attitudes, and voting behavior even of self-identified LGB voters. Fortunately, however, within the past few years, we have obtained the sound data necessary to begin work on this topic. That being the case, let us delay no further.

TWO

From "Lavender" People to "Lavender" Voters

The case of lesbians, bisexuals, and gay men bears particular interest in a number of ways for those of us interested in why, and for whom, Americans vote. Like African Americans and indigenous Americans, homosexual and bisexual Americans have been subject not merely to widespread social rejection and disapproval, but also to mandatory legal disabilities, and unlike African Americans and indigenous Americans, they remain subject to such legal disabilities throughout the country today. The "mark of oppression" remains upon them in numerous ways discussed below, and alienation (see Almond and Verba 1963; Easton 1965) from both the system of government and its policies might be taken to be the norm. But sexuality, unlike race or sex, never has been used in a formal or informal way to disqualify any person from voting. Unlike litigation, lobbying, or various forms of protest, which often require more openness about their sexuality than many desire or feel safe enough to show, the secret ballot always has been open to LGB Americans as a potential means of effecting both substantive and symbolic social change.

Regrettably, we cannot examine the voting behavior of homosexuals and bisexuals who will not identify themselves as such on survey forms. As discussed below, there is considerable evidence from sex research that the proportion of the population who will identify themselves as LGB is a rather small fraction of those with romantic and sexual feelings and actions directed toward persons of the same sex. This is the result of a combination of negative legal and social consequences, which the LGB movement describes as oppression, and the ability to "pass" for heterosexual. The discreet, self-aware bisexual or homosexual can avoid most, perhaps all, legal and social difficulties if she or he pretends to be heterosexual, at least so far as the family, the people at work, and heterosexual friends are concerned (Sherrill et al. 1990; Sherrill 1991).

In this study I consider whether LGB self-identification has a significant independent effect, be it direct or indirect, on the decision to vote and on vote choice. In doing so, I consider whether we can hypothesize that self-identified LGBs constitute a social group with distinctive voting behavior as defined by Campbell et al. (1960). Some additional questions of interest, therefore, are why certain LGB Americans "come out of the closet" and identify as bisexual, gay, or lesbian, why such a group identity should carry over from the sphere of personal relations into that of politics, and why distinctive group voting might be expected of self-identified LGBs.

Group Affiliation and Voting Behavior

The framework of social group affiliation and its effects on voting behavior laid out in *The American Voter* (Campbell et al. 1960, chap. 11) provides us with a model against which we can examine openly LGB American voters and with a set of questions, the answers to which will allow us to hypothesize about what sort of fit with the model we can expect.

According to Campbell and his colleagues, social groups, encompassing racial and ethnic, religious, and class affiliations,[1] are "secondary groups" with respect to their influence on an individual's political behavior; "primary groups," those with the greatest direct influence, are made up of the personal circles of family, friends, neighbors, and coworkers. Objective membership in a "secondary group," therefore, is not sufficient for that group to exercise significant influence over those who belong to it. One must have a psychological identification with the secondary group, and the degree of the group's influence correlates directly with the strength of identification on the part of the individual member. Both the fact of identification and the strength thereof develop through an acculturation process, by which a member becomes aware of the group's history, values, norms, and political agenda. The greater the share of objective group members who identify themselves as group members, and the stronger their degree of identification, the more cohesive the group is—that is, the more likely it is that members will act in the voting booth in a way consistent with the group's collective perception of its interests.

Group effects on voting behavior may be measured by the distinctiveness of the total vote by group members compared with that of their neighbors of similar background and status who do not belong to the group. Several factors will increase or decrease group distinctiveness. Strength of identification among group members increases distinctiveness; that is, those who identify strongly with the group will vote differently from nongroup members more often than will those who identify with the group weakly. A second factor affecting distinctiveness is what Campbell and his colleagues call the "transmission of group political standards" to its members, which is a direct function of the relative unity of or division among group leaders: the more the group's acknowledged leaders disagree, the less likely it is that the group's aggregate vote will differ much from that of the rest of the voters. Finally, distinctiveness is affected by the "political salience" of group membership, the degree to which the group and its issues are important or "hot" in an election; this can be manifested either in a group member's candidacy for office against a nonmember or in an election fought in part on issues of special concern to the group's members.

It is in the interest of practical politicians to bring groups into and cement them in permanent coalitions, usually through political parties. It is not necessarily in the interest of any particular group, however, to so limit its room for maneuver. Once partisan habits become ingrained among the mass of members they are difficult to shift, even in situations in which the group's interests would objectively be better served by such a shift.

Campbell et al. (1960) make clear that factors affecting the degree and strength of self-identification are those most likely to promote group cohesion and/or distinctive voting between members of any social group and the rest of the population. Because of the degree to which self-identification is an issue for LGB people in their daily lives, let alone for the purpose of assessing their degree of group identity and distinctiveness in the voting booth, the next section of this chapter concentrates largely on the connection between self-identification and oppression. I first define oppression and assess the LGB movement's claim that it represents an oppressed group. I then examine psychological and sociological studies relating to the development of group identity and positive self-assessment among individuals belonging to oppressed groups.

The third section looks at why members of any oppressed group should wish to participate in the political system, and why voting would be seen as a fruitful means of achieving relief from their conditions. This section concentrates on the work of Easton (1965) in differentiating among types of political system support, Almond and Verba (1963) in defining America as a "participatory political culture" and comparing it to others, and Edelman (1964) in setting forth "symbolic" purposes for political participation.

The fourth section defines and discusses "group consciousness" (Verba and

Nie 1972; Miller et al. 1981; Shingles 1981), a concept that marries group identification to a set of conceptions of the group's place in the political world that, together, make participation in the political process seem desirable and likely to be effective. Because Cass's seminal study (1984) appears to find a direct connection in time between the willingness to "come out" to persons whose expected reactions are unknown or likely to be negative and the development of what, among blacks and feminists, would be described as group consciousness, I then take up the question of whether, among LGBs, group identification for political purposes is necessarily equivalent to the existence of group consciousness.

The fifth section will examine the development of the postwar LGB movement. This section will suggest the strength of particular issue concerns or ideological orientations, and any differences that may be expected among subgroups within the community in attitudes and voting behavior, particularly between LGB women and men. From this we can assess the likely success of transmission of shared group political norms by LGB political leaders, which directly affect group distinctiveness in voting.

The complete thesis will be summarized at the end of the chapter in the form of nine specific hypotheses to be tested in the rest of the book.

Group Identification and the Claim of Oppression

It is the central claim of the LGB movement today that its members constitute an oppressed cultural minority (Marotta 1981; Adam 1987). It will be helpful to first define the concepts of group identification and oppression, and their applicability to the situation of LGBs.

Miller et al. (1981) define group identification as "a perceived self-location within a particular social stratum, along with a psychological feeling of belonging to that particular stratum." Group identification is essentially the outward expression of a psychological feeling of belonging to a particular subset of a population, a sense that one's essential identity is bound up with that of other people who share some common attribute, characteristic, or belief. It differs from objective group membership in that, unlike objective membership, it is a matter of choice that occurs *a posteriori* — or, in rare instances, group identification may occur among those with a psychological desire to belong, but who lack the characteristics that would give them objective membership in the group.

A particularly clear example of the separation between objective group membership and group identification is found in the attitudes of persons who, by their income levels and job status, clearly belong objectively to the working class. A sizable percentage, ranging from a quarter to half of those in this classification, prefer to identify themselves with the middle class (Bailey 1992). As individuals identify psychologically with the middle class rather than their own, their political attitudes and voting behavior come to reflect those of the middle class far more than those of their working-class neighbors who identify with their objective class. The increasing trend toward working-class members identifying as middle class, therefore, spells trouble for those on the left seeking to build a coalition of feminists, social minorities, and working-class whites.

With regard to oppression, several working definitions are available to us, going back to the Pentateuch and, in the nineteenth century, Marx. The numerous definitions of oppression in use have in common the notion of the exercise of authority or power in an "unjust," "cruel," and/or "burdensome" manner, or in a manner that "pushes others down" or "holds them down." The numerous and various definitions may be summarized as the deliberate stratification of society by one or more dominant groups for the purpose of accumulating an undue share of economic, political, social, and/or psychological benefits by placing an undue share of economic, political, social, and/or psychological burdens on the subordinated classes.[2]

The first American to define gay men, lesbians, and bisexuals as "an oppressed cultural minority" was Harry Hay, founder of the Mattachine Society, the first gay organization in postwar America, in 1950 (D'Emilio 1983; Timmons 1990; Marcus 1992). Earlier gay movements, centered in pre-Hitler Germany, had called merely for toleration and compassion (Adam 1987), so Hay's assertion was something quite new.

The concept of oppression in the nineteenth and twentieth centuries often has been laid over with Marxian notions of historical materialism, and Hay, a lifelong Marxist, based his application of oppression to homosexuals on the notion that insuring sexual control—limiting the release of sexual energies to procreation—was in the strong interest of capitalists seeking to insure that labor's energies were focused on production, and thereby on maximizing surplus value. Thus was an alliance formed between Christian moralists (who sought sexual continence for other reasons) and the capitalist class, which in his view has continued to the present (Adam 1987; Timmons 1990).[3]

However, as Mattachine cofounder Chuck Rowland (in Marcus 1992) notes, the majority of the members they brought into Mattachine were simply men[4] tired of police entrapment and harassment, men who wanted to meet, socialize with, and discuss issues of common interest with other gay men in peace.

"They didn't want to be part of an oppressed cultural minority," Rowland recalled, and they argued that gay people were "just like everybody else except for what we do in bed." This rejection of Hay's analysis and its implications, along with the former Communist Party ties of Hay, Rowland, and some other founders, led to the founders' resignation from the group in 1953 (D'Emilio 1983; Timmons 1990). The claim of oppression also likely would have been dismissed at the time by virtually all nongays, as homosexuality was deemed to be either a grave sin or a psychological disorder or (interestingly) both, and consensual homosexual acts in private were criminal offenses in every state of the Union.[5]

However, a few influential activists in the vanguard of the early "homophile" movement discussed later in this chapter, including Frank Kameny of the Mattachine Society of Washington, D.C. and Barbara Gittings of the Daughters of Bilitis, did accept the notion of oppression, if not Hay's Marxist basis for it; the basis for oppression more commonly accepted in the movement was that LGB people were simply the subject of unjust and mindless intolerance because of misunderstanding, ignorance, and fear, as were blacks (Marotta 1981;D'Emilio 1983; Marcus 1992).

The oppression argument was explicitly adopted by the Gay Liberation movement and by lesbian feminism following the Stonewall riots of June 1969 (Marotta 1981). The explanations offered for this oppression are numerous and remain the subject of debate; I shall not attempt a comprehensive survey here. But acceptance and explication of the *fact* of oppression—the undue denial of social benefits and placement of undue social burdens on those romantically attracted to persons of the same sex—has become universal among LGB activists (Adam 1987; Marcus 1992). Hay's "oppressed cultural minority" idea, with or without (usually without) its Marxian underpinnings, has become the standard of the movement.

It is, of course, the contention of the proponents of legal restrictions on homosexuals and bisexuals, including on their private, consensual sexual activity, that such measures are not oppressive at all, but are necessary to "protect" families from the possibility that any one of their members, particularly their pubescent and teenage children, may become homosexual. Levels of public disapproval have not been altered in the last ten years; now as then, opinion polls find that less than 45 percent of Americans consider homosexuality "an acceptable alternative lifestyle,"[6] and that consistently for twenty years now, roughly 70 percent have said that homosexual activity is "always wrong" (Bowman and Ladd 1993).

Who/What Is "Gay"? The Measurement Problem

There is considerable ambiguity in the term "homosexuality." First, we must distinguish among three disparate, but often confounded, measures of sexuality: sexual attraction, sexual behavior, and sexual identity. In particular, the extent to which a person is attracted to men, to women, or to both has been confounded with LGB self-identification.

The first published random-sample study of any national population to distinguish among a population's location on these elements was Laumann et al. (1994), most commonly called the NORC or Chicago sex survey.[7] The researchers' face-to-face interviews with 3,432 respondents found that 10.1 percent of U.S. men and 8.6 percent of U.S. women showed either same-sex attraction, behavior, or self-identification, or some combination thereof. Of these, however, only a quarter of the men (2.7 percent of all men surveyed) and one-sixth of the women (1.4 percent of all women surveyed) self-identified as gay, lesbian, or bisexual. The remainder reported either same-sex desires or behavior, or both, but self-identified as heterosexual.

This mirrors the results of an interesting study (Miller and Bukolt 1990) of undergraduate students at Notre Dame University at the behest of its governing board. A survey on general issues of sexuality on campus was mailed to every fourth undergraduate, about two thousand total. Seven hundred five surveys were mailed back. The survey asked about both same-sex sexual behavior and self-identification. On the first of these questions, 6.5 percent of the students responding who said they were sexually active at Notre Dame reported having had relations solely with members of the same sex, whereas 2.4 percent had had relations with both sexes. This adds up to 8.9 percent, not too far from Kinsey's much-used number of 10 percent, Janus and Janus's estimate (1993) of 7 percent, and the 9.3 percent found by Laumann et al. (1994). (We must remember that each study used a different definition of homosexuality and a different sampling method.) But when asked how they identified themselves, only 1 percent said they considered themselves homosexual, and 2.5 percent bisexual. In other words, a majority of those who reported they were homosexual or bisexual behaviorally still *identified* themselves as heterosexual.

A fourth term, used increasingly commonly in discrimination law, is "sexual orientation," sometimes iterated as "affectional preference," "affectional orientation," or "sexual preference" (Editors of the Harvard Law Review 1990). "Sexual orientation" — or any of these substitute terms — is used in discussions of those who are either attracted to or have sex with persons of the same sex, or both, or those who identify themselves as homosexual or bisexual. For purposes of the law, the three aspects of homosexuality have been piled into one.

Social Impediments to Self-Identification

The results of the NORC and Notre Dame surveys make considerably more sense when one considers the strong forces arrayed against a person identifying as gay, lesbian, or bisexual. In this section I list principally extralegal forces; in the next section I turn to legal forces, with which we are principally concerned. In the upshot, it may surprise the reader that anyone at all would choose to self-identify.

Lack of family socialization. Although recent evidence points to a physiological connection with homosexuality or bisexuality (LeVay 1991; Allen and Gorski 1992; Bailey and Pillard 1991; Bailey et al. 1993; but see Barinaga 1991; King and McDonald 1992; Byne and Parsons 1993), there is at the same time no evidence that LGB parents are more likely to have LGB children than are the rest of the population (Polikoff 1990; Patterson 1992). An extremely small number of lesbians, bisexuals, and gay men grew up in families in which one or both of the parents was openly, or even implicitly, the same way, or even in which a close family member could serve as a "role model." A second element usually is present: strong parental and familial disapproval of homosexuality, reflected in the survey results across time noted above (Bowman and Ladd 1993).

The information gap. The absence of role learning appropriate to LGB youth, and the likelihood of family hostility to the child's developing interest in persons of the same sex should that interest become known, translate as well into the classroom. Outside the central cities of major metropolitan areas, little or no information about homosexuality is taught even in high school classrooms. Where proposals are made to teach the subject in a more than cursory way, severe objections often are raised, principally that the very discussion of the subject in the classroom will promote homosexuality (Editors of the Harvard Law Review 1990).[8] Most students' education about homosexuality is confined to rumor, misinformation, and abusive epithets directed at suspected homosexuals and bisexuals. It is therefore almost uniformly true that lesbian, gay, or bisexual young people grow up without any exposure to other LGB people or LGB culture, save for occasional appearances in the popular media (Sherrill 1991; Alyson 1991).

A report commissioned by the U.S. Department of Health and Human Services in 1989 estimated that as many as 30 percent of teenage suicides and suicide attempts were related to an inability to accept one's sexual orientation, that half of gay and lesbian teenagers had attempted suicide at least once, and that suicide was the leading cause of death among homosexual youth. The report was rejected by the Secretary, Dr. Louis Sullivan, because of objections to its findings by Republican Representative William Dannemyer of California, a notable figure in the Religious Right wing of the president's party (Maguen 1991).

Fear of personal rejection. For those who do develop an understanding of their sexuality, three great fears cloud the horizon (discussed in Challandes 1992; Sherrill 1991). The most powerful, apparently, is the fear of personal rejection by family and friends, especially parents. Negative reactions are far from the uniform response, but these fears are not unfounded. Studies of teenage runaways estimate that as many as half have left home because of physical or emotional abuse related to their sexual orientation; a considerable number were thrown out of the house by the parents (Galst 1992). Among adults, the instances of parents cutting off their children, emotionally or financially, because the children have "come out" to them are legion (Sherrill et al. 1990).

Fear of material or personal loss. Even if the family and friends are accepting and/or supportive, a second set of substantial fears looms: fears of material or personal loss. Two predominate: loss of a job or career opportunities and loss of child custody (see Stoddard et al. 1983; Editors of the Harvard Law Review 1990). Again, neither is uncommon, and, as discussed below, the law often mandates or strongly encourages the termination of employment or custody rights based on sexual orientation.

Fear of physical violence. Finally, even those with completely supportive families, friends, and employers, living in states or cities in which antigay bias is unlawful, are subject to random, unprovoked physical attack at a significant rate (Comstock 1991). Although such attacks occur in all areas, they are predominately directed against gay and bisexual men in major cities, and are committed predominately by younger men (Shapiro 1990; Comstock 1991).

Legal Barriers to Self-Identification

Our principal concern, of course, is with conscious use of the law to repress homosexual and bisexual behavior and/or self-identification. This is not the place for a thorough recapitulation of antigay laws and policies on the books. Clearly, however, the law reinforces the fears noted above (see Editors of the Harvard Law Review 1990).

"Sodomy" laws. As noted earlier, in twenty-two states, sex between consenting adults of the same gender in private remains a criminal offense, often a felony (Murdoch 1993). The U.S. Supreme Court, in *Bowers v. Hardwick* (1986), which challenged Georgia's felony law, ruled five to four that such private sexual acts are not protected under the right to privacy enunciated in *Griswold v. Connecticut* (1965) with respect to use of contraceptives, and in *Roe v. Wade* (1973) with respect to obtaining an abortion.[9]

Mandatory exclusion from employment. Public school teachers and counselors in many jurisdictions (Stoddard et al. 1983) and members of the U.S. armed forces (Humphrey 1990; Steffan 1992; Shilts 1993) are subject to mandatory, summary dismissal if found to be homosexual or bisexual. As noted earlier, President Clinton failed early in his administration to convince Congress to support his plan to permit gay men, lesbians, and bisexuals to serve openly in the military.

Family law. As of this writing, in no state, as in none but three foreign countries (Denmark, Norway, and Sweden), are same-sex couples permitted legally to marry.[10] Open LGBs are forbidden, by law or (more often) by regulation or informal policy, from adopting children. Further, in the majority of states there is a rebuttable presumption in custody law that a gay father or lesbian mother is an unfit parent for his or her own children (Gibson and Risher 1977; Bagnall et al. 1984; Suseoff 1985; Gottsfield 1985).[11]

Permissible discrimination. Where discriminatory practices are not written into law, such practices nonetheless are permitted in most of the country. One may be fired from one's job, evicted from one's home or denied a lease or contract, denied credit or insurance, refused service in a place of business, or otherwise affected in numerous aspects of one's daily life, solely because of one's actual or perceived sexual orientation. The cases of such discrimination are legion and do not warrant repeating here (see Stoddard et al. 1983; Editors of the Harvard Law Review 1990; Sherrill 1991).

In only nine states and the District of Columbia, and in scattered localities in other states, is any legal redress available for discrimination based on sexual orientation. The voters of Colorado in November 1992 amended their state constitution positively to *forbid* any such protection; the vote repeals antidiscrimination ordinances in Denver, Boulder, and Aspen and an executive order of the governor banning discrimination in state employment.[12] No state, and only a scattering of cities, provide any legal protection to persons in long-term same-sex relationships with regard to property rights, insurance, health care, and inheritance.

Even where laws exist protecting the jobs and homes of lesbians, gay men, and bisexuals, large numbers of offenses go unreported, for three reasons: lack of confidence that the enforcement authority will do anything to redress the situation; inability or lack of willingness to devote the time, psychological energy, and (sometimes) money needed to pursue redress; and, in many cases, the unwillingness to be identified as homosexual or bisexual for fear of other repercussions such as discovery by unknowing family members or friends, verbal or physical abuse, and the like (Sherrill 1991; Powell and Mitrovich 1992).

Are Homosexuals and Bisexuals Oppressed?

Oppression was defined earlier as the deliberate stratification of society in which one set of persons obtains or holds undue benefits by placing undue burdens on another set of persons. The LGB movement has submitted to the nation a claim that it constitutes an oppressed group. We have before us a synopsis of laws and practices grounded in sexual orientation that are cited frequently by LGB leaders in support of this claim. One may test the "oppressiveness" of the same by asking whether heterosexuals would find such laws and practices acceptable, or even tolerable, if applied to them by bisexuals and homosexuals, rather than the other way around. If they would be deemed unacceptable or intolerable—and there is every indication that they would be—then the argument that bisexual and homosexual Americans are an oppressed group has, at the very least, too much weight to be dismissed out of hand.

Clearly the conditions faced by LGB Americans differ substantially from the challenges faced by women, persons with disabilities, and members of racial, ethnic, and religious minorities. We see that conditions within and without the individual militate strongly in most cases against self-identification as gay, lesbian, or bisexual. It is no surprise, therefore, that the very few random-sample studies of bisexual, gay, and lesbian self-identification prior to the Chicago study, all conducted within the past few years (Harry 1990; Miller and Bukolt 1990; Rensberger 1993), found that 1.0 to 1.5 percent of a given population will self-identify as gay or lesbian, and an additional 2 to 3 percent will self-identify as bisexual—substantially lower than Kinsey's figure of 10 percent, and Janus and Janus's figure of 7 percent, who in practice are exclusively or predominately homosexual.

We then add to this matrix the option of "passing." Whereas nearly all women, most African Americans and Asian Americans, and many indigenous Americans and Latinos are readily identifiable by their external appearance, most LGBs are not, and in the context of the disabilities discussed here, the optimal pragmatic solution might appear to the casual observer to be to "pass" for heterosexual in contexts in which disclosure of one's sexual orientation could provoke conflict. "Passing," in addition, can be justified to oneself on a ground often used early on by gay rights supporters, and still used when politically convenient today (Samar 1991): what one does in private, they argued, is one's own business and does not need to be the concern of anyone else (D'Emilio 1983; Marcus 1992). Sexuality being one's own business, many persons who are open with LGB friends and have reached the stage of "identity acceptance" (Cass 1984) may refuse to identify generally as LGBs or to involve themselves with the organized LGB community.

What is of interest, then, is to discover why, given all these barriers and the opportunity to escape them by "passing," anyone would choose to identify as a member of a sexual minority.

In this context, a brief look is warranted at the response to oppression among African Americans, a group most of whose members are unable to "pass." Although the forms of oppression faced by blacks differ in many ways from those faced by LGBs, blacks are the most similar to LGBs in having endured wide-ranging discrimination mandated, until the 1960s, by law. Taken together, these studies suggest a broad menu of potential responses, leaving much up to the individual and her or his circumstances.

Kardiner and Ovesey (1962), in their ground-breaking psychodynamic study of twenty-five black Americans (a number of whom had sought treatment for psychiatric disorders or difficulties), laid out evidence of a tremendous beating down of self-esteem and indeed of active self-hatred and self-destructiveness among blacks, with a variety of neurotic and pathological consequences. This is the result, the authors reported, not of inferior morals or values or an inability to adjust to stress on the part of blacks, but of the breadth and intensity of racial animosity of white society toward them and the *internalization* of that animosity.

This internalization did not appear to be confined, as in the Kardiner-Ovesey study, to black people who had active psychological problems. Clark and Clark (1947) found evidence of such effects in young black children in early studies in which a child was given a black doll and a white doll and asked to choose one to play with; most black children, like nearly all white children, chose to play with the white doll.

However, later black researchers have criticized these findings. Jenkins (1982), in particular, classifies these findings as one-dimensional and mechanistic, and notes that they fail to account for the effect of "humanistic" factors — actions taken based on a conscious direction adopted by the individual (to become a good baseball player or to go to law school, for instance)—on subsequent adjustment and behavior. Summarizing research from the 1970s, Jenkins finds that, although relatively negative *racial* images still could be found among African Americans, these often did not carry over into other aspects of self-assessment and self-esteem.

White (1984) looks to cultural bias in interpretation of black responses. He delineates what he calls an "Afro-American psychological perspective," which differs in significant respects from the European-based perspective of American psychology and which is essential to understanding the way black Americans respond to an oppressive dominant culture.

Both Jenkins and White also note the central role of the civil rights and Black Power movements of the 1960s in bringing to the fore a more positive self-image among many African Americans and reestablishing conscious connections with black African history and culture. As discussed later in this chapter, this led to a rise in levels of "black consciousness" in politics during the same period.

Thus evidence exists that internalization of a negative self-image because of membership in a despised group need not carry over into all aspects of the personality. Those centers of positive self-esteem within the individual, coupled with the presentation (however meager) of positive attitudes toward her group membership, can help her reorient her feelings about belonging to that group.

The Development of Group Self-Identification among Members
of Sexual Minorities

We have examined the elements of self-identification and why gay men, bisexuals, and lesbians might not self-identify, but have yet to answer *why* or *how* certain people acquire the psychological attributes of self-identification while others do not. The question of why and how—the question of identity formation—is essential with respect to LGBs.

Cass (1984), in her study pulling together the work of several other researchers, points out the fundamental fact that homosexual children grow up not only unaware that they are homosexual, not only often unaware until late in childhood of what homosexuality actually is, but *grow up believing that they are heterosexual.* Children are socialized into strictly bifurcated sex roles, with the expectation that when the time comes a boy will fall in love with a girl (and vice versa), they will marry, and they will have and raise children together.

This differs from the situation of black or female children. It is the case that there is no preexisting race or sex consciousness[13] in very young children; this awareness is inculcated, directly and indirectly, by adults and by older children.

The studies above show that young children, after becoming conscious of these differences, then often look to whites, or men, as the "reference" for what is best and tend to negate their own race or sex as a result. But once this consciousness of difference is established, black children grow up knowing that they are "black," and female children grow up knowing that they are "girls," with each over time learning the attitudes and behavior expected of them by society in these roles. Further, the development of Afrocentrism and feminism has offered a countervailing, positive black or female "reference." Homosexual and bisexual children[14] do become conscious of differences in sexual identity, and develop affects (usually negative) toward homosexuality, but all the while they believe, and are constantly reinforced in the belief, that they are heterosexual.

The discovery that one is attracted to others of the same sex, therefore, is a most profound shock to the psyche. It is just such a shock to the psyche, caused by some potent external event, that Cross (1971) and Downing and Roush (1985) cite as the keystone to the identity development of African Americans and feminists, respectively. In the absence of such an event, it is unlikely that the existing social order will be questioned or that the process of personal transformation will begin.

After the development of several different theories of identity formation, Cass (1984) devised a six-stage hypothesis, tested it, and found support, rather, for a four-stage process of development in gay people:

1. *Identity confusion.* The homosexual person, having expected to be heterosexual, faces the critical realization of not being what one has been trained to be all one's life. Here one asks oneself repeatedly whether one really is homosexual. At the point at which the answer seems to be affirmative, several options are open: denial and suppression of homosexual feelings, leading to other psychological difficulties; attempts to change to heterosexuality, at least on the surface; or suicide. Provided that none of these options are taken, or that none are deemed workable, an individual may proceed to the next stage.

2. *Identity tolerance.* In order to meet one's social, sexual, and emotional needs, one begins seeking out the company of other homosexuals. However, one has not at this point accepted oneself as homosexual, and what happens next depends on the extent to which one comes to view one's homosexuality in a negative or positive light, often depending largely on one's gay contacts and the reactions of the few trusted straight friends to whom one's secret is revealed. All during this stage, in most of one's life one continues to "pass" for heterosexual, and consciously so. If the assessment is negative, the individual is likely to keep to

limited encounters with the gay world when necessary and to maintain the heterosexual facade.

3. Identity acceptance. If, however, one's assessment of gay life is positive, and particularly if straight confidants are supportive, one is likely to accept one's sexuality and immerse oneself more into gay life, developing a network of gay friends and the firm sense that one "belongs" in the gay community. One further discloses one's sexuality selectively to friends and family members. However, at this stage, one still feels it prudent to "pass" and fit in with the heterosexual majority, and to avoid confrontation over the issue of homosexuality; there remains the notion that being gay is less good than being straight, but that one might as well be happy with what one is. As will be seen later in this chapter, this is roughly the degree of development that characterized the early "homophile" movement, and that characterizes certain assimilationist gays today (for example, see Bauman 1986).

4. Identity pride and synthesis. There may, however, develop a fierce loyalty to one's gay friends and community that outweighs and nullifies these ideas. At this point, negative feelings develop toward antigay heterosexuals (if not all heterosexuals), along with a sense that "straight" society—not one's sexuality and not the LGB community—is the problem. These changes are consonant with and essential to the development of "group consciousness," as will be discussed later in this chapter. The gay person comes out to virtually everyone, often at first in a confrontational way to force others to face and deal with their negative feelings. As time goes on, if reactions are not overwhelmingly negative, disclosure and its ramifications become a nonissue and hard feelings toward straight society soften, as one becomes fully comfortable with one's identity regardless of the reaction of others. The identity so jarred by the discovery of youth becomes fully, happily integrated again.

Cross (1971) and Downing and Roush (1985) present somewhat different patterns for blacks and feminists, but they bear some small resemblance to the four stages Cass presents for lesbians and gay men. At baseline, absent parental guidance to the contrary, blacks and women grow up accepting the existing social order, the authors hypothesize, placing these people at the level equivalent to Cass's "identity acceptance" stage, with the obvious exception of having neither the need nor the ability to hide their sex or race.

Development proceeds from this baseline condition. In the first stage, one is catalyzed by some event or events that anger one, making one question the social order, and resulting in "polar affect," negative feelings toward the "oppressor" group. In the second, one withdraws from contact with members of the "oppressor" group and immerses oneself with other women or blacks, developing a sense of pride and affirmation, which leads eventually to more flexible perceptions and lessens the blanket condemnation of men or whites. In the third, one's new, positive self-image is internalized, and one finds oneself transcending traditional ideas of race and sex roles, adopting a pluralistic perspective. Finally, one makes a commitment to meaningful action on behalf of the nonsexist/nonracist view of the world one has adopted.

These studies inform each other. Cass's "identity acceptance" stage is very similar to the situation in which blacks and women find themselves in the two studies cited above just before the catalyzing event that causes the questioning of society and results in group consciousness. In other words, it may be that, having gone through the process of establishing gay identity, one must then go through a second process, similar to that described in the studies above, before the flowering of gay consciousness (compressed by Cass into her "identity pride and synthesis" stage) can occur.

The catalyzing event will vary from person to person. In the case of an LGB person, it may be the positive affirmation of attending a Gay Pride Day for the first time, or it may be the negative of the queer-bashing of a friend, the slow death of another from AIDS, or the loss of one's own job.

At the outset I suggested that it did not appear to be in the interest of homosexuals and bisexuals to identify themselves as such in public and on survey forms, other than sex surveys completed in absolute privacy. This was because of the legal and social disabilities imposed on them—*prima facie* evidence for the movement's claim that homosexuals are an oppressed minority—and their ability to avoid these disabilities by "passing" for heterosexual. However, it appears that environmental effects can catalyze "closeted" people into reorienting their personal attitudes toward their own sexuality and toward society's treatment of their kindred spirits, in a way that, as will be seen later in this chapter, is equal or equivalent to the development of group consciousness in the political context. If this is the case, we can expect that self-identified LGBs, though small in number, will have the strongest sense of identification with the group.

Oppressed Groups and Electoral Politics

The question that then arises is *why* groups long excluded from positions of power, such as African Americans, Latinos, and, in our case, open LGBs, should accept the mores of the dominant political culture and play by its rules rather than becoming alienated from it. Why should previously excluded groups look to participation in the "mainstream" political process, rather than separatism or rebellion—be it violent or not—as a means of achieving relief from their isolation and suffering?

This question is especially pertinent in the American electoral system, with its single-member districts, plurality voting, and the duopoly of the Democratic and Republican parties; American general elections (though not always the party nominating processes) emphasize the need to compromise and reach toward the center, wherever it may lie. In this context, what is the allure of voting to a member of a marginalized and oppressed group? What makes voting worthwhile, as opposed to recusing oneself from the electoral process or confronting it by other means?

The literature offers three answers. First is the divorcement of "diffuse" support for the nation and its form of government, which is high and relatively stable, from "specific" support for policies and politicians (Easton 1965; Abramowitz in Almond and Verba 1980). Second is the "participatory" nature of American political culture and the value that culture places on voting as an affirmation of the form of government and democratic ideals (Almond and Verba 1963; Elazar 1965; Abramowitz in Almond and Verba 1980). Third is the usefulness of voting to achieve symbolic goals even when the connection between voting and substantive policy change is tenuous (Edelman 1964; Browning et al. 1990).

One answer is supplied by Easton's model (1965) separating "diffuse" support for the nation and its forms and institutions of government from "specific" support for policies and public officials. At the time he wrote, both "diffuse" and "specific" support for the United States government were quite high. In the succeeding years of Vietnam, Watergate, economic troubles, and social unrest, "specific" support for government plummeted (Abramowitz in Almond and Verba 1980), although, as Abramowitz points out, general questions on "specific" support appear to elicit responses based on evaluations of the president and executive branch. In the 1980s, "specific" support climbed again during the height of the Reagan administration, though not to anywhere near its levels in the early 1960s, then fell again as the 1980s came to a close. In the meantime, levels of support for both the nation and the basic system of government remained remarkably high; the pessimism about politics, politicians, and policies did not translate into an erosion of confidence in our constitutional framework.

Similar results, interestingly, were obtained across racial groups. This may not be difficult to understand. Even members of disinherited groups are raised on the promises of the Declaration of Independence, and are taught American history filled with examples of groups overcoming poverty, hardship, oppression, and degradation, if only by degrees and only after a long, hard struggle against entrenched power, through appeals to underlying fairness and the creative use of a flexible Constitution. The successful transmission of participatory and egalitarian ideals to members of minority groups who had access to the ballot is attested to empirically as far back as *The American Voter* and *The Civic Culture,* a landmark five-nation study by Almond and Verba (1963).

In *The Civic Culture,* Almond and Verba enunciated the concept of a civic or political "culture," a set of attitudes toward the political system and its component parts, and toward one's own personal participation in the system. This set of attitudes is generally shared by and characteristic of a particular political community or subdivision. The notion of a shared civic culture goes back at least to Plato; Almond and Verba rework and operationalize that notion for the present day.

The authors characterize the United States as having predominately a "participatory" political culture as opposed to a "subject" culture. In the latter, the citizen is aware of the basic political structures and functions of her society, and has opinions about its legitimacy, but is concerned with watching and evaluating only what it does and not *how* it does so, and is not concerned to participate herself. In the former, the citizen has a direct interest in the doings of the various players—elected officials, interest groups, parties, and the like—and feels that she should be a participant in the process herself. Voting, therefore, is seen as especially important as one effective means, and for many in their American sample the only effective means, of influencing the actions of government "elites."

Elazar (1965) expands on this and lays out a (largely impressionistic) schema of intranational political cultures, which are discussed, and applied to an analysis of gay and lesbian voting in three states, in chapter 4. It is notable, however, that in the Southern states, which Elazar classified as having "traditional" political cultures in which governing was expected to be left to elites (see chapter 4), black citizens were expected to refrain from participation in affairs of state and faced serious extralegal consequences, sometimes inflicted by law enforcement officials, if they violated this unofficial code. As a result, Almond and Verba found among Southern blacks the only significant remnant of a "subject" political culture in the United States. As Elazar's book was in press, the Voting Rights Act of 1965 was being passed; it effectively removed this barrier. Within a few years, Southern blacks were voting at rates not too far below those of whites—higher rates, indeed, when one controlled for socioeconomic status (Verba and Nie 1972)—and Southern blacks classifiable as holding "subject" rather than "participatory" political mores nearly vanished within a few years (Abramowitz in Almond and Verba 1980). The mere accessibility of the ballot, combined with acceptance of the political mores of the dominant culture with respect to the importance of voting, led to significant levels of voting among citizens who previously were mere "subjects" of the system.

The question arises in this context: Why should any group turn to the ballot box rather than to some other means of effecting its ends, especially when the connection between mass voting and the substantive decisions of elected and appointed officials is attenuated at best? The answer lies less in any substantive nexus between voting and specific public policy than in the symbolic effects of (1) affirming the political system and one's allegiance to it— what Almond and Verba (1963) and Easton (1965) call "allegiant" behavior, (2) helping to gain an audience for one's concerns with those in power, and (3) serving as a political counterweight to the demands of opposing "reference" groups—in other words, showing the official that a political benefit accrues from supporting one's own group and a political cost accrues from supporting the "reference" group.

A long-deprived group appears to act cohesively and mobilize politically for both the redress of specific grievances—that is, to accomplish specific *substantive* policy goals—and for the *symbolic* purpose of placing members of the group in positions of authority, as a means of increasing the self-esteem and "internal political efficacy" (Shingles 1981) of individuals in the group, and making the rest of the community take notice of them and *deal with them with respect* (Edelman 1964). In fact, both "substantive" and "symbolic" goals have been seen to be important to enhancing the social standing and economic condition of racial minorities. Perry writes:

Some observers seem to feel that symbolic benefits are not important. Symbolic benefits that confer an aura of legitimacy, respect, and equal standing to a previously disadvantaged, discriminated against, and subordinate group are very important. (Perry in Browning et al. 1990, 149)

Edelman identifies three kinds of "symbolic" uses of politics. One is the use of politics as a means of "object appraisal," the determination of where one stands with those in power or those seeking power; for example, the use of a political party's platform to appeal to certain groups of voters, rather than as a crystal ball in which the future policies of government may be seen should the party win. Two others relate to more deep-seated psychological causes: the use of politics for the externalization of unresolved inner problems, and, more important to us, the use of politics as a means of social adjustment. In this last context, the mere act of making demands on the system and causing them to be heard makes the system recognize and legitimize the person(s) making the demands, and whether the individual's or group's aims have any substantive chance of being adopted is of relatively small importance, as recognition and legitimation are the principal symbolic goals. The symbolic goal of "object appraisal" also is served when the individual or group, having made the demand, can determine a public official's positive, negative, or neutral orientation toward itself.

Because members of racial minorities have both substantive and symbolic goals, the question is whether voting is a satisfactory means of obtaining either or both kinds of goals. Edelman (1964, 27–28) notes that public officials themselves anecdotally see little relation between the public's votes and their own. Fenno (1978) and Kingdon (1989), studying members of Congress, modify this understanding by distinguishing issues based on their salience within a member's district and their relative complexity, and noting the degree to which members tailor their voting behavior to avoid controversy. They find, then, that some nexus exists between the electorate's votes and the member's, although these cases appear largely to be restricted to high-salience, "easy" issues used by voters for the purpose of "object appraisal."

The Problem of Developing Group Consciousness

Having established that previously disinherited groups with access to the ballot can see its use as advantageous to achieving symbolic and substantive political goals, we now turn our attention to whether self-identified LGBs specifically are likely to do so in any numbers, and whether they are likely to base their votes at least in part on a perception of oppression or disadvantage because of their sexual identity.

This raises again issues related to the studies of identity formation discussed earlier (Cross 1971; Cass 1984; Downing and Roush 1985). These teach us that a woman, an African American, or an LGB person must go through a process of shedding society's predominant ideas about herself and her place in society before becoming fully committed to her identity and asserting political demands based on that identity. A lesbian or gay man, Cass tells us, in the stage of "identity pride and synthesis," develops the willingness to identify him- or herself as LGB even in situations in which the revelation is likely to provoke confrontation. It appears then that in the case of LGBs, acceptance of one's identity is insufficient to prompt one to behave politically as an open LGB. Public self-identification likely occurs only once one has developed the psychological qualities constituting *group consciousness.*

Browning et al. (1990), studying political incorporation of racial minorities in American cities, examined the composition of cross-group coalitions, be they two sets of minorities (black-Latino coalitions, for example) or coalitions between a minority group and some segment of the dominant majority (usually white). Their model posits that political *mobilization* of a group was essential to its success in building electoral coalitions with other groups, winning office, and enacting favorable policies.

Previous research (Verba and Nie 1972; Miller et al. 1981; Shingles 1981) suggests that among these groups, the force that mobilizes them is *group consciousness,* as distinct from group identification. Miller et al. (1981) define group consciousness as "identification with a group *and* a political awareness or ideology regarding the group's relative position in society along with a commitment to collective action aimed at realizing the group's interests."

Group consciousness has not been shown to exercise an independent effect on group members' attitudes or their consistency with one another, or on members' cohesion in voting or other political behavior. However, group consciousness appears to be a central element in motivating individuals to act politically, and to do so through certain specific channels they deem effective. In the case at hand, then, group consciousness, though it would have no discernible effect on *how* they voted, may induce LGBs *to* vote.

The empirical study of group consciousness as an essential element in group political mobilization goes back to Verba and Nie's seminal discussion (1972, 149–73).[15] These researchers operationalized black consciousness rather simply, using as their indicator whether, and how many times, a black respondent mentioned race or racial issues as a problem in the country in an open-ended question. They found that the 64 percent of African Americans who did so— those conscious "of race as a problem or a basis of conflict" (158)—were slightly more likely to vote or otherwise participate politically than were whites, and that after controlling for socioeconomic status, the "group-conscious" blacks were very considerably more likely to participate than similarly situated whites (159–63).

Since the Verba-Nie study, the meaning of the term and the indicators used to measure the concept have been sharpened considerably. Group consciousness research in this country principally has focused on African Americans, but a few studies also have been done on the factors leading to group consciousness among women, the poor, different age groups, and even within dominant groups such as whites and businesspeople.

Miller et al. (1981) identify four elements constituting group consciousness. The first is *group identification,* as they have defined it above.

The second is a strong positive feeling for one's own group and a similar negative feeling for an opposing "reference" group, what the authors call *polar affect.* This concept usually has been measured with relative placement of these groups on a "feeling thermometer," with a rating of 100 representing the "warmest" possible feeling toward the group, 0 representing the "coolest," and 50 representing absolute neutrality. In certain instances the "opposing" groups have been easy to identify: whites and blacks, businessmen and workers, and so forth. In others, identifying the appropriate "reference group" is difficult; indeed, it may be argued that the mere existence of relative antipathy between the identifiers of two groups can be equated with the existence of a "reference group" relationship.

The third is a sense of discontent with the relative power of one's own group compared to the opposing "reference group," called *polar power.* This concept can be measured with questions relating to relative group influence in society, or questions that require the respondent to place the two groups on a continuum of relative power. A dominant group that feels its position threatened by a subordinate group would score high on a measure of polar power, just as would a group with a strong feeling of oppression.

The final element, *system blame,* we may call a sense of societal fault, a belief that the power structure, rather than individual behavior, is responsible for the relative conditions of one's own group and the reference group. This has been a particularly important factor studied in the group consciousness literature: the extent to which African Americans or working-class people come to believe that, whether they work hard and follow the rules or not, barriers to their progress remain because of reference group prejudice or perceptions of threat; the extent to which women come to believe that the home is not the place for them, or that working women come to perceive "glass ceilings." The direct relevance of this concept to LGBs will be assessed later in this chapter.

Shingles (1981) adds to the equation a fifth element, which he calls *internal political efficacy.* Gamson (1968) posited that the optimal combination of elements to induce political participation consisted of high political efficacy (a strong belief that one's political participation can make a difference) and low political trust. Shingles distinguishes between "external efficacy," the degree to which environmental or systemic factors impede the individual in achieving political goals, and "internal efficacy," the degree to which the individual believes in her or his own abilities, given a relatively level playing field, to score points.

An important finding of group consciousness research has been the significant correlation of group consciousness with education level, age (younger people being more "conscious"), partisanship, and degree of political interest. Tate (1991) also found that, among older and less-educated blacks, membership in a politically active black church was an important inducement to group consciousness.

There is no way to measure these additional elements of LGB consciousness in any of the existing political data bases that allow LGB self-identification. However, if in fact LGB self-identification is concomitant with the development of LGB group consciousness, we can expect to find that the self-identified LGBs in these samples will display the same correlates with group consciousness found among African Americans and feminist women. That is, at the minimum we should find that self-identified LGBs are significantly younger, more educated, and more partisan than the rest of the population.

Electoral Cohesion and the Several LGB Movements

It appears obvious that, if a group is to have a strong influence as a group on elections, it should be relatively united around a set of candidates, principles, or specific substantive or symbolic goals. We return to the point raised by Campbell et al. (1960) that group distinctiveness in voting is in large part a function of the transmission of group political norms, which in turn is a function of the relative unity of the group's political leaders. How united are self-identified and, we presume, group-conscious LGBs likely to be, and, therefore, how distinctive is a "lavender vote" likely to be?

Having chosen the channel of electoral activity (alone or with other channels of political activity), a political leader within a group usually is obliged to work with others. The extent to which those others, and the leader her- or himself, are willing to put aside personal and philosophical differences to achieve the common end is essential to success. This potentially is very problematic in the LGB community, which has had to be built up from scratch within the last few decades and into which its members are not socialized until adulthood, if at all.

Within the LGB community, there have been a succession of practical and theoretical responses to their social condition in the period since World War II. These are discussed in especially good detail by Marotta (1981) and Adam

(1987), and also by D'Emilio (1983), Timmons (1990), and Marcus (1992). A brief review of these movements will guide us in determining the likely extent of group cohesion and distinctiveness in voting.

The Homophile Movement

As noted before, the first postwar organization to promote fairer treatment for homosexuals in the United States was the Mattachine Society, founded in Los Angeles in 1950 by longtime Communist Party activist Harry Hay, his then lover, fashion designer Rudi Gernreich, and a small number of others (including Chuck Rowland, mentioned earlier). The name Mattachine came from medieval court entertainers who hid behind masks to speak unpleasant truths,[16] which gives the reader a clue to the basic line taken by the first gay movement, known as the "homophile" movement. As noted earlier, Hay and the early Mattachine founders got too far ahead of their members and resigned under pressure in 1953; it is principally the more conservative LGBs who carried on the movement that I discuss here.

Facing absolute societal hostility toward homosexuality, the homophile movement sought to stress that, except for their sexual orientation, LGB people were "just like everybody else." The term "homophile" was adopted in preference to "homosexual" in order to counteract the prevailing stereotype that LGB people were obsessed with sex. Much was made of the idea that people did not choose to be gay or bisexual, and therefore should not be punished for it—agreeing implicitly with the notion that heterosexuality was "better" than homosexuality. The argument also was advanced that the sexual acts of consenting adults in private had no bearing on any other facet of their lives, that homosexuality in essence was private behavior and should be beyond the questioning of the state.

The question "Why are we gay?" also received considerable attention in homophile discussion groups and conferences. Considerable controversy arose in 1965 when Washington activist Frank Kameny proposed that a convention of the East Coast Homophile Organizations (ECHO) adopt a formal statement that homosexuality was not a mental illness, as it was then generally considered by medical professionals.[17]

The principal sociopolitical aims of the homophile movement, then, were (1) to desexualize the issue of homosexuality, (2) to make the issue one of privacy, (3) to convince the public that gays could not help how they were and were simply trying to make the best of their situation, and (4) to further convince the public of their essential sameness. The recipe was, through public education and occasional protest and lobbying, to convince straight society to remove the barriers to assimilation. There was, at this point, no talk of "gay pride," much less of "gay power," and no sense of common cause with other groups facing social oppression. There was merely a desire for an end to the constant threat of police raids and beatings, entrapment, psychiatric commitment, official blackmail, and other uses of the blunt force of the state to persecute those who loved others of the same sex.

The Gay Liberation Movement

The counterculture ethic that arose in the mid- to late 1960s, however, introduced a drastically different point of view, which was crystallized in the Stonewall riots. The new thinking, encouraged by the militancy of the African American civil rights movement and the budding feminist movement, held not only that LGB people were as good and moral as straight people, but that the dominant culture had much to learn from the gay subculture and, indeed, that the dominant culture had become thoroughly corrupted and needed to be altered in radical ways.

The Gay Liberationist vision took much from the Black Power movement of the late sixties. Like Black Power, and the similar Black Consciousness movement then arising in South Africa, Gay Liberation sought to define the good and build up a positive sense of humanity in LGB people in a context independent of the dominant culture's values and mores. Indeed, the ultimate goal of Gay Liberation was subversive of the dominant culture: it sought to break down the dominant mores of sexual monogamy, strict gender roles, and the postwar ideal of the nuclear family with the father at its head (Tobin and Wicker 1975; Jay and Young 1977; Richmond and Noguera 1979).

Marotta (1981) and Adam (1987) divide the early Gay Liberationists into two principal groups, "political" and "cultural" reformers. The political reformers, according to Marotta, sought to achieve LGB freedom through changes in the law and social institutions, particularly the media. They sought redress through litigation, lobbying, electoral politics, and protest demonstrations with specific political aims, and therefore wished to keep the debate focused squarely on equal rights and ending stereotypes without diversion into "side issues."

The cultural reformers, on the other hand, sought through social activities and public visibility demonstrations without (necessarily) specific political purposes to help skittish LGB people become comfortable with, and proud of, what they were. They viewed personal liberation as the fundamental goal, eschewed political game playing, and stressed making all LGB people welcome, accepted, and visible, including drag queens, leatherfolk, prostitutes, and others excluded from the homophile movement.

The basic tension was between what we may call putting institutional change first and putting personal transformation first. This resulted in constant bickering between the factions in the early days of Gay Liberation, but eventually a sort of "cross-fertilization" allowed each side in the dispute to adapt many means of the other for its own ends and to exist in an acceptable *modus vivendi*.

Lesbian Feminism

However, the women's movement at first made little impact on the gay and bisexual men active in Gay Liberation. Lesbians and bisexual women complained of having to remind the men that they were there, and that they were not especially concerned with police entrapment (one issue that was stressed by the gay movement) but were concerned about achieving equal opportunities, financial independence, and an end to violence against women (issues that were not then stressed by the movement). They were underrepresented in decision making and, it was claimed, found the men often assuming that they would make the coffee and put out refreshments at meetings (Marotta 1981). The suspicion arose among some women that the men were interested solely in gaining access to the privileges of male heterosexuals and were perfectly willing to ignore their concerns as women.

At the same time, lesbians who had found shelter in the women's movement, and who had had a disproportionate role in running it, were beginning to be run out of it. Betty Friedan, whose book *The Feminine Mystique* made her the founding mother of modern American feminism, decried lesbians as "a lavender menace" who threatened the credibility of the movement, and led a 1970 purge of lesbians from the board of the New York chapter of NOW. Kate Millett's book *Sexual Politics,* published the same year, was well received until Millett publicly said that she was bisexual, at which time her usefulness to the movement was deemed ended.[18]

As feminist theory and consciousness-raising developed in the early 1970s, many lesbians deemed it necessary to curtail or break off joint efforts with men and to form separate groups that would address their concerns both as lesbians and more generally as women. Thus was born lesbian feminism as a separate and important development (see especially Phelan 1989).

The influence of lesbian feminist thought and practice often is underestimated. All feminist thinkers sought means to undo the cultural conditioning that kept women in psychological as well as material subjection. One of the distinctive contributions of lesbian feminism has been its experimentation with new "woman-identified," nonhierarchical forms of social interaction in which an egalitarian process is emphasized. The most prominent example is consensus decision making, ditching *Robert's Rules of Order* and other formal regulations and making no final decision until firm consensus has been reached after thorough (often very lengthy) discussion. Another experiment, with varying degrees of success, was "leaderless" organization, in which tasks are assigned by lot or rotation and no one person or body of persons speaks for the group on a permanent basis (Marotta 1981).

A rift developed in the early 1970s between the lesbian feminists, who came to predominate in the lesbian movement and identified in particular with feminism, and those lesbians who remained in Gay Liberation and identified principally with the gay rights movement. The latter initially were denounced and ostracized by the former as being "male-identified." This rift, although far less intense as lesbian feminists rejoined common efforts with gay men, seems to remain important in perceptions of differences and in some issue priorities between lesbians identified with the feminist movement as opposed to those identified with the LGB rights movement but not with feminism (Kristiansen 1990).

Lesbian separatism, another strand of feminist thought, developed when certain lesbian feminists came to believe, indeed, that the problem was not with the aggressive, violent, domineering mores of men and the culture they had constructed, but with men themselves: men were biologically incapable of being anything other than aggressive, violent, and domineering, and no amount of feminist consciousness-raising of men was going to do any good. Even were it theoretically possible, men would never give up their privileged position. It was necessary, therefore, for women to completely separate from men and have no interaction with them at all, to build separate all-woman communities where they would be safe and self-sufficient. There remain a small but committed number of lesbian separatists.

Responses to the New Right and AIDS

The divisions in the movement resulting from the split between Gay Liberationists and lesbian feminists began to heal as united efforts to achieve national change began to be mounted. The National Gay Task Force was founded in New York in 1973 to try to provide a united front for the "political" arm of the movement; early on its practice was to have two co-executive directors, one a woman, one a man (Marcus 1992). The NGTF—

later renamed the National Gay and Lesbian Task Force (NGLTF)—together with other movement groups helped score an early victory when the American Psychiatric Association voted in 1973 to remove homosexuality from its list of mental and emotional disorders. At the same time, gay and lesbian bookstores and newspapers appeared in major cities and on some college campuses, usually as joint efforts between lesbians and gay men. (Bisexuals, at the time, were given little recognition or acceptance within the movement.)

This trend toward healing and reunion within the movement took on steam in the late 1970s and early 1980s because of two related developments. The first was the rise of the "New Right" movement, much of which became what today is called the Religious Right or Christian conservatism, which included an initial spurt of antigay activity. The second was the onset of the AIDS epidemic and the government's seemingly feeble response to it, largely related to fear of offending President Reagan's "New Right" constituency (Pressman 1983).

The first notable antigay electoral campaign, a referendum drive to repeal a recently passed gay rights ordinance in greater Miami, Florida, in the spring of 1977, was led to victory by singer and orange juice spokeswoman Anita Bryant. Copycat measures were passed within months in Wichita, Kansas, and St. Paul, Minnesota. A repeal measure also reached the ballot in Seattle, Washington, but failed there. In each case, the impetus to overturn the gay rights laws came mainly from fundamentalist Christian churches (Adam 1987).

Most notably, California's statewide ballot in November 1978 included an initiative measure to mandate the firing of homosexual schoolteachers (Zonana 1978). Led by state senator John Briggs, whose base of support again was fundamentalist churches, the measure failed after leading in the polls during most of the year, after LGB organizers won over Ronald Reagan and Gerald Ford, among others. The statewide LGB effort to raise funds to fight the "Briggs Initiative" was cochaired by Sally Gearhart, an openly lesbian college professor and activist, and San Francisco Supervisor Harvey Milk, the state's first (and, at the time, only) openly gay elected official (Shilts 1982; Epstein 1986).

The "New Right" gained a national foothold when it aided in the election of Ronald Reagan and the Republican takeover of the Senate in 1980. The following year, the first report of a strange "gay cancer" appeared in the *New York Times*. The emerging unity among lesbians and gay men in response to the antigay backlash of the late 1970s was redoubled when large numbers of gay and bisexual men began to succumb to acquired immune deficiency syndrome.

Initial efforts to educate the public to avoid behavior associated with AIDS were stymied by strong reluctance among social conservatives to have the government advertise ways to make gay sex and intravenous drug use "safer"; they believed such campaigns would signal approval of and encouragement to engage in what they deemed immoral behavior. In addition, a low priority was attached to research into the causes and possible cures or treatments for the syndrome until it started to appear in the "general population"—that is, beyond the identified "high risk" groups of Haitians, intravenous drug users, and gay and bisexual men (Shilts 1987). Indeed, some New Right leaders opined that AIDS was just desserts for immorality; the Reverend Jerry Falwell, founder of the Moral Majority movement, called AIDS "God's punishment on homosexuals."

Faced with a national administration seemingly unwilling to halt the spread of the disease within the gay community, numerous local efforts to provide education, treatment, and counseling sprung up, beginning with Gay Men's Health Crisis, founded in playwright Larry Kramer's living room in New York (Shilts 1987). In turn, the national LGB organizations born since Stonewall made government action on AIDS a significant priority.

By the mid-1980s there were several national movement organizations in place. In addition to the NGLTF, the Human Rights Campaign Fund was formed in 1979 to raise money for progay congressional candidates and, later, to engage in professional and grassroots lobbying (it absorbed the Gay Rights National Lobby in 1985). Four other groups centered on litigation: the Lambda Legal Defense and Education Fund, the National Center for Lesbian Rights, Gay and Lesbian Advocates and Defenders, and the ACLU's Gay and Lesbian Rights Project. The AIDS Action Council, to lobby on AIDS issues specifically, was formed at the national level in 1985. Shortly thereafter came the first chapter of the Gay and Lesbian Alliance Against Defamation (GLAAD), to concentrate on improving the portrayal of LGBs in the mass media. The Gay and Lesbian Victory Fund, which raises money for openly LGB candidates for public office, was formed later, in 1991.

ACT UP and the Rise of the "Queers"

However, by the end of the Reagan administration, after what was seen as several years of government neglect of AIDS largely on political grounds (Dejowski 1989), patience with the "insider" methods of the national groups was wearing out among those whose friends and lovers were dying, or who were HIV-positive themselves. In 1987 Larry Kramer—who had been expelled from GMHC, the organization he cofounded, on the ground that his angry, belligerent style was alienating potential benefactors and damaging the group internally—once again organized a group of New Yorkers into the first chapter of the AIDS Coalition To Unleash Power, far better known by its acronym, ACT UP.

A mass action group that quickly spread to other cities, ACT UP used (mostly) nonviolent confrontation tactics, such as "sit-ins" and "die-ins" at the offices of government agencies, pharmaceutical companies, and others, to force expedited testing and approval of AIDS treatments and to lower the often exorbitant cost charged for those treatments by drug companies (Crossen 1989).

ACT UP's structure was quite loose. Mass meetings were held weekly. Anyone attending could propose a direct action, which the group would discuss and endorse by consensus. A number of committees were set up, but all were deemed responsible to the total membership rather than to officers. There were informal ties with chapters in other cities, but no means were exercised to control the use of the ACT UP name, either externally or internally. This led eventually to controversial episodes and the splintering or dissolution of several ACT UP chapters.[19]

This coincided with a new wave of antigay activism in Congress and the states. In 1989 Senator Jesse Helms of North Carolina succeeded in his effort to place content restrictions on artists subsidized by the National Endowment for the Arts, specifically ruling out government funding for "homoerotic art." Four performance artists had their NEA funding cut off in 1990 for violating the rules, among them a lesbian and two gay men who treated of their sexuality in their art. Also in 1989, as noted previously, Health and Human Services Secretary Louis Sullivan suppressed an HHS report that one-third of teenage suicides and suicide attempts in the United States were related to an inability to deal with one's sexual orientation, after Representative William Dannemyer of California objected that the report would promote acceptance of homosexuality.

However, the initial successes of ACT UP in some of its battles with the government and business (most notably the "fast tracking" of AIDS treatment approval by the Food and Drug Administration) and in channeling the energies of many LGBs sparked a new LGB militancy at the end of the 1980s. Again in New York, a new direct action group arose, organized along the lines of ACT UP but this time to promote "queer visibility," and called itself Queer Nation. Again, Queer Nation chapters—connected to the mother group in spirit only—popped up in major urban areas around the country. Chanting their trademark slogan, "We're here! We're queer! Get used to it!" members conducted "queer-ins" in shopping malls, government offices, and public gathering places, as well as outside meetings of antigay organizations and the offices of antigay businesses and officials (Browning 1993).

Like ACT UP, the "queer movement" was distinguished by a rejection of the "insider" or "mainstream" tactics of the national lobbying and litigation groups. It was felt that efforts to integrate LGBs into mainstream American life and to convince their fellow citizens of their essential sameness had been ineffective, especially with respect to people with AIDS, and also served to deny the right of less conventional LGBs to look, dress, speak, act, and be different from the heterosexual norm. Thus, like the lesbian feminist movement, the queer movement eschewed hierarchy and structure. It also encouraged visible action to shock heterosexual society into "getting used to it."

The adoption of the word "queer" by the movement was deliberate. In prior years the LGB movement had converted the pink triangle, the Nazis' symbol for homosexuals in the concentration camps, into a symbol of pride. The queer activists appropriated one of the most provocative insults hurled at LGBs of both sexes to neutralize painful memories of rejection and abuse and imbue the term with a positive connotation for LGB people. At the same time, the happy adoption of the insulting and abusive term for themselves would shock heterosexuals into paying attention. Connected to this was the all-inclusive nature of "queer." Used by heterosexuals to encompass nonviolent sexual outcasts of all kinds, including transvestites and transsexuals, "queer" was thought to embrace all such persons as the word "gay" once did but could no longer. Finally, given the sense of "queer" meaning anything odd or different, its use was meant to embrace and promote the acceptance of oddities and differences (Signorile 1993; Browning 1993).

The New Assimilationists

At the same time as the queer movement took off, so did a reaction against its "in-your-face" confrontationalism, its celebration of sexual freedom and glaring difference, and its embrace of liberal or left-wing politics. A small but increasingly vocal group of LGB conservatives and libertarians argued that LGBs must live in the "real world," that the dominant culture had much to recommend it in preference to the "gay subculture," and that LGBs had to accept much of the dominant culture against which many of their leaders had been rebelling if the dominant culture was to accept them as equals. These voices ranged from Camille Paglia, a lesbian scholar who critiqued feminism from a libertarian perspective in provocative language and held much LGB scholarship to be second-rate, to Marvin Liebman, a longtime "movement conservative" ally of William F. Buckley who came out as gay in 1990.

Expositions of this "new assimilationist" viewpoint are found in the work of Kirk and Madsen (1989) and Bawer (1993). Kirk and Madsen argued that gay "misbehavior," as they viewed it, was largely responsible for the failure of the LGB movement to reach the hearts of middle America. They advocated both a national advertising campaign to stress the similarities between LGBs and the rest of society, and changes in the personal lifestyles of LGBs (especially men) immersed in the urban subculture to better fit in with the societal norm.

Bawer later argued that LGB people living next door in the suburbs who looked, sounded, and acted just like their straight neighbors were far more psychologically threatening to heterosexual society than are flamboyant folk in feathers or leathers living in distant big cities who are seen by heterosexuals only on television in Gay Pride parades. Therefore, Bawer asserted, it was assimilated LGBs living and working and playing among their neighbors who would do the most difficult, and at length the most successful, work in breaking down ancient hatreds and fears and bringing about real equality.

There was a dramatic shift in philosophy and strategy following Stonewall from the essential assimilationism of the early homophile movement to the flamboyant radicalism of Gay Liberation, which asked for nobody's permission to be whatever one was and demanded equality. In like manner, the assumptions of Gay Liberation were flipped on their head by the withdrawal of the lesbian feminists, who demanded a more fundamental challenge to what they saw as a fundamentally oppressive culture, not merely with respect to sexuality.

The community eventually grew back together in response to the AIDS crisis and political challenges from the right. Yet some of the old conflicts reemerged in new guises, especially that between the militant street activists of the late 1980s and early 1990s and the new assimilationists whose response it engendered. Between these poles were numerous national, state, and local LGB political organizations seeking to hold the movement (and, sometimes, themselves) together and change the country's mind and heart at the same time.

Nine Hypotheses

At this point we can draw this long discussion together in the form of nine hypotheses, the questions to be answered to the extent possible with the empirical exit poll data in the succeeding chapters.

In doing this, I must note again the inherent disadvantages of the absence of empirical data on LGBs up to now. First, there is no group of nonvoters who self-identify as LGBs against whom one can compare those self-identifiers who do choose to vote. Second, as noted throughout, there is no way to compare "closeted" homosexuals and bisexuals with self-identified LGBs with respect to their political attitudes or voting behavior, and our demographic information about people in the closet is sketchy at best.

With these caveats in mind, here are the hypotheses upon which I shall base the empirical tests:

Hypothesis 1: Rate of Identification

Lesbians and gay men will self-identify in political surveys at rates equivalent to those found in previous random-sample research, about 1.0 to 1.5 percent of the population. When bisexuals are included, the share of self-identifiers will increase by an additional 2 to 3 percent.

Hypothesis 2: Demographic Characteristics

LGBs who do self-identify will be possessed of the equivalent of "group consciousness." Therefore, the demographic correlates of group conscious-ness found among women and African Americans—youth, high educa-tion levels, and strong partisanship—should be disproportionately great among self-identified LGBs. Also, given the results of prior sex surveys, men may significantly outnumber women among self-identifiers.

Hypothesis 3: Political Attitudes

The general political orientation of LGB voters will be liberal or leftist and Democratic, in keeping with the pattern found among African Americans, feminists, and non-Cuban Latinos, and will be highly distinc-tive from that of non-LGB identifiers.

Hypothesis 4: Gender and Feminism

Lesbians and bisexual women, whether feminists or not, will be more opposed to the use of force in politics, and therefore will be more likely to vote for Democrats than are gay and bisexual men. In addition, lesbian feminists will hold different issue priorities from LGB men and women who do not identify with feminism, and thus are far more likely to hold liberal positions on abortion and other feminist issues; they will be more inclined to vote for Democrats than will other women.

Hypothesis 5: Voting Blocs within the Community

Given the divergent concepts of group identity among LGBs, and their differing notions of what the goals of the LGB movement should be and the best means for achieving them, LGB voters will not be monolithic; although the large majority will vote for Democrats, significant minorities will support Republicans or leftist third candidates.

Hypothesis 6: The "Sexuality Gap"

LGB voting will be sufficiently distinctive as to have an independent effect on vote choice after controlling for attitudes, partisanship, incumbency, and demographic factors significantly correlated with LGB self-identification. Thus, there will be an authentic "sexuality gap," meaning that self-identified LGBs will be more liberal and Democratic in their voting than will their liberal, Democratic cohorts who do not identify as lesbian, bisexual, or gay.

Hypothesis 7: Results in Specific Contests

LGB voting will remain highly distinctive in particular individual contests, not merely in aggregated national partisan results for governorships and seats in Congress, and will be particularly distinctive in high-salience contests.

Hypothesis 8: Symbolic versus Substantive Voting

LGB voters will seek both substantive and symbolic gains. Therefore, in a high-salience contest between a "progay" and an "antigay" candidate, they will vote for the "progay" candidate; and in a contest in which there is little difference between the candidates on LGB issues, substantive issue differences will be of greater concern.

Hypothesis 9: Role of Political Leadership

The extent of LGB voting cohesion in any given contest will depend on the unity of LGB political leaders, who, if united, should be able to mobilize LGB voters independently of any outside political force.

Having thus laid out a theory of LGB self-identification and its manifestation in the voting booth, I proceed to test that theory in the succeeding chapters.

 THREE

The Sexuality Gap: The 1990 National Exit Polls

This is the first of four chapters presenting the results of the study of LGB voting behavior. The first two of these chapters present data from the 1990 midterm general elections for members of Congress and for state governors. The present chapter discusses the results of two simultaneous versions of the national exit poll, which give us the first look ever at lesbian and gay (though not bisexual) voters across the land. Chapter 4 goes on to look at the aggregated results from twenty-one states in which the gay/lesbian self-identification question was asked, and at three states in particular for which the lesbian and gay sample size was large enough to conduct more in-depth analysis.

Chapter 5 looks at a Democratic primary race in New York City in September 1990 that is distinctive both for having a strong, openly lesbian candidate in the contest and for being the subject of an exit poll developed by local political scientists that measures not only the demographics and political attitudes of the voters, but the effect of newspaper and magazine endorsements, support of political clubs, and contact by specific campaign organizations, and how all of these together affected the voters' decisions. Using these data we can assess the effect of LGB political activists on LGB voters.

Chapter 6 gives us our first look at LGB political behavior in a presidential race, the 1992 contest among Bill Clinton, George Bush, and Ross Perot. It also marks the first time that bisexuals are included in the LGB identification category in a general election survey.

Two things should be noted at the outset. First, chapters 3 to 5 do not include bisexuals, because the self-identifier questions did not include bisexuals; I shall be discussing in those chapters only the voting behavior of self-identified lesbians and gay men.[1] In those chapters, therefore, I will usually not refer to "LGBs." Second, all the surveys discussed here are *exit polls,* which differ in certain respects from pre- and postelection polling done either door-to-door or by telephone.

A thorough discussion of the study methods is found in the appendix, but a brief introduction to exit polling is in order here. All the polling places (usually called precincts) in the country are *stratified* by their geographic location. Then, within each geographic "sampling unit" a number of precincts are selected at random. Precincts with more voters assigned to them have a greater chance of being chosen, but small and middle-sized precincts get included as well.

On election day, a trained polltaker goes to each sample precinct and asks every *N*th voter (the number varies according to her instructions) leaving the polling place to participate. Each selected respondent who agrees to participate is handed a single sheet of paper printed on one or both sides with questions. All questions are in a check-the-box format; there are no "open-ended" questions in which the respondent writes out an answer. The respondent completes the form either at an adjacent table or booth, or on a clipboard provided by the polltaker. She then folds up her survey and deposits it, unsigned, in a "ballot box."

At the end of her shift, the polltaker either transports the completed forms to a data-entry location or telephones a data-entry operator at the central office and reads the answers off each form. The results are tabulated on a mainframe computer and are made available to the broadcast networks that commissioned the poll, which announce the results as the polls close in each state (unless the contest is, according to the poll, too close to call).

The disadvantages to exit polling are that researchers cannot compare the results among voters with those among nonvoters, and that the check-the-box format does not allow researchers to probe respondents' answers or observe tone of voice, body language, and the like that may be important in interpreting responses, as they can do in a telephone or face-to-face poll. Exit polls, however, offer the great advantages of allowing for the polling of very large numbers of people in a very short time frame; assuring that only those people who actually voted are included in the sample (leaving out those who did not vote but later claim they did, a constant problem with postelection surveys); and getting the voter's attitudes and impressions of the candidates and campaigns immediately after she leaves the polls.

With these things in mind, let us proceed to look at the national results from 1990. In this chapter, I present first comparative demographic data, then comparative attitudinal and voting behavior data. As this study is the first of its kind of this group of voters, I necessarily shall devote a substantial portion of the chapter to these "baseline" statistics. Following this, I shall attempt to develop an initial causal model to account for differences between the self-identified lesbian and gay voters and nonidentifiers, and any differences between lesbians and gay men.

The 1990 national exit polls allow us to assess the first six of the nine hypotheses set forth at the end of chapter 2; the remaining three will be addressed in chapters 4 and 5. This chapter is organized in the order in which the hypotheses appear in chapter 2. At each stage, I shall refer back to these hypotheses and note whether the data confirm or fail to confirm them.

Throughout this discussion I refer to the CBS, VRS, and U.S.A. data bases. As mentioned in chapter 1, CBS wrote a separate version of the national exit poll, whereas a joint version of the survey was written for all four participating networks: CBS, ABC, CNN, and NBC. Both were administered by Voter Research and Surveys, Inc. (VRS), and some questions on each poll were identical to those on the other poll. Data from the CBS version alone make up the CBS data base; data from the four-network joint version alone are called the VRS data base; and the combined responses to identical questions on both versions are called the U.S.A. data base.

Hypothesis 1: Rate of Identification

> Lesbians and gay men will self-identify in political surveys at rates equivalent to those found in previous random-sample research, about 1.0 to 1.5 percent of the population. When bisexuals are included, the share of self-identifiers will increase by an additional 2 to 3 percent.

Of the 19,888 respondents to the U.S.A. poll, 221, or 1.1 percent, identified themselves as being gay or lesbian. Exactly the same percentage so identified themselves when the total unweighted responses from the twenty-one state exit polls were added together (see chapter 4). One percent of the respondents to the VRS form, and 1.2 percent of those to the CBS form, said they were lesbian or gay. If we compare this to rates of exclusively or predominantly homosexual behavior, using either the Kinsey figure of 10 percent or the Janus and Janus figure of 7 percent (3 percent being self-identifiers), we find that only a minority of lesbians and gay men in the United States are willing to identify themselves as such on a political survey that was anonymous and self-adminis-tered, although not completed in absolute privacy. These findings conform to

Hypothesis 1; self-identification falls in the range between 1.0 and 1.5 percent found in other random-sample surveys not completed in absolute privacy.

Edelman (1991, 1993) notes that there is a substantial drop-off in responses to the "grab-bag" questions, among which the self-identification item was included, which means this figure is likely an underestimate. The discussion of Hypothesis 1 in chapter 6 sets forth Edelman's findings on this issue in greater depth.

Hypothesis 2: Demographic Characteristics

LGBs who do self-identify will be possessed of the equivalent of "group consciousness." Therefore, the demographic correlates of group consciousness found among women and African Americans—youth, high education levels, and strong partisanship—should be disproportionately great among self-identified LGBs. Also, given the results of prior sex surveys, men may significantly outnumber women among self-identifiers.

The Essential Differences and Similarities

The essential demographic differences and similarities between the homosexual and heterosexual samples are set forth in table 3.1 (at the end of the chapter). The reader's attention may be directed to the following differences in particular.

Age. Self-identification appears to be largely a function of age. Random-sample data indicate that the rate of homosexual behavior reported by any given age group among men is statistically identical to that at any other, save for a slight dip in reporting among those aged sixty-five and older (Fay et al. 1989).[2] We see, however, that among those aged eighteen to twenty-nine (born in 1961 or later), 2.6 percent checked the "gay or lesbian" box, whereas only 1.5 percent of those between ages thirty and forty-nine (born between 1941 and 1960) did so, and a paltry 0.3 percent of those aged fifty or older (born before World War II).[3]

It is worth noting that there was no significant difference between the gay and nongay samples in the share of first-time voters, usually persons eighteen or nineteen years of age. Given the data above, it would be expected that a larger share of first-time voters would self-identify. This finding, along with the data on education discussed below, indicates that the predominant age for "coming out" is not eighteen or nineteen but sometime in the twenties.

Education. Another significant correlate with high levels of group consciousness is education, and the lesbian/gay sample certainly scores exceedingly high on this indicator. The VRS survey sample as a whole is, as expected, more educated than is the population (Wolfinger and Rosenstone 1980), according to concurrent census data. However, although the sex studies cited previously indicate that college-educated respondents were far more likely to report having had a homosexual experience than were those without college, there is no theoretical or anecdotal reason to suppose that homosexual and heterosexual voters would have significantly different levels of education. They do. Eighty-nine percent of the lesbian and gay sample reported having some college education, as against two-thirds of the rest of the voters and a bit over one-half of the total adult population in the 1990 census. An absolute majority of self-identified lesbians and gay men (53 percent) had received at least a bachelor's degree. Most notably, two gay voters in seven reported having attended postbaccalaureate graduate or professional schools.

As noted above, the sample is predominately young. However, even controlling for age, the gay sample was far more highly educated than were the rest of the voters (data not shown).

Sex. Gay men consistently were found to outnumber lesbians significantly. In the U.S.A. data, men constituted 59 percent of the gay and lesbian respondents, as against 49 percent of the nongay respondents.[4] This imbalance is found in the state surveys as well: in only four of the twenty-one state-level studies did women outnumber men (see table 4.1, chapter 4).

Why this should be so is beyond the scope of this work to determine, but should be touched upon here. The early studies (Kinsey et al. 1948; Institute for Sex Research 1953) indicated that about twice as many men as women were homosexual. The Janus and Janus (1993) findings confirm this, as do the Chicago findings on sexual self-identification (Laumann et al. 1994).[5] It has been postulated that differences in gender role training — the greater permissibility of emotional and physical closeness between women than between men, and the stronger social forces directing women toward marriage and motherhood — may lead women to comprehend their feelings as lesbian later in life than is the case with gay men. It is possible as well that a large number of lesbians have custody of children, which, they feel, would be endangered were they to identify themselves as lesbian, even in a self-administered exit poll, because of the lack of total privacy.[6]

An additional hypothesis that may be worthy of investigation was generated by the finding of considerable "lesbian bisexuality" in the Glick poll (see chapters 5 and 7 for further explication).

As predicted in Hypothesis 2, the gay and lesbian self-identifiers are disproportionately young and highly educated; these are two demographic correlates of group consciousness, and indicate a likelihood of especially strong identification with the group. Further, we find that gay men do significantly outnumber lesbians, by rates equivalent to those found in previous sex research on sexual behavior and identity.

Other Demographic Findings

Race. It is interesting that the one significant difference found among the races in self-identification was that a considerably larger proportion of Latinos than whites self-identified. It also is of interest that rates of self-identification among blacks, Asians, and persons of "other" races did not differ significantly. If group consciousness and group identification overlap, as I have hypothesized, one would expect based on overall education levels that Latinos and African Americans would self-identify at a much lower rate than would whites in the sample. The lack of difference among African Americans may be attributable to the higher levels of partisanship and politicization among blacks who do vote; these levels, as noted in chapter 2, are not necessarily dependent on education level. I am not sure, however, what to make of the significantly higher self-identification rate of Latino voters, who have the lowest education levels in the sample.

Residence. A major difference among the groups was found with respect to both region of residence and the size of the locality of residence. Twice as many lesbians and gay men as nongays, indeed almost half of the subsample (43 percent), lived in the Western states. There were no significant differences in residence patterns between the groups in the Northeast and, interestingly, in the South. It is in the Midwestern states that the lowest level of self-reporting is found, half the national rate. These findings were confirmed precisely in the twenty-one state surveys when the totals from the states in each region were added together (see table 4.1, chapter 4).

This apparent Western migration was not confined to California. Nor, apparently, was it dependent on state laws regulating sexual activities or the existence of state gay rights laws. No significant differences in self-reporting were found between states with and without "sodomy" laws (data not shown), and none of the states in the continental West had statewide civil rights laws protecting sexual minorities in 1990.[7]

Significant differences also were found in the size of localities in which lesbian and gay respondents resided, and in this particular instance significant differences between the lesbians and the gay men were found. The lesbian/gay sample as a whole was considerably more urban than the rest of the respondents, with about one-third living in a major city. The urban residents, however, were disproportionately male; although more lesbians lived in the cities than did similarly situated nongay women, they tended to reside in the suburbs.

Income. It is interesting that there are no statistically significant differences between the incomes of the gay sample and the rest of the sample. There are somewhat more gay/lesbian respondents in the lowest income category, but this appears to be caused by the substantial tilt toward youth in the sample; controlling again for age, the gay group if anything does better than its nongay counterparts. It also is worthy of note that a gender gap appears between the incomes of lesbians and those of gay men.

Occupation. The gay/lesbian sample, again, disproportionately falls within the highest occupational categories. An absolute majority report holding professional or managerial employment, and five in seven are white-collar workers of some sort. The categories in which the group we are studying is underrepresented include retirees (10 percent, versus 21 percent for the rest of the sample), homemakers (no respondents, versus 10 percent), and farmers and farm workers (no respondents, versus 2 percent). It is well to note that, in spite of prohibitory laws and practices, one in twelve self-identified lesbians and gay men reports being a school teacher, although the great majority presumably do not disclose their sexuality to their students or employers. Identical shares of the gay and nongay samples are government employees (12 percent) and labor union members (11 percent).

Religion. The CBS form asked voters what their religion was currently, the conventional survey question. The VRS form, however, asked voters the religion in which they were raised; it is possible that some voters answered the latter question as they would have the former. Nonetheless, significant comparisons do emerge.

Half of American heterosexuals who voted in 1990 were raised as Protestants, and nearly half call themselves Protestant today. In contrast, only about a third of self-identified homosexuals were, or are, Protestant. The number raised as Catholics does not differ between the groups, but only about 15 percent of gay men and lesbians, as against 25 percent of nongay voters, consider themselves Catholics today. A somewhat larger share of the gay sample (16 percent versus

11 percent) said it was raised in "other Christian" denominations; only 9 percent, however, identified with such denominations today.[8]

Most notable is that twice as many open gays and lesbians as heterosexuals (20 percent versus 10 percent) reported having been raised as non-Christians, and today, fully three gay or lesbian voters in seven (versus one nongay voter in seven) report being non-Christian. It is not difficult to propose, although here it is impossible to test, a hypothesis that the differences in religious affiliation are the result of long-standing condemnation of homosexual behavior by most Christian denominations, leading to a rejection of Christianity in favor of more accepting faiths, or the abandonment of religion altogether. Given the hostility to or discomfort with homosexuality of most Christian denominations, it may be more surprising that 59 percent of openly gay and lesbian voters still identify with the Christian faith, that the same share of both groups (11–12 percent) identifies as "fundamentalist or evangelical Christian," and that about a quarter of the gay/lesbian sample reports attending religious services at least once a month (24 percent, versus 43 percent of nongay voters). Eighteen percent of the gay sample (versus 8 percent) hold no religious preference, while 19 percent (versus 5.5 percent) identify with religions other than Christianity and Judaism.

It also may be postulated, given the difference in religious upbringing between homosexual and heterosexual identifiers reported in the VRS poll— particularly the larger share of non-Christians and the small percentage of Protestants—that one's religious upbringing has a direct effect on willingness to identify as a gay man or a lesbian. In effect, a Christian, particularly Protestant, upbringing may make a lesbian or a gay man far more likely to stay in the closet, or not to admit his or her homosexuality even to him- or herself.[9] The surprising finding here is that being raised in certain religious traditions, particularly the Protestant tradition, appears to have a significant effect on acknowledgment of one's sexual orientation. Those raised as Catholics, for instance, may leave their church in disagreement with its stand on the state of their souls; but being raised as a Protestant appears to suppress even one's self-acknowledgment.[10]

Miscellaneous demographics. The fact that numerous gay and lesbian couples and singles have children, whether by previous opposite-sex marriage, adoption, or alternative methods of parenthood (artificial insemination, surrogate parenthood, etc.), is well known. The data confirm that, among those lesbians and gay men who vote, childrearing is not at all uncommon, although considerably more women—18 percent, versus 6 percent of gay men (and 32 percent of non–self-identifiers)—had children under eighteen living with them at the time of the survey. More notable is that 10 percent of the gay sample stated they were presently married!

It is interesting, and perhaps a cause for concern, that 12 percent of openly gay and lesbian voters report having been crime victims within the last year, as against 5 percent of nongay voters. Some of this effect may be explained by the disproportion of lesbians and gay men living in large cities; but it is possible that some also may be attributable to antigay violence. Given this fact, it is interesting that slightly fewer gay voters own guns than nongay voters, although again this likely is a function of urban residence; the survey data show that gun owners are disproportionately found in small-town and rural America.

Despite the armed services' continued efforts to exclude and expel lesbians and gay men from the service, exactly the same share (18 percent) of both the gay-lesbian sample and the rest of the sample reports being military veterans. Equal percentages also report currently having relatives in the military or reserves (12 percent).

The differences between the two groups perhaps may best be seen by building a hypothetical "median" voter, one heterosexual (or, at least, not self-identified as homosexual), one self-identified as "gay or lesbian." The demographic differences noted here may presage differences in attitudes and voting behavior.

The median heterosexual voter in 1990 appears to have been a forty-six-year-old white woman living in the suburbs of a medium- to large-sized city somewhere in middle America. She was raised as a Christian, almost certainly a Protestant, and still calls herself one today, but does not go to church even once a month. She is married, with children either grown or of college age; she has taken some college-level courses; and she works at least part-time outside the home in a white-collar job, probably administrative.

The median openly homosexual voter in 1990, meanwhile, appears to have been a thirty-six-year-old white man with a college degree and a full-time professional or managerial job, living and working in a central city of at least fifty thousand, most likely in the West. He is unmarried and has no children. Raised as a Christian, he still considers himself one, but is far less likely even than our median nongay voter to attend services.

Hypothesis 3: Political Attitudes

The general political orientation of LGB voters will be liberal or leftist and Democratic, in keeping with the pattern found among African

Americans, feminists, and non-Cuban Latinos, and will be highly distinctive from that of non-LGB identifiers.

Ideology and Partisanship

Table 3.2 presents the party affiliation, ideology, and attitudes on issues of
the two groups. Briefly, the results confirm in essence the finding of Jay and
Young's self-selected sample (1979), and confirm the ideological prediction of
Hypothesis 3: self-identified lesbians and gay men are very liberal indeed.

When asked directly about their ideological leanings in the VRS survey, five
gay/lesbian voters in nine call themselves liberals, as opposed to fewer than one
in five nongay voters; and while more than one-third of nongay respondents
call themselves conservatives, only one-eleventh of lesbian and gay respondents
do so. Part of this is attributable to the strong feminism of an extraordinary
percentage of the women: five lesbians in eight call themselves "strong feminists," as opposed to a mere one in eight nongay women. However, even
controlling for this factor and for the demographic correlates of gay/lesbian
self-identification, homosexual self-identification in and of itself makes one
statistically more likely to be liberal (see discussion under Hypothesis 6).

Perhaps more interesting is the fact that, although the size of the localities
in which they reside is a factor in the liberalism of gay men and lesbians, the
percentages of liberals remain high and relatively even from the cities down to
the countryside. Thus, city dwellers, both gay and straight, similarly tend to
be liberal, with gay people tending to be somewhat more so; but in the
suburbs, small towns, and rural areas, gay voters are far more liberal than their
nongay neighbors.

Because the CBS form did not ask the respondents their ideology, I built a
0–6 scale, based on responses to six issue-related questions in which a liberal-
conservative dichotomy reasonably could be established,[11] with 6 being "most
liberal," 0 "most conservative." Forty-six percent of gay and lesbian respondents
fell into the two most "liberal" categories, versus 13 percent of heterosexuals;
24 percent of nongay voters, versus 8 percent of gay/lesbian voters, fell into the
two most "conservative" categories.

This consistent liberalism, however, did not automatically translate into
more support for the Democratic Party. The U.S.A. results find that only 12
percent more gay men and lesbians than nongay men and women identify with
the Democrats (48 versus 36 percent). It does translate, however, into a general
aversion to the Republican Party (19 percent of the gay sample versus 34
percent of the nongay sample reported a Republican affiliation). The rate of

identification with neither major party is equivalent for both groups (33 percent of gay men and lesbians versus 30 percent of the remainder).

Thus, the element of especially strong partisanship predicted in Hypothesis 2 is *not* confirmed in this data set. The partisan tilt of lesbian and gay self-identifiers is distinctive, as predicted in Hypothesis 3, but given the extremely distinctive liberalism of the self-identifiers, it may be surprising that these attitudes did not more strongly translate into a preference for the more liberal political party in 1990.

An example of why this might be the case is given in Messina's study (1985) of the attitudes of the major British party candidates for office toward racial minorities in a multiracial London borough. In essence, the Labour Party's candidates, who were pledged in principle to equality for all Britons, and spoke to that effect to the borough's minority group members, were observed to distance themselves strongly from any concrete measures on behalf of minority groups for fear of losing the white support needed to win the election. Such may be said to have been the general attitude of the national Democratic Party toward lesbians and gay men until 1992; it sought to include gay and lesbian voters in its base of support with sympathetic words, without alienating socially conservative voters who supported the Democrats on economic and historical grounds.

Issue Stands and Priorities

It is well to remind the reader of the circumstances in the country in November 1990. George Bush was midway through his single term of office, and the issues dominating the public consciousness at that point reflected his perceived strengths and weaknesses, the relative effects of which would result in his defeat two years later.

Three months before the 1990 election, Bush had sent 250,000 American troops to Saudi Arabia and the Persian Gulf in order to prevent seizure of the Saudi oil fields by Iraq's dictator, Saddam Hussein, who had invaded and conquered the emirate of Kuwait days before. Later, Bush was the principal organizer of an international coalition that imposed an economic and military embargo on Iraq to force its withdrawal from Kuwait. It was widely anticipated that war might be necessary to accomplish this latter goal.

At the same time, the U.S. economy was sliding into a recession, and a principal factor cited in the country's economic sluggishness was the inability of Bush and the Congress, controlled by the Democrats, to make substantial cuts in what were then more than $200 billion annual deficits. After much public and private wrangling, the parties agreed on a deficit reduction package, as part of which Bush agreed to a tax increase, breaking his principal campaign pledge of 1988.

Other issues had come to be prominent during this period. Bush had pledged to be the "education president" and the "environmental president" during his 1988 campaign, and in 1989 declared "war on drugs" and "zero tolerance" of drug importation and use. The U.S. Supreme Court's decision in *Webster v. Reproductive Health Services* (1989), which gave states increased latitude in restricting certain abortions, returned abortion to the forefront of social issues. The savings and loan failure crisis of the late 1980s reached full fruition during this period of Bush's term.

The first issue of *Time* for 1991, two months after the election, reflected the public's apparent mixed feelings about its president: it named as its "Men of the Year" "the two George Bushes," one a strong, astute leader in foreign affairs without recent precedent who sought to create a "new world order" from the ashes of Soviet communism, the other one essentially uninterested in affairs in his own country, weaving from issue to issue without clear focus or vision.

In either case, issues of specific concern to lesbians and gay men — gay civil rights, AIDS, and violence against women and minorities being paramount — were not high on the agenda of the Republican president, the Democratic Congress, or the greatest number of heterosexual American citizens as the country went to the polls, and questions on these topics were included in neither the CBS nor the VRS version of the survey.

Approval ratings. There was a seventeen-point divergence in the ratings of President Bush's performance between the gay and nongay samples; 60 percent of nongays approved; 57 percent of open homosexuals did not. At the same time, there was an eleven-point difference in assessment of whether the country generally was headed in the right direction; 59 percent of nongay voters, and 70 percent of lesbian and gay voters, said the nation was "seriously off on the wrong track." The fact that Bush's personal approval rating was relatively high given this degree of voter pessimism is remarkable.

There was no significant difference in the voters' overwhelmingly negative opinions of Congress, or in how often they felt they could trust "the government in Washington" to do the right thing (two-thirds of each group said "only sometimes" or "never"). A somewhat smaller majority of lesbians and gay men (63 versus 72 percent) thought an answer was to limit the number of years members of Congress may serve.

The important issues. The most notable divergence between straight and gay was the evaluation of the importance of the environment as a campaign issue. One-fourth of gay voters in the CBS version of the survey considered this the most important issue in their vote for members of Congress in 1990, second only to the economy, versus 8 percent of nongay voters; and 45 percent in the VRS version of the poll named it one of their top "one or two" issues, far and away the most important, as against 21 percent of nongay respondents, who ranked it behind education, the federal deficit, and the combined category of crime and drugs. Moreover, when the CBS form asked whether voters considered preserving the environment or preserving jobs the more important, even in the face of a looming recession, 55 percent of the nongay voters opted for the ecology—and so did 77 percent of gay and lesbian voters.

It is notable that the situation in the Persian Gulf did not register highly in the minds of the voters, gay or straight, when it came to casting their votes for members of Congress; only the savings and loan crisis ranked *lower* in determining individuals' votes.

The economy. No significant difference was found between the groups in their assessment of the state of the economy (either on the day of the election or projecting a year ahead from then), whether they considered themselves better off financially than two years before, their concern about the federal deficit, or their (lack of) approval of the federal deficit package recently turned down by Congress. Slightly more gays and lesbians listed unemployment as a greater economic concern than inflation; rather fewer in the CBS version listed the state of the economy as their chief concern in casting their votes for Congress. Minimal, similar numbers of both groups listed the savings and loan crisis as important.

Differences were seen, however, when voters were asked to assign economic responsibility to a particular party. (This is not surprising given the twenty-nine-point party identification gap among gay voters, versus 2.6 percent among nongays.) Nine-point pluralities of nongay identifiers thought the Democratic-controlled Congress would make better decisions about deficit reduction than would Bush, and gave Republicans more blame than Democrats for the savings and loan mess. Gay and lesbian voters, however, trusted Congress more on the deficit by a three-to-one margin; 40 percent blamed the Republicans, and only 13 percent the Democrats, for the savings and loan crisis.

Abortion. Both the VRS and CBS polls found that 66 percent or more of homosexual voters essentially supported abortion on demand, as against 43–45 percent of nongays. With the question worded somewhat differently, 77 percent in the VRS version, and 66 percent in the CBS version, indicated that abortion should always be legal. In the CBS form, 41 percent of nongay voters indicated that abortion should be either outlawed or allowed only in cases of rape, incest, or endangerment of the mother; only 20 percent of gay and lesbian voters agreed. As noted below, significantly more lesbian and gay voters named abortion as one of their *two* most important issues, but lesbians were far more likely than gay men to name it the most important (also see the next section, on gender and feminism).

Crime and drugs. Lesbian and gay voters, it appears, believed the "war on drugs" as pursued by the administration was a dismal flop. Straight and gay agreed that more emphasis should be given to education and treatment rather than law enforcement; but the margin among nongay voters was four to three, indicating a strong base of support for Bush's "zero tolerance" policy, whereas among homosexual voters, the margin for education and treatment was seven to one.

The groups parted company as well on the death penalty. Asked in the CBS version to name their preferred penalty for first-degree murder, heterosexuals opted for capital punishment by a two to one margin over life imprisonment without possibility of parole; only 5 percent opted for the possibility of parole. Homosexual voters split almost exactly down the middle between life without parole and death, and 15 percent supported the possibility of parole.

Defense and the Persian Gulf. As noted above, at the time of the election, a quarter-million American troops were stationed in what became the Persian Gulf War zone, and President Bush had ordered the doubling of this force. The United Nations, however, had not approved military action against Iraq or set a deadline for Iraqi withdrawal from Kuwait. While Saddam Hussein was on the minds of the voters, therefore, he did not loom as large as issues at home; only about 7 percent of nongay voters and 5 percent of gay voters (no significant difference) indicated the Persian Gulf as a major factor in their vote in 1990.

Opinions on the conflict did diverge, however. Lesbian and gay voters were less likely to approve of Bush's commitment of American forces to the Gulf (59 versus 70 percent); and when asked whether U.S. forces should remain there, even if there might be American casualties, a 54 percent majority said no, whereas a five to three majority of nongays said yes. Although no later data are available broken down by sexual orientation, these numbers suggest that a substantial majority of lesbians and gay men, perhaps three out of five, probably supported the war when it came to pass, but not the overwhelming majorities of three, four, or five to one found among the rest of the population.

Gay and lesbian voters believed that the Defense Department was getting far too large a share of the federal budget. While 39 percent of nongay respondents believed the defense budget should be cut — 45 percent believing it should be kept at about its present level — 60 percent of gay and lesbian voters favored cuts.

Our median heterosexual voter in November 1990 was a political independent, ideologically moderate but leaning more toward conservative than liberal. She saw the economy and federal deficit reduction, along with education, crime, and drugs, as the most important issues in casting her vote for Congress. She voted for George Bush and generally approved of the job he was doing, but thought the country was seriously off track and was not sure whether she would vote for Bush or for the Democratic nominee in 1992. She loathed Congress's performance and thought members' tenure should be limited by law — but trusted it slightly more to deal with the deficit than she did Bush. On specific issues, she supported the Persian Gulf deployment and was inclined to support our staying there, even at the risk of war; she favored some restrictions on legal abortion, but not those proposed by pro-lifers; she favored the death penalty for first-degree murder and, while supporting education and treatment to deal with drugs, thought law enforcement was an important second element; she thought both parties must share the blame for the savings and loan crisis; she opted for preserving the environment over preserving jobs if need be, but hesitantly.

Our median self-identified homosexual voter was for all practical purposes a liberal Democrat: he voted for Michael Dukakis in 1988, disapproved of Bush's conduct as president, thought the country was seriously off track, and probably would vote for the president's Democratic opponent two years hence; he blamed both parties, but the Republicans more than the Democrats, for the savings and loan mess and trusted the Democrats in Congress far more to deal with the deficit than the president. He thought we were right to send the troops to the Middle East, but not to keep them there if war became likely, and that defense spending generally should be cut substantially. He too distrusted the federal government, strongly disapproved of Congress and favored tenure limits, although not quite as enthusiastically. While not a strong feminist himself, most of his lesbian friends were, and he joined in their strong support of legal abortion. His principal concern, after the economy, was the environment, and he strongly favored the ecology over economic growth when the two conflict. He favored life without parole over the death penalty, and thought drug law enforcement essentially should be abandoned in favor of drug education and treatment.

Voting Behavior

Table 3.3 displays the breakdown between the groups on the dependent variables, voting behavior. The data for the House of Representatives show the percentages of respondents in all fifty states, including those in which the incumbent representative was unopposed; whereas those for the Senate and for state governors reflect total percentages of the vote only from those states in which such elections were being held.

It is in the returns for chief executives of the states that Democratic dominance in gay and lesbian voting behavior is most fully expressed. Non–self-identifiers gave Democrats a six-point margin over Republicans; self-identified homosexuals gave Democrats a forty-two-point margin. (Seven percent of nongay voters, and 5 percent of gay voters, cast ballots for third candidates.)

In U.S. Senate elections, heterosexual voters split almost exactly down the middle, at about 49 percent for each party. Gay and lesbian voters, in contrast, split five to three for the Democrats. One may note the complete absence of voting for independent or third party candidates, and the comparatively strong showing for Republicans, compared to the gubernatorial and House returns.[12]

Two particular differences are notable in the House returns. First, heterosexuals gave the Democrats a fifty to forty-three margin, while homosexual voters gave them a margin of fifty-eight to twenty-six. Second, a remarkable 16 percent of lesbian and gay voters cast their ballots in House races for independents and third party candidates, compared to 7 percent of nongay voters. This independent bloc voted almost unanimously for Democrats for governor in states in which such elections were being held. This raised the possibility that among lesbians and gay men in the United States there was a leftist vote of about 15 percent that went to the Democrats in major statewide and national elections, but splintered off to third candidates in House races, and perhaps at the local level as well. This possibility will be tested in the section on Hypothesis 5 later in this chapter.

The Democratic dominance was reflected in the (obviously inaccurate) self-reporting of the presidential vote in 1988, and the (more likely accurate) statement of how the voters likely would cast their ballots in 1992. Of those who reported they had voted in 1988, 63 percent of nongays said they had voted for Bush; only 33 percent admitted to having voted for Michael Dukakis.[13] Among self-identified gay men and lesbians, these numbers were almost reversed: 60 percent said they voted for Dukakis, only 33 percent for Bush.

As noted above, however, support for Bush at this point appeared to be weak. Despite the relatively high approval rating and claimed 1988 support, only 34 percent of nongay voters, just over half of those who claimed to approve of Bush's performance, said they probably would vote for Bush in 1992; 31 percent said they probably would vote for the Democratic nominee, and 35 percent did not know. Among lesbian and gay voters, an absolute majority (52 percent) said they probably would vote for the Democrat; only 10 percent said they probably would vote for Bush.

Certain factors were more influential than others in the vote choice of gay and lesbian voters. They were significantly less likely to see the ability to get things done as the most important quality in a congressional candidate, and more likely to view stands on the issues as the most important factor. Partisan labels also were cited as principal reasons for voting for a given candidate far more by lesbian and gay voters (17 percent, versus 8 percent among nongays). These results may be explained by the very high education level of the gay and lesbian sample. Although there were great differences in opinion about President Bush, about two-thirds of both groups indicated that the president was not a factor in their congressional voting decision. There were no significant differences between the groups in their assessment of the tone of the 1990 campaigns; about half of each group opined that the year's campaigns were more negative than in the past.

Respondents to the VRS version also were asked to assess several possible Democratic presidential contenders, more than fifteen months before the first 1992 presidential primary or caucus was held. (In the event, only two of the seven potential candidates listed entered the race, along with four other "major" candidates not listed.) In our analysis, avowed Republican respondents were excluded.

Although the differences between the groups were not statistically significant, certain differences were manifested. About one-third in each group named New York's governor, Mario Cuomo, as their first choice. Then they split. The Reverend Jesse Jackson, who actively had courted gay and lesbian voters in 1984 and 1988, placed second with these voters, but at 21 percent, rather anemic given the strong support he had sought from the community. New Jersey Senator Bill Bradley ran third among gays and lesbians at 15 percent; four others trailed in the single digits. One of those four, moderate-to-conservative Texas Senator Lloyd Bentsen, Dukakis's 1988 running mate, garnered the support of one out of six nongay Democrats and independents, putting him second; Jackson ran third, with most of his support coming from black voters, and Bradley a close fourth. In each group, about one voter in six preferred someone other than the seven candidates listed.

Bill Clinton, the then governor of Arkansas, got the support of 2 percent of nongay voters—and none among self-identified gay men and lesbians![14]

Hypothesis 4: Gender and Feminism

Lesbians, whether feminists or not, will be more opposed to the use of force in politics, and therefore will be more likely to vote for Democrats than are gay men. In addition, lesbian feminists will hold different issue priorities from LGB men and women who do not identify with feminism, and thus are far more likely to hold liberal positions on abortion and other feminist issues; they will be more inclined to vote for Democrats than will other women.

I next compared gay men with lesbians to determine whether any significant differences existed in attitudes or voting behavior.[15] The items in which a statistically significant difference was found are shown in table 3.4.

Hypothesis 4 is based in part on Gilens's finding (1988) that foreign policy, rather than pocketbook issues or even "women's issues," was a principal source of the "gender gap" among American voters in the 1980s. Additionally, however, we see an extremely high share of lesbians who called themselves "strong feminists." This confirms the existence and predominance within the open lesbian community of lesbian feminism (Marotta 1981; Phelan 1989). Given this, one would expect to find that abortion and, perhaps, economic issues would cause a cleavage between the sexes.

Although there are significant differences on certain indicators, it does not appear that a great divide exists between lesbians and gay men on any domestic issue. Gay men support abortion rights as strongly as do lesbians, and when asked the one *most* important issue in the election, the sexes did not differ notably. The finding that three times as many women as men considered abortion one of the *two* most important issues, therefore, must be read with some caution.

Equally mixed messages are found in gender differences regarding the state of the economy. Although gay women viewed the state of the economy as worse, and were extremely unlikely to approve of the recently passed bipartisan deficit reduction plan, only a third as many women as men named the deficit plan as a top issue, and other indicators relating to the economy showed little or no gender differences.

The most notable difference attributable to sex was found—as Gilens would have predicted—in the questions on U.S. intervention in the Persian Gulf. Gay men supported the sending of American troops to Saudi Arabia, and their potential use in battle, by margins equal to those of heterosexuals. It was lesbians, more than perhaps any other demographic category, who most strongly objected both to the initial deployment and to any further use of force in the region.

There is, however, a strong "feminism gap" within the lesbian and gay community. Even taking only variables used in the VRS form (the only one to ask the feminism question), table 3.5 displays a variety of issues on which *strongly feminist* lesbians differed from gay men and from lesbians who did not identify strongly with feminism.[16] Although feminism in and of itself does not eliminate the gap between gay/lesbian self-identifiers and the rest of the population, nonfeminist gays and lesbians are far closer on many issues to the heterosexual population than are lesbian feminists (see tables 3.2 and 3.3); indeed, the nonfeminist lesbians are considerably less likely to vote for Democrats or to oppose any restrictions on abortion, and more likely to rate their personal situation as better than two years ago, than are the gay men. An additional issue on which nonfeminist lesbians diverged both from gay men and their feminist sisters was the importance of education in the election: this was named the most important issue by nonfeminist lesbians, whereas it got middling importance from the other two groups.[17]

On two issues a joint effect of gender and feminism can be observed. For our purposes the most important issue is attitudes on the Persian Gulf deployment. Five gay men in seven supported it, compared to fewer than half of the nonfeminist lesbians and only a third of feminist lesbians. The other issue is the importance attributed to the deficit plan: only half as many nonfeminist lesbians as gay men named the deficit plan as a top issue; lesbian feminists rated it lower still.

Yet on the cutting-edge feminist issue of abortion rights, the feminism gap was readily apparent: 48 percent of lesbian feminists, but only 18 percent of nonfeminist lesbians and 9 percent of gay men, rated abortion one of the two most important issues in the election. In addition, whereas lesbian feminists were nearly unanimous in opposing any restrictions on abortion rights, only three in five nonfeminist lesbians agreed, fewer than the three-fourths of gay men who held this position.

It is of interest that feminism appeared to have an independent effect on one's economic perceptions as well: twice as many lesbian feminists as gay men or nonfeminist lesbians described the current state of the economy as "poor," and whereas a majority of lesbian feminists rated themselves worse off than two years before, an absolute majority of nonfeminist lesbians rated themselves better off!

It is of additional interest that 44 percent of lesbian and gay feminists were not raised as Christians, as against 11 percent of the nonfeminist lesbians and gay men, and 10 percent of the heterosexual population (table 3.1). Being raised as a non-Christian (as opposed to one's present religious activity) also was a significant contributing factor to strong feminism (see table 3.9).

It is not possible to test the CBS data for the effects of feminism. This strong relationship between feminism and non-Christian upbringing, however, warrants exploration in a future study.

Perhaps the most notable finding with regard to lesbian feminists was that it was they, more than any other group, who deserted Democratic nominees for third candidates in the contests for the House of Representatives; two in seven did so. Possible explanations for this phenomenon are discussed and tested in the next section of the chapter, on Hypothesis 5.

The findings here appear to confirm our hypothesis that a gender gap exists within the lesbian and gay community, as among heterosexual voters, with respect to foreign policy, at least with respect to the use of military force. The hypothesis that an additional "feminism gap" exists with respect to abortion and economic issues also was confirmed. In addition, feminism appeared to augment the comparative military dovishness of the lesbians in the sample.

With respect to the economic issues, it is interesting that although lesbian feminists perceived economic conditions to be much worse than did gay men or nonfeminist lesbians, and although they almost unanimously opposed the deficit reduction plan hammered out by President Bush and Congress, they were the group least inclined to see the deficit plan as important in the election; to these women, abortion was the key issue. The priorities of gay men (the economy and the deficit), nonfeminist lesbians (education), and lesbian feminists (abortion rights) were considerably different.

Hypothesis 5: Voting Blocs within the Community

Given the divergent concepts of group identity among LGBs, and their differing notions of what the goals of the LGB movement should be and the best means for achieving them, LGB voters will not be monolithic;

although the large majority will vote for Democrats, significant minorities will support Republicans or leftist third candidates.

Two questions need answering in order to confirm Hypothesis 5. First, do those gay and lesbian voters who support Democrats differ significantly in their demographic characteristics or their attitudes from those who do not? Second, are there consistent and identifiable blocs of votes within the lesbian and gay community that hold together from contest to contest?

There were few significant demographic indicators of what will cause self-identified lesbians and gay men to identify with the Republican Party or to vote for its candidates. The most important one appeared to be religiosity: 32 percent of those attending religious services at least once a month identify as Republicans, as against 15 percent of secular gays and lesbians. Related to this was the finding that, of the small share of the CBS gay sample who called themselves fundamentalist or evangelical Christians, 72 percent (ten of fourteen respondents) called themselves Republicans, versus 16 percent of the rest, and this group makes up more than a third of gay and lesbian Republicans in the CBS poll. A third significant factor, as may be expected, was race: 21 percent of European-American self-identifiers were Republican, versus 8 percent of people of color. Finally, region approached statistical significance (at .089): 26 percent of Southerners and 22 percent of Westerners identified with the GOP, as against 13 percent of Midwesterners and 9 percent of Easterners.

The attitudes of gay and lesbian Republicans did differ significantly from those of the Democrats and independents, but their attitudes do not resemble those of heterosexual Republicans; they are self-described, and can be objectively described, as moderates rather than conservatives. In the VRS data, only three of fifteen Republican identifiers labeled themselves conservative, whereas eight of fifteen called themselves moderate, and the remaining four called themselves liberal. This distinguishes gay/lesbian Republicans from the absolute majorities of Democrats (70 percent) and independents (56 percent) who called themselves liberal, but puts their ideological self-identification closer to that of nongay independents than to nongay identifiers with either party.[18]

In the CBS data, although they were more likely to take conservative positions than Democrats or independents, large majorities of lesbian and gay Republicans supported environmental protection over jobs and supported drug treatment and education, rather than law enforcement, to solve drug abuse. The most significant differences were found on maintaining the military force in the Persian Gulf (73 percent supported it, versus 31 percent of Democrats) and on defense spending (59 percent opposed cuts, versus 25 percent of Democrats). In addition, 57 percent of Republicans, as against 23 percent of Democrats, favored some restrictions on abortion, and a narrow majority of Republicans (55 percent) supported the death penalty—almost equal to the 52 percent support found among gay and lesbian independents. The scaled responses show that only one Republican respondent held no liberal positions, and only seven of twenty-four held just one, whereas six of twenty-four held liberal stands on all or nearly all issues. The plurality (ten respondents) fell in the middle, with two, three, or four liberal responses out of six.

Interestingly, when gay Republicans were broken out into religious categories, the "born-again" Republicans were no more conservative, either in the aggregate or on any individual issue, than were the rest, and the churchgoing Republicans were more *favorable* to cutting defense spending than were the secular Republicans (significant at .05).

The principal finding regarding voting behavior among self-identified gay and lesbian Republicans is that they split their tickets considerably more than do gay and lesbian Democrats. Thirty-nine percent of gay/lesbian Democrats, and 36 percent of nongay Democrats, voted a straight ticket for House, Senate, and gubernatorial elections where all three were contested. But although 31 percent of nongay Republicans did the same, only 18 percent (five of twenty-seven) of gay/lesbian Republicans in these states supported their party's entire ticket. This was most evident in contests for governor: about half of gay and lesbian Republicans voted to put Democrats in their statehouses.

As for lesbian and gay self-identifiers who affiliated with neither major party, in most respects they did not differ significantly from self-identifiers who called themselves Democrats.[19] Demographically, people of color were somewhat less likely to be independents than were European-Americans. However, the principal difference appears to be regional: half of Midwesterners and 41 percent of Easterners gave no major-party identification, as against about one-quarter of those from the South or the West (significant at .089).

Ideologically, independents are somewhat less liberal than are self-identified Democrats. As noted above, in the VRS poll an absolute majority of independents call themselves liberal, and it is notable that half of the "strong feminists" identify as independents as well (significant at .076). In the CBS questions, however, only a third of the independents, as against two-thirds of the Democrats, fall into the most liberal categories; another one-third gave liberal responses to four of the six questions, and the remaining one-third gave two or three such responses. They are as liberal as the Democrats on abortion, environmental protection, and drugs, but unlike the Democrats they split down the middle on defense spending, the Persian Gulf, and the death penalty.

It is in their voting behavior that gay and lesbian independents are most likely to be confused, on the surface, with Democrats. Nearly a quarter (thirteen of fifty-four respondents) voted for Democrats in every one of three contests, whereas only two of fifty-four voted for Republicans across the board. The thirty-nine independents (of fifty-four) who split their tickets, however, behaved like "true independents," with Democrats receiving rather small pluralities in the House and gubernatorial contests and the Republicans a small plurality in the Senate races; fully 35 percent of independent ticket-splitters (fourteen of thirty-nine) voted for third candidates in the House races. This distinguishes them from Democratic ticket-splitters, who appear to have splintered away mostly in the House races.

One other gay and lesbian subgroup demands our attention: the 16 percent who reported voting for a third candidate for the House of Representatives. We have clues to the composition of this group. An absolute majority of lesbian and gay Democrats who split their tickets voted for third candidates for the House, whereas only three of twenty Republican ticket-splitters did so. Also, as noted earlier, all but one of this group voted for Democratic candidates for governor; and a disproportion of lesbian feminists are found among the third candidate voters.[20]

An examination of their issue positions tends to confirm the initial impression that this group is significantly more liberal than were voters for the Democrats. On the CBS issue scale nearly two-thirds of third candidate voters (65 percent) fell into the top two categories for liberalism, and 90 percent took liberal stands on at least four of the six issues in the scale. The third candidate voters were significantly more liberal on cutting defense spending and on abortion rights than were the Democratic voters. However, oddly, they were more conservative on the death penalty; this is an anomalous finding that I cannot now explain. This group maintained the strong liberalism of all lesbian and gay self-identifiers on the weighing of environment against jobs and on the solution to drug abuse, and was as opposed to continuing the presence in the Persian Gulf as were the Democratic voters.

However, in the VRS data, only 38 percent of third candidate voters, as against 68 percent of Democratic voters, identify as liberals; the plurality of third candidate voters (45 percent) identify as moderates. This result approaches statistical significance, at .077. Further, and of greater importance, no significant differences were found between the Democratic and third candidate voters on issue priorities that would account for a splitting away from the Democratic candidate. Finally, after party and incumbency were controlled for, no difference was found in voting for a third candidate whether the seat had a Democratic or Republican incumbent, or no incumbent seeking reelection. My initial impression that liberals were voting for third candidates against Democratic incumbents who were insufficiently liberal was not confirmed.

Why, then, would liberally inclined voters who almost unanimously support Democrats for governor, and about half of whom are self-identified Democrats, vote for third candidates for the House? The only clue remaining is the interesting, indeed peculiar, finding that third candidate voting was confined almost exclusively to the Northeastern and Western states. In each of these regions, just under a quarter of all gay and lesbian House voters chose third candidates, as against one respondent apiece from the Midwest (4 percent of gay/lesbian Midwestern voters) and the South (2 percent of gay/lesbian Southern voters) (significant at .01). No other demographic differences help us explain this phenomenon.

Whatever the explanation may be, it appears that there is not a "green" vote after all, merely a gaggle of Democrats and independents of liberal temper who have yet to be persuaded or integrated into voting for a straight Democratic ticket.

A surprising finding was the existence of significant differences in voting for the Senate and for state governors based on the original age clusters. The basis of the differences was made more clear when these clusters were compressed into the three shown in table 3.6: ages eighteen to twenty-nine (the "post-boom" generation), thirty to forty-four (the "baby boomers"), and forty-five and up (those born during or before World War II). The baby boomers were significantly (or near significantly) more likely to support Democrats and oppose Republicans than were either the generation before them or the generation after.

This is not a mere reflection of relatively weak partisan commitment among the younger generation. As seen in the table, the youngest cohort, although apparently more mindful of the environment than were the baby boomers, were significantly more likely to approve of President Bush's performance in office, were less sanguine about the prospect of cutting the defense budget (although there were no significant differences in support for the Persian Gulf engagement), and were more inclined to support some restrictions on abortion. Taken together, the youngest self-identifiers also were the least liberal.

The older cluster was notably more moderate than the boomers as well, but the reasons for this are not readily discernible. Those forty-five and older in

1990 include the largest share of self-identifiers without college educations—and the largest share with postgraduate educations; the largest share with low incomes—and the largest share with higher incomes, but, interestingly, the lowest share with white-collar employment. This group also was distinguished from all voters under forty-five in its rate of religious attendance, which was equal to that of nongay identifiers (43 percent); 81 percent of those under forty-five, in contrast, were secular. However, controlling for education, income, employment status, and religious attendance did not produce any consistent patterns that might explain the greater relative conservatism of this group.

The principal differences in the voting booth between self-identified gay and lesbian Americans and the rest of the population are as follows:

This group of voters has a distinctive tilt toward the Democratic Party. Whereas among nongay respondents 18 percent voted a straight Democratic ticket and 15 percent straight Republican, 26 percent of gay and lesbian respondents voted straight Democratic and only 7 percent straight Republican.

Preference for the Democrats alone does not explain the degree of distinctiveness of lesbian and gay voters. Independents, a majority of whom are self-described liberals, also tend to support Democrats; but whereas nongay independents split almost evenly between the parties, 23 percent of gay and lesbian independents voted straight Democratic, as against 4 percent who voted straight Republican. In addition, the gay and lesbian Republican minority tends to fracture: only 18 percent of gay/lesbian Republicans voted a straight ticket, as against 39 percent of gay/lesbian Democrats.

That said, the gay and lesbian electorate is *not* monolithically Democratic. This group splits its tickets at exactly the same rate as nongay voters—two-thirds do so. The independent ticket-splitters are very much independent in behavior and up for grabs. And what appeared at first blush to be a leftist or "green" vote appears merely to be liberal Democrats and independents in the Northeast and West who split from their party in the House races for unexplained reasons. It is probable, therefore, that moderate or liberal Republicans sympathetic to lesbian and gay concerns could receive majorities, even large majorities, of gay and lesbian votes.[21]

Finally, there is an important generational difference within the gay and lesbian sample. Baby boomers are significantly more liberal and more inclined to vote for the Democrats than are the generation that preceded them or the generation that followed them. The pre- and post-boom generations are not conservative, but middle-of-the-road. If this trend continues, the distinctiveness of gay and lesbian voting may *decrease* as the years go on, even as the share of the population that openly identifies as lesbian and gay is likely to increase.

Hypothesis 6: The "Sexuality Gap"

LGB voting will be sufficiently distinctive as to have an independent effect on vote choice after controlling for attitudes, partisanship, incumbency, and demographic factors significantly correlated with LGB self-identification. Thus, there will be an authentic "sexuality gap," meaning that self-identified LGBs will be more liberal and Democratic in their voting than will their liberal, Democratic cohorts who do not identify as lesbian, bisexual, or gay.

Despite the actual and potential divisions within the community discussed in the preceding two sections of this chapter, it is clear from the preceding pages that there are fundamental differences in the demographics, political attitudes, and voting behavior of self-identified lesbians and gay men as against the rest of the population. I now look at the extent to which gay or lesbian self-identification can assist in explaining and predicting voting behavior for Congress or for state governors after we have controlled for other variables.

Table 3.7 shows the hypothesized demographic correlates with gay/lesbian self-identification, as determined from table 3.1. In addition, because of the extraordinarily distinctive liberalism of this group, and the extraordinarily strong feminism of most of the lesbians, I tested whether the demographic correlates would "wash out" any independent effect of sexual self-identification on liberalism or feminism. The results showed that, even when we control for all demographic correlates, sexual self-identification retained a potent, independent effect on identification as a liberal (table 3.8) and as a strong feminist (table 3.9) (significant in both cases at .0001). Indeed, in the case of feminism, gay/lesbian self-identification was the third strongest factor (measured by the Wald statistic) after gender and education.

I then tested the elements of Hypothesis 6 in this order:

1. Sexual self-identification standing alone has a statistically significant effect on vote choice and party affiliation.

2. Sexual self-identification has an independent effect on vote choice after controlling for demographic variables on which gay and lesbian self-identifiers differ from the rest of the population.

3. Sexual self-identification has an independent effect on vote choice after

controlling for these demographic variables, plus party identification and the party of the incumbent seeking reelection (if any).

4. Sexual self-identification has an independent effect on vote choice after controlling for the strong liberalism and feminism shown by the gay and lesbian self-identifiers, in addition to the demographic and partisanship indicators included above.

For the purposes of logistic regression analysis, seven "yes-no" dependent variables were created to measure vote choice: a vote for or against a Democrat for the House, Senate, or governor's office, for or against a Republican for the same, and for or against a third candidate for the House alone.

The results are abstracted in table 3.10. Briefly, self-identification as gay or lesbian had an independent effect on each of the seven dependent variables. Following the addition of the demographic correlates, however, the effect of self-identification clearly was eliminated in the Senate races, and only approached significance in the governor's contests; only in the House races was an independent effect found after controlling for demographics.

At the next stage, controls were added for the party affiliation of the voter and of the incumbent official seeking reelection, if any. The addition of partisanship indicators eliminated any remaining independent effect of self-identification in the gubernatorial races, as well as in voting for a Democrat for the House. Yet even after the inclusion of party affiliation, incumbency, and the demographic correlates with self-identification, the gay/lesbian self-identifiers retained independent power to explain a vote for or against a Republican or independent candidate for the House.

Finally, ideology and feminism were added to the mix. These elements eliminated the independent explanatory power of self-identification on voting for or against a Republican.[22] The independent effect, however, was retained with respect to voting for a third candidate. Thus, after liberalism, feminism, party affiliations, and several demographic correlates are accounted for, self-identification as lesbian or gay in and of itself made a person more likely to vote for a third candidate for the House of Representatives.

What These Results Tell Us

The distinctive voting behavior of gay/lesbian self-identifiers cannot be explained away on the basis on demographic correlations. In the House races, and possibly in the gubernatorial races, a gay or lesbian citizen votes differently from her or his heterosexual neighbor who shares the same demographic characteristics. In the House races, it also is evident that the self-identified gay

or lesbian voter differs in the booth from the heterosexual neighbor who
shares not only demographic characteristics, but party affiliation and the same
incumbent officeholder. It is only once one controls for the strong liberalism
and feminism of the group that these differences are eliminated—almost.
There remains a chance that if you are a nongay liberal feminist, then a liberal,
feminist copartisan neighbor who is demographically like you in every way
except for identifying as gay or lesbian will still be voting for a third candidate
in the House election, rather than for the Democrat.

Are we making too much of a small thing? In most cases, ideology and
feminism wipe out any independent effect remaining after partisanship and
demographics have been entered into the equation. One cannot say, therefore,
that as a rule gay and lesbian self-identification has an independent effect on
vote choice after controls have been applied.

Yet we have seen that self-identification as gay or lesbian has an independent
effect on liberalism and feminism after controlling for numerous demographic
correlates. These in turn exert an independent effect on party affiliation, issue
stands, and evaluations of incumbent officeholders and government performance, which together determine vote choice (Campbell et al. 1960). We can
say, therefore, that because of its effect in augmenting liberalism and feminism,
gay/lesbian self-identification has important indirect effects on voting behavior
in the United States.

A Look at the Retrospective Model

In this subsection I shall examine these direct and indirect effects of the gay
and lesbian vote in the context of the principal model of voting behavior
accepted today, the "Michigan model" (Campbell et al. 1960)[23] as refined by
the "retrospective model" (Fiorina 1981).

The Michigan model, briefly alluded to above, holds that the principal
factor in determining one's vote is party affiliation, which results from a
combination of family socialization (especially the party affiliations of one's
parents), historical forces within the community in which one grows up,
current socioeconomic status, and (in Campbell's day of the one-party South, at
least) region of residence. Various "short-term" forces also influenced the final
voting decision; in presidential elections, these forces principally were personal
evaluations of the candidates, evaluations of their issue stands, and assessment
of the performance of the incumbent party—all of which were influenced by
one's party affiliation.

The retrospective model's principal refinement of the Michigan model is
its discovery that short-term forces are manifested principally in presidential

performance ratings and, interestingly, in retrospective evaluations of *economic* performance. Initial modeling during the 1980s sought to predict presidential vote choice using objective indicators of economic health, either at the aggregated national level or at the individual, personal level (Morin 1989). Such modeling failed, however, in the 1992 presidential election, in which perceptions of the state of the national economy were considerably gloomier than either voters' assessments of their personal economic conditions or the objective economic indicators. Thus, it was discovered that the voters' perceptions of whether the *country's* economy is better off now than it was four years ago appears to be the most accurate indicator.

Retrospective modeling is most notable for its predictive power in two-candidate presidential contests. By knowing the voter's party affiliation, evaluation of presidential performance, and retrospective assessment of the nation's economy,[24] one can determine the aggregate popular vote, within three percentage points, *and* predict how between 80 and 90 percent of individual voters will cast their ballots (Morin 1989).[25]

This modeling, as noted above, has been used principally in analyzing presidential elections rather than off-year congressional races. Therefore, I attempt some small modifications to the usual indicators. In addition to the measure of the president's performance, I include an indicator of congressional performance;[26] and I add the element of incumbency in the House races, which is a particularly significant influence on congressional voting (Mayhew 1974; Jacobson 1983).

Table 3.11 shows the result of specifying a classic retrospective model, modified as noted above and adding gay/lesbian self-identification to the mix. As one may expect, party affiliation and House incumbency were by far the two greatest determinants of voting for members of the House. It is interesting that Bush's performance as president exercised a greater independent influence on House voting than did the evaluation of Congress as an institution. As expected, no independent effects of gay/lesbian self-identification were found.[27]

It is worth noting that the individual-level percentage predictive power of these retrospective models in the House races consistently fell in the low seventies, as against the high eighties and low nineties found in predicting presidential elections.

Conclusion: The Gay or Lesbian American Voter

The fundamental question for the practical national politician or her advisers is, of course, whether this small number of voters really matters. The answer is yes. Although gay and lesbian self-identification did not have a direct independent effect on voting behavior, self-identifiers were significantly more liberal and feminist than were nongay identifiers who shared the same demographic characteristics. Ideology and feminism, in turn, influence the factors that the Michigan model, and its refinement in the retrospective model, tell us determine how all but a few citizens will vote: party affiliation, issue positions, retrospective evaluations, and personal judgments about the candidates.

We are left with the chicken-or-the-egg question of which came first. Does one's life experiences as a homosexual in America make one more socially liberal and nonconformist, or are socially liberal, nonconformist homosexuals the most likely to self-identify, and therefore be reflected in the poll? The soundest answer is that we do not know, and we cannot tell from these data. Anecdotal evidence suggests that the answer may be both. In chapter 2 I discussed the psychological process of self-acceptance and, later, a sort of conscientization that leads to group consciousness. I have hypothesized that one "comes out," or self-identifies, in settings that may lead to confrontation only during the period in which this conscientization is taking place, but not before it has begun.

The 1990 national exit polls reveal to us for the first time a numerically small community of self-identified gay and lesbian voters who are far younger, better educated, more urban, more white-collar, less religious, less inclined to affiliate with Christianity, and more liberal and feminist than are the rest of the voting population. Demographically this group could fit easily into any portrait of "yuppie" twenty- and thirtysomethings at the beginning of the 1990s, save for the fact of its distinctive liberalism and, among lesbians, their strong feminism.

This distinctiveness, however, did not uniformly benefit the Democratic Party. Compared to the strong culturally liberal tendencies of the gay and lesbian population, party identification with the Democrats remains relatively weak. These voters on the whole do have a pronounced aversion to identification with the Republican Party, but fewer than half of the lesbian and gay voters identified with the Democrats, a share far lower than that among African Americans and nonlesbian feminists. About one in six lesbian and gay voters, nearly all of whom were liberal or leftist, abandoned the Democrats for third candidates in races for the House of Representatives. Thus, the limited evidence we have regarding the concurrence of self-identification with group consciousness is inconclusive.

There is, nonetheless, a "sexuality gap" in American politics. Homosexual self-identification correlates with and augments liberalism and feminism. These two variables, in turn, affect voting behavior and positions on external affairs issues. Further, as noted above, with respect to cultural issues lesbian and gay voters are significantly more liberal in their attitudes than are heterosexuals with identical demographic backgrounds. Within the gay/lesbian community itself, the principal gender-based division appears to be not between men and women, but between strong feminists and the rest, although on questions of military force a clear "gender gap" is manifested.

What is perhaps of the greatest importance to the practical-minded is that, although the voting behavior and issue attitudes of gay and lesbian self-identifiers are distinctive compared with the rest of the population, lesbians and gay men are just as likely to split their tickets as are other citizens. Thus, the "gay and lesbian vote" is up for grabs. As of 1990, it had neither been lost to the Republican Party nor integrated into the Democratic Party to anywhere near the extent to which the African American vote had been.

This much we know from the results so far. Several questions, however, remain unanswered. In the next two chapters I seek both to confirm the results obtained in these aggregated results at the level of individual contests, and to test the remaining three hypotheses: whether lesbian and gay voting remains distinctive, or as distinctive, in individual contests; whether a cohesive bloc of gay and lesbian voters can be turned directly to a specific candidate based on issue concerns or a "progay" political orientation; and whether local gay/lesbian political organizations effectively can mobilize a bloc vote for a favored candidate. In short, we have to determine whether, aside from generally liberal gay and lesbian *voters,* there is a liberal gay and lesbian *vote* in America.

TABLE 3.1.
Demographic comparison of gay and lesbian voters with other voters, 1990 U.S. general election

Data base	Variable	Nongay (%)	Gay/lesbian (%)
U.S.A.	Age[c]		
	18–29	13.8	31.3
	30–39	22.3	28.3
	40–44	12.2	16.8
	45–49	9.3	12.1
	50–59	15.2	4.3
	60 or older	27.2	7.2
VRS	Education[c]		
	Not high school graduate	6.7	2.3
	High school graduate	27.8	8.6
	Some college	27.7	35.7
	College graduate	22.5	25.1
	Postgraduate work	15.3	28.3
U.S.A.	Sex[c] (% male)	49.0	58.9
U.S.A.	Race[a]		
	White	90.6	86.8
	Black	5.3	5.7
	Hispanic/Latino	2.4	5.1
	Asian	1.0	.7
	Other	.8	1.8
U.S.A.	Region[c]		
	East	22.7	18.5
	Midwest	28.8	15.4
	South	27.6	22.1
	West	20.9	43.9
U.S.A.	Size/type of locality[c]		
	500,000 or more	12.9	17.8
	250,000–499,000	4.1	13.6
	50,000–249,000	13.0	20.8
	Suburbs	38.5	31.7
	10,000–49,000	3.3	2.1
	Rural area	28.2	13.8
VRS	Household income		
	Less than $15,000	12.5	17.0
	$15,000–29,999	25.0	25.5
	$30,000–49,999	34.1	29.0
	$50,000–99,999	23.5	25.5
	$100,000 or more	4.9	3.0
CBS	Type of employment[c]		
	Professional manager	30.2	50.6

Data base	Variable	Nongay (%)	Gay/lesbian (%)
	Schoolteacher	5.4	8.4
	Other white-collar	11.7	12.3
	Blue-collar	12.4	13.4
	Farm	1.8	—
	Full-time student	3.1	2.4
	Homemaker	9.7	—
	Retired	21.1	9.6
	Unemployed/looking	4.7	3.1
CBS	Government employee	11.8	11.9
VRS	Labor union member	11.3	10.8
VRS	Religion *raised in*		
	Protestant	49.2	31.6
	Catholic	30.0	32.1
	Other Christian	10.8	16.1
	Jewish	3.8	6.3
	Other religion	3.1	7.4
	No religion	3.2	6.6
CBS	Religion *today*[c]		
	Protestant	46.7	34.5
	Catholic	25.2	15.3
	Other Christian	11.9	8.9
	Jewish	3.2	4.8
	Other religion	5.5	19.0
	No religion	7.6	17.6
U.S.A.	Attend religious services at least once a month[c]	43.4	24.4
CBS	Fundamentalist or evangelical Christian	10.7	11.7
VRS	Married	62.0	10.4
CBS	Have children under 18[c]	31.6	11.4
U.S.A.	First-time voter	3.2	3.5
CBS	Military veteran	18.1	17.5
VRS	Have family member in armed forces or reserves	11.7	12.2
CBS	Crime victim within last year[b]	5.3	12.3
CBS	Gun owner[a]	28.5	21.6

NOTE: Data are presented as weighted percentages. "U.S.A." indicates combined responses to identical questions from both the VRS and CBS polls.

[a] Significance level (chi²): = .05.

[b] Significance level = .01.

[c] Significance level = .001.

TABLE 3.2.
Comparison of political attitudes of gay and lesbian voters with other voters, 1990 U.S. general election

Data base	Variable	Nongay (%)	Gay/ lesbian (%)	Data base	Variable	Nongay (%)	Gay/ lesbian (%)
General				VRS	Economy next year will be		
U.S.A.	Party affiliation[c]				Better	14.0	12.5
	Democratic	36.4	47.8		About the same	31.7	32.2
	Republican	33.8	19.0		Worse	54.3	55.3
	Independent, other	29.8	33.1				
				CBS	More important economic problem[a]		
U.S.A.	Bush approval				Unemployment/jobs	15.7	19.3
	rating[c]	60.3	43.4		Inflation/prices	28.6	23.5
VRS	Ideology[c]			CBS	Saving environment more important than		
	Liberal	19.0	55.5		saving jobs (% "yes")[c]	54.9	76.8
	Moderate	46.5	35.2				
	Conservative	34.5	9.3	*Federal spending*			
				CBS	Better able to handle deficit[c]		
VRS	Approval of Congress	19.6	25.6		Bush	45.5	25.4
					Congress	54.5	74.6
CBS	Single most important issue						
	Economy	44.0	35.0	VRS	Approve of 1990 bipartisan		
	Drugs	8.3	4.8		deficit reduction plan	44.6	36.1
	Environment[c]	7.6	25.3				
	U.S. deficit plan	19.5	16.9	*Social issues*			
	Abortion	10.4	8.9	VRS	Abortion should be legal[c]		
	Persian Gulf	7.4	5.3		Always	39.5	77.4
	Savings and loans	2.8	3.8		Sometimes	45.3	21.9
					Never	15.2	.8
VRS	Among top two issues						
	Environment[c]	20.9	44.9	CBS	Abortion should be legal[c]		
	Education	25.9	19.7		Always	42.7	66.4
	Crime and drugs[a]	21.9	16.6		In most cases	16.7	13.0
	U.S. deficit plan	24.9	25.9		Rape/incest/life of		
	Abortion[a]	13.4	21.0		mother	31.2	13.6
	Federal taxes[a]	14.6	10.2		Never	9.4	6.9
	Persian Gulf	6.5	4.5				
	Savings and loans	4.6	6.4		First-degree murder penalty should be[c]		
	National economy	13.9	12.9		Death	62.5	42.1
					Life without parole	32.4	42.5
VRS	Country is seriously				Prison, possible		
	off track[b]	59.0	70.2		parole	5.1	15.4
The economy					Better way to fight drugs[c]		
VRS	Condition of economy				More law		
	Excellent or good	20.4	14.4		enforcement	43.7	12.5
					Education, treatment	56.3	87.5
VRS	Compared to two years ago am						
	Better off	28.5	38.8				
	About the same	44.9	38.2				
	Worse off	26.5	23.0	VRS	Strong feminist[c]	8.4	26.0

Data base	Variable	Nongay (%)	Gay/ lesbian (%)	Data base	Variable	Nongay (%)	Gay/ lesbian (%)
Defense and foreign affairs				*Institutional trust*			
VRS	Right to be in Gulf[b]	69.7	58.9	CBS	Federal government can be trusted to do the right thing		
CBS	Should stay in Persian Gulf even at risk of				Almost all the time	3.1	2.8
					Most of the time	30.0	31.6
					Only sometimes	58.4	60.5
	U.S. lives[c]	61.9	46.1		Never	8.4	5.0
CBS	Defense spending should[c]			CBS	Most members of Congress deserve reelection	21.1	27.3
	Increase	15.5	4.1				
	Stay about the same	45.1	35.5	VRS	Support Congressional term		
	Decrease	39.3	60.4		limits[a]	72.0	62.5

NOTE: Data are presented as weighted percentages. "U.S.A." indicates combined responses to identical questions from both the VRS and CBS data bases.
[a] Significance level (chi^2): = .05.
[b] Significance level = .01.
[c] Significance level = .001.

TABLE 3.3.
Voting behavior and 1992 presidential preferences of gay and lesbian voters compared with other voters,
1990 U.S. general election

Data base	Variable	Nongay %	Gay/ lesbian %	Data base	Variable	Nongay (%)	Gay/ lesbian %
U.S.A.	Vote for governor[c]			CBS	Most important factor in making		
	Democratic	49.4	68.8		Congressional vote choice[c]		
	Republican	43.5	26.4		Effectiveness	45.1	26.0
	Other	7.1	4.8		Stands on		
					issues	46.8	57.2
U.S.A.	Vote for U.S. Senate[c]				Party	8.1	16.8
	Democratic	48.8	59.7				
	Republican	48.0	37.6	CBS	Which party do you blame more for		
	Other	3.2	2.8		the savings and loan crises?[b]		
					The Democrats	16.9	12.6
U.S.A.	Vote for U.S. House[c]				The Republicans	26.0	40.3
	Democratic	50.0	58.1		Both equally	43.4	38.0
	Republican	43.2	25.8		Neither	13.7	9.1
	Other	6.8	16.1				
				CBS	Campaigns this year were		
VRS	Self-reported 1988 presidential vote[c]				More positive	10.3	12.9
	Bush (R)	62.5	33.2		More negative	49.5	52.0
	Dukakis (D)	33.3	60.1		About same as		
	Other	4.2	6.7		in past	40.2	35.2
VRS	Probable presidential vote in 1992[c]			VRS	Preferred Democratic nominee in		
	Bush	33.7	10.3		1992 (Republicans excluded)		
	The Democrat	31.2	51.7		Lloyd Bentsen	16.5	7.3
	Not sure	35.1	37.9		Bill Bradley	11.6	15.0
					Bill Clinton	2.4	0
CBS	Congressional vote today[c]				Mario Cuomo	31.0	33.9
	Pro-Bush	19.7	11.8		Jesse Jackson	12.4	20.8
	Anti-Bush	16.0	29.2		Sam Nunn	8.2	3.1
	Bush was not a				Douglas Wilder	1.3	2.4
	factor	64.3	59.0		Someone else	16.6	17.5

NOTE: Data are presented as weighted percentages. "U.S.A." indicates combined responses to identical questions from both the VRS and CBS data bases.
[a] Significance level (chi[2]): = .05.
[b] Significance level = .01.
[c] Significance level = .001.

TABLE 3.4.
Significant differences between lesbians and gay men, 1990 national exit polls

Item	Men (%)	Women (%)	Significance
VRS data			
Abortion a top issue	12.2	36.4	.001
Deficit plan approval	45.8	20.0	.05
Favor Gulf deployment	71.1	37.0	.01
Country off track	64.3	80.5	.05
Economy excellent/good	22.6	0	.05
Strong feminist	6.2	61.2	.001
CBS data			
Should stay in Gulf	59.9	32.5	.01
Neared statistical significance			
Environment a top issue	51.5	33.2	.08
Deficit plan a top issue	33.6	12.3	.051

TABLE 3.5.
*Significant differences among gay men and feminist and nonfeminist lesbians, 1990 VRS
national exit poll form*

Item	Gay men %	Nonfeminist lesbians %	Feminist lesbians (%)	Significance
Abortion a top issue	9.2	18.3	47.9	.001
Deficit plan a top issue	34.9	16.1	9.8	.05
Economic state (% "poor")	18.5	22.5	44.1	.05
Senate vote (% Democratic)	58.1	26.8	77.0	.01
Deficit plan approval	48.5	41.4	6.5	.01
Favor Gulf deployment	71.2	45.0	31.7	.01
Bush approval	41.9	52.3	4.6	.01
Probable Democratic voter 1992	45.3	19.8	80.8	.01
Compared to two years ago am				.01
Better off	37.0	55.2	35.1	
About the same	46.0	41.5	12.1	
Worse off	17.0	3.3	52.7	
Neared statistical significance				
Education a top issue	15.7	43.4	19.3	.064
Voted for Bush 1988	39.0	53.0	9.9	.070
Country off track	62.4	68.5	88.1	.076
House vote				.099
Democratic	70.0	61.2	64.3	
Republican	21.7	27.7	7.1	
Other	8.3	11.1	28.6	
Abortion always legal	74.1	59.8	95.7	.104

TABLE 3.6.
Differences among self-identified lesbian and gay respondents, based on revised age cluster

Data base	Item	18–29 (%)	Age 30–44 (%)	45 + (%)
Demographics				
U.S.A.	Attend religious services at least once a month[b]	18.5	18.7	43.0
VRS	Education[c]			
	Not high school graduate	0	0	11.9
	High school graduate	5.9	6.3	19.2
	Some college	55.7	26.7	17.3
	College graduate	24.4	32.4	10.1
	Postgraduate work	14.0	34.7	41.5
VRS	Household income[b]			
	Less than $15,000	20.4	7.6	33.2
	$15,000–29,999	41.1	20.4	3.7
	$30,000–49,999	18.6	39.8	24.8
	$50,000–99,999	14.1	30.5	38.3
	$100,000 or more	5.8	1.6	0
CBS	White-collar employment[a]	82.3	76.6	51.8
Attitudes				
U.S.A.	Bush approval[a]	54.1	35.0	45.4
CBS	Single most important issue[b]			
	Economy	31.5	46.3	18.6
	Drugs	0	7.1	6.2
	Environment	31.8	20.0	27.5
	U.S. deficit plan	16.5	10.8	28.1
	Abortion	5.6	14.0	3.6
	Persian Gulf	1.6	1.7	15.9
	Savings and loans	13.0	0	0
CBS	Abortion should always be legal[b]	58.5	81.1	48.6
CBS	Defense spending should be decreased[b]	36.5	67.9	71.3
CBS	0–6 issue scale (number of liberal stands)[d]			
	0 or 1 liberal	6.3	5.4	13.2
	2 to 4 liberal	64.8	36.2	43.1
	5 or 6 liberal	28.9	58.3	43.7
VRS	Among top two issues			
	Environment[d]	58.9	38.0	33.3
	Federal taxes[a]	9.8	4.0	24.8

Data base	Item	Age 18–29 (%)	30–44 (%)	45 + (%)
Voting behavior				
U.S.A.	Vote for governor[a]			
	Democratic	65.6	77.3	57.4
	Republican	34.4	17.2	32.5
	Other		0	5.4
U.S.A.	Vote for U.S. Senate[a]			
	Democratic	51.2	75.6	49.6
	Republican	48.8	22.6	40.8
	Other	0	1.8	9.6
U.S.A.	Vote for U.S. House[d]			
	Democratic	60.8	63.1	44.7
	Republican	22.8	18.8	35.3
	Other	10.4	18.1	20.0

NOTE: Data are presented as weighted percentages. "U.S.A." indicates combined responses to identical questions from both the VRS and CBS data bases.

[a] Significance level (chi2): = .05.

[b] Significance level = .01.

[c] Significance level = .001.

[d] Relationships significant at .051 to .099 (approaching statistical significance).

TABLE 3.7.

Logistic regression of factors with significant relationship to self-identification as gay or lesbian

Variable	B	S.E.	Wald	Significance
U.S.A. data				
Age	−.3606	.0428	70.9608	.0000
Sex	−.3424	.1385	6.1162	.0134
Race	−.0248	.2085	.0141	.9053
Church attendance	−.6411	.1589	16.2793	.0001
Region				
East	.4038	.2359	2.9300	.0869
South	.4413	.2304	3.6687	.0554
West	1.1276	.2079	29.4077	.0000
Size of locality				
500,000 or more	.8147	.2463	10.9404	.0009
250,000–499,999	1.5397	.2645	33.8869	.0000
50,000–249,999	.9484	.2347	16.3292	.0001
Suburbs	.4065	.2182	3.4697	.0625
10,000–49,999	.1525	.4939	.0953	.7575
Constant	−3.7423	.3316	127.3746	.0000
VRS data				
Age	−.4239	.0746	32.3141	.0000
Sex	−.6325	.2171	8.4912	.0036
Race	.0656	.2911	.0509	.8215
Region				
East	.4154	.3763	1.2186	.2696
South	.8988	.3551	6.4056	.0114
West	1.2127	.3350	13.1021	.0003
Size of locality				
500,000 or more	1.1353	.3804	8.9093	.0028
250,000–499,999	1.6382	.4019	16.6163	.0000
50,000–249,999	.7595	.3794	4.0089	.0453
Suburbs	.5105	.3464	2.1717	.1406
10,000–49,999	−.0617	.8380	.0054	.9413
Church attendance	−.6713	.2428	7.6468	.0057
Religion raised in				
Catholic	.2324	.2689	.7471	.3874
Other Christian	.4358	.3265	1.7822	.1819
Jewish	.5706	.4654	1.5034	.2201
Other religion	.8503	.4388	3.7544	.0527
No religion	.2424	.4522	.2874	.5919
Education	.3737	.1061	12.4032	.0004
Income	−.2913	.1058	7.5789	.0059
Constant	−4.2311	.6669	40.2486	.0000

NOTE: Sex: Men are coded "1," women "2." Race: People of color are coded "1," whites are coded "0." Region: The Midwest is the baseline. Size of locality: Rural areas are the baseline. Religious upbringing: Protestants are the baseline.

TABLE 3.8.

Logistic regression of effect of self-identification as gay or lesbian, after its demographic correlates are controlled for, on self-identification as a liberal

Variable	B	S.E.	Wald	Significance
Age	−.1313	.0164	64.4386	.0000
Sex	.2704	.0560	23.2710	.0000
Race	.5240	.0887	34.9306	.0000
Region				
East	.1183	.0775	2.3297	.1269
South	−.3218	.0816	15.5441	.0001
West	−.0233	.0806	.0837	.7724
Size of locality				
500,000 or more	.1714	.0938	3.3419	.0675
250,000–499,999	.3575	.1358	6.9317	.0085
50,000–249,999	.3038	.0936	10.5240	.0012
Suburbs	−.0007	.0745	.0001	.9925
10,000–49,999	−.0664	.1853	.1284	.7201
Church attendance	−.6947	.0602	133.0346	.0000
Religion raised in				
Catholic	.2138	.0675	10.0395	.0015
Other Christian	.1894	.0954	3.9447	.0470
Jewish	1.2081	.1254	92.8383	.0000
Other religion	.1322	.1582	.6987	.4032
No religion	.6327	.1379	21.0579	.0000
Education	.1139	.0273	17.3966	.0000
Income	−.0710	.0290	5.9839	.0144
Gay/lesbian	1.3324	.2186	37.1534	.0000
Constant	−1.5399	.1663	85.7483	.0000

SOURCE: VRS data base.

NOTE: Sex: Men are coded "1," women "2." Race: People of color are coded "1," whites are coded "0." Region: The Midwest is the baseline. Size of locality: Rural areas are the baseline. Religious upbringing: Protestants are the baseline.

TABLE 3.9.
Logistic regression of effect of self-identification as gay or lesbian, after its demographic correlates are controlled for, on self-identification as a strong feminist

Variable	B	S.E.	Wald	Significance
Age	−.0534	.0229	5.4233	.0199
Sex	1.7870	.0948	355.4827	.0000
Race	−.1511	.1353	1.2475	.2640
Region				
East	.1541	.1099	1.9669	.1608
South	.1089	.1103	.9750	.3234
West	.1053	.1146	.8449	.3580
Size of locality				
500,000 or more	.4716	.1297	13.2187	.0003
250,000–499,999	.2158	.1987	1.1794	.2775
50,000–249,999	.4723	.1292	13.3663	.0003
Suburbs	.1940	.1068	3.2960	.0694
10,000–49,999	−.1766	.2724	.4204	.5167
Church attendance	−.0280	.0804	.1213	.7276
Religion raised in				
Catholic	.1255	.0929	1.8266	.1765
Other Christian	−.0244	.1432	.0289	.8650
Jewish	.5269	.1695	9.7330	.0018
Other religion	.6097	.2145	8.0785	.0045
No religion	1.0346	.1811	32.6465	.0000
Education	.4904	.0386	161.0552	.0000
Income	.0347	.0397	.7626	.3825
Gay/lesbian	1.3406	.2634	25.9036	.0000
Constant	−7.7284	.2822	665.4474	.0000

SOURCE: VRS data base.
   NOTE: Sex: Men are coded "1," women "2." Race: People of color are coded "1," whites are coded "0." Region: The Midwest is the baseline. Size of locality: Rural areas are the baseline. Religious upbringing: Protestants are the baseline.

TABLE 3.10.

Logistic regression analysis of effect of gay/lesbian self-identification on voting behavior when controlled, in succession, for demographic variables, party affiliation and incumbent's party, and ideology and feminism, 1990 general elections

	Explanatory measures				Predictive measures	
	B	S.E.	Wald	Significance	Mean	% Correct
House contests (N = 8,239)						
Voted for Democrat					53.19	
Self-identification alone	.8368	.2411	12.0494	.0005		52.99
Add demographics	.6948	.2495	7.7564	.0054		59.45
Add party identification, incumbency	.2420	.2691	.8085	.3686		72.52
Add ideology, feminism	−.0076	.2730	.0008	.9779		72.88
Voted for Republican					43.85	
Self-identification alone	−1.2096	.2745	19.4176	.0000		55.98
Add demographics	−1.0696	.2827	14.3110	.0002		60.51
Add party identification, incumbency	−.6364	.3029	4.4136	.0357		73.04
Add ideology, feminism	−.3816	.3079	1.5353	.2153		73.83
Voted for third candidate					6.92	
Self-identification alone	.8711	.3001	8.4229	.0037		93.32
Add demographics	.7357	.3102	5.6266	.0177		93.32
Add party identification, incumbency	.6431	.3128	4.2252	.0398		93.32
Add ideology, feminism	.6388	.3174	4.0515	.0441		93.32
Senate contests (N = 4,587)						
Voted for Democrat					48.98	
Self-identification alone	.6475	.3193	4.1135	.0425		
Add demographics	.3445	.3326	1.0728	.3003		
Add party identification, incumbency	.3116	.3739	.6945	.4046		
Add ideology, feminism	.0178	.3813	.0022	.9628		

TABLE 3.10. *continued*

	Explanatory measures				Predictive measures	
	B	S.E.	Wald	Significance	Mean	% Correct
Voted for Republican					48.11	
Self-identification alone	−.7934	.3333	5.6686	.0173		51.76
Add demographics	−.5282	.3460	2.3299	.1269		60.03
Add party identification, incumbency	−.5126	.3819	1.8014	.1795		72.28
Add ideology, feminism	−.2341	.3899	.3606	.5482		73.11
Gubernatorial contests (N = 6,661)						
Voted for Democrat					50.01	
Self-identification alone	.7950	.2440	10.6147	.0011		50.42
Add demographics	.4675	.2534	3.4022	.0651		60.65
Add party identification, incumbency	.2841	.2781	1.0434	.3070		72.61
Add ideology, feminism	.0149	.2840	.0027	.9582		73.68
Voted for Republican					42.95	
Self-identification alone	−.8609	.2636	10.6628	.0011		57.04
Add demographics	−.5000	.2723	3.3709	.0664		62.74
Add party identification, incumbency	−.3022	.2945	1.0533	.3047		72.53
Add ideology, feminism	−.0696	.3000	.0539	.8165		73.04

SOURCE: VRS data base.

TABLE 3.11.

Logistic regression of vote for U.S. House according to the retrospective model, adding the variables of incumbent party, evaluation of Congress, and self-identification as gay or lesbian

Variable	B	S.E.	Wald	Significance
Voted for Democrat for House				
(72.88% correct)				
Democratic identification	.9468	.0640	218.5561	.0000
Republican identification	−.7870	.0642	150.1569	.0000
Democratic incumbency	.6305	.0921	46.8756	.0000
Republican incumbency	−.8062	.0934	74.4559	.0000
Bush approval	−.6855	.0580	139.6852	.0000
Congressional approval	.2489	.0675	13.5920	.0002
Retrospective evaluation of national				
economy	.1168	.0434	7.2596	.0071
Ideology	−.4234	.0386	120.2243	.0000
Gay or lesbian	−.0571	.2691	.0450	.8320
Constant	.1307	.2040	.4105	.5217
Voted for Republican for House				
(73.34% correct)				
Democratic identification	−.9006	.0662	184.8204	.0000
Republican identification	.8519	.0642	175.9151	.0000
Democratic incumbency	−.7816	.0935	69.9195	.0000
Republican incumbency	.7345	.0941	60.9713	.0000
Bush approval	.7838	.0593	174.9790	.0000
Congressional approval	.2150	.0687	9.7842	.0018
Retrospective evaluation of national				
economy	−.2002	.0441	20.5983	.0000
Ideology	.4237	.0395	115.2897	.0000
Gay or lesbian	−.3269	.3044	1.1536	.2828
Constant	.2031	.2072	.9604	.3271
Voted for third candidate for House				
(no "yes" answers predicted)				
Democratic identification	−.5819	.1061	30.0614	.0000
Republican identification	−.4422	.1103	16.0678	.0001
Democratic incumbency	1.3302	.2498	28.3602	.0000
Republican incumbency	.8540	.2544	11.2682	.0008
Bush approval	−.1807	.0977	3.4205	.0644
Congressional approval	−.2962	.1272	5.4189	.0199
Retrospective evaluation of national				
economy	.3093	.0733	17.8211	.0000
Ideology	.0819	.0641	1.6332	.2013
Gay or lesbian	.5905	.3131	3.5581	.0593
Constant	−5.3030	.4218	158.0968	.0000

SOURCE: VRS data base.

NOTE: Retrospective evaluations were coded on a 1-to-4 scale, with 1 being "excellent" and 4 being "poor."

FOUR

A View from the States

It was established in the preceding chapter that in November 1990 there was a distinctive "gay and lesbian vote" in America. Self-identified lesbians and gay men were significantly more liberal, particularly on domestic social issues, than were other voters with the same demographic characteristics, and lesbian self-identifiers were profoundly more likely still to call themselves "strong feminists" than were women who did not identify as lesbians. This augmented liberalism and feminism in turn directly affected party affiliation, retrospective evaluations of the president and the economy, and vote choice in contests for both houses of Congress and for state governorships.

At the same time the national exit polls analyzed in the last chapter were taken, VRS conducted a statewide exit poll in each of forty-two of the forty-three states (Virginia excluded) in which either a governor or a U.S. senator, or both, was being elected in November 1990. Each state survey was a version of the four-network VRS form of the national poll adapted to the circumstances in each state. In only twenty-one of these states did VRS employ the two-page "long form" survey (see appendix) that included the question permitting self-identification by lesbians and gay men. Nearly all the second-page questions were identical in each state, as were a number of demographic questions asked on the first page of each survey.

In this chapter I seek to confirm at the state level the results found at the national level, and also to test two additional hypotheses that were not possible to test using the national polls, relating to the distinctiveness of voting in individual contests (as opposed to the aggregated results found in the national polls) and the extent to which results differ given the relative closeness or polarization of candidates in high-salience contests on LGB issues. In addition, I seek to determine whether the "political culture" of each state appears to have an effect on lesbian and gay voting behavior, and to reach initial inferential conclusions about the role of LGB political leaders in mobilizing a cohesive bloc vote among lesbian and gay self-identifiers (to be tested more thoroughly in chapter 5).

In this chapter I first compare the pooled results of the twenty-one-state data with the results of the national data, to determine whether they are sufficiently similar that the national numbers can be confirmed as a reliable baseline for future study.

It is extremely important to caution the reader that a substantial share of the respondents to the state exit polls also were respondents to one or the other of the national surveys. As many as 70 percent of the respondents to the "VRS" national poll form also answered a state-level survey (Murray S. Edelman, personal communication).

Although this does not preclude all comparative analysis, given that the large majority of respondents to any given state survey did not complete the national VRS poll, a substantial minority of state-level respondents did complete both surveys. Some built-in correlation on that account must be expected, and the national-state comparisons must be read with great conservatism. It has not been possible for me to isolate those respondents who completed the national survey from those who did not.

It will be of special interest, then, when looking at the comparative results, to find those areas in which a trend found in the national polls was *not* confirmed in the state-level data.

Then, in the same manner as in the national study, I seek to establish baseline measurements for each of three particular states. As shown in table 4.1, in only three states were there as many as thirty gay and lesbian self-identifiers—California ($N = 86$), Texas ($N = 50$), and Massachusetts ($N = 33$). I take 30 as the absolute minimum number of cases with which any meaningful analysis may be done.

The three-state analysis begins with an assessment of Elazar's typology (1965) of "political cultures" as applied to each of the three states, and the likely effect of political culture on gay and lesbian voters in those states. Then follows a thumbnail description of the political situation in each state at the time of the 1990 general election. This is followed by simple comparative crosstabulations of attitudes, demographics, and voting behavior in that election, as were presented at the national level in chapter 3.

Once this has been done for all three states, I then will assess, both state by state and comparatively among the three of them, how the conclusions initially reached using the national data bases hold up in individual contests. This will involve determining (1) the extent to which sex, feminism, and party affiliation are responsible for divisions among self-identified lesbians and gay men, (2) the independent effect of gay/lesbian self-identification after controlling for demographic correlates, partisanship, ideology, and feminism, and (3) the independent effect, if any, of gay/lesbian self-identification on vote choice in retrospective models in statewide elections. The answers to these questions constitute the answer to Hypothesis 7, which postulates that distinctive gay/lesbian voting will be maintained in individual contests at the levels found in the national polls, and will be especially distinctive in high-salience contests.

In addition, my speculations in the next few pages about the effects of political culture on lesbian and gay self-identifiers in each state will be tested using crosstabular data. I shall compare the vote choices of self-identifiers with the rest of the sample as broken down by race and by strong identification (or not) with feminism.

I shall also be testing Hypothesis 8, relating to the role of symbolic versus substantive voting. In two of the three gubernatorial contests, one candidate clearly was perceived as "progay," the other "antigay," and in one of these (Massachusetts), the "progay" candidate was the Republican. In the third statehouse contest (California), both candidates attempted to present themselves as gay rights supporters. Hypothesis 8 would predict, then, that the "progay" candidates, regardless of party, would win over the lion's share of lesbian and gay self-identifiers in Texas and Massachusetts, whereas in California the contest would be decided on the basis of substantive issue concerns, and the gay and lesbian vote might therefore be fragmented, unlike in the other two states. The results of this inquiry will allow us to make initial inferences about the ability of LGB political leaders independently to mobilize "their" voters, which is the subject of Hypothesis 9; this hypothesis will be tested empirically in the next chapter.

Comparing the National and Twenty-One-State Results

Edelman (1991) previously reported some of the findings from pooled results from the twenty-one state polls. These results, and some additional ones, are set forth in tables 4.1 (pooled, unweighted data compared with nongay respondents) and 4.2 (comparison with lesbians and gay men in weighted national data). These pooled results are consistent with the findings of the national random samples, and therefore confirm the first three hypotheses in several respects.

Table 4.1 breaks down the raw number of respondents in each of the twenty-one "long form" states by sex and by sexual self-identification. The total share of self-identifiers is 1.1 percent, precisely the same as in the national polls. The regional patterns of self-identification are the same as well; Westerners are nearly twice as likely to self-identify as are Northeasterners or Southerners, and these in turn are twice as likely to do so as are Midwesterners. The breakdown by sex shows a substantial majority of gay men over lesbians; gay men made up 64 percent of the pooled state respondents. These levels are found in most of the states; in only four of the twenty-one do women constitute a majority, whereas women are in the majority among the rest of the voting population in all but one state and in both national polls.

Table 4.2 compares the findings of the national polls and the pooled twenty-one-state data on the demographics and attitudes of the gay and lesbian respondents. In nearly every respect the findings of the pooled state samples closely corroborate—although they do not precisely mimic—the findings of the simultaneous national polls. Of particular note is that the pooled state-level data confirm the findings of the national polls that self-identifiers are disproportionately young, well educated, liberal, and feminist—but not as strongly identified with the Democrats as their liberalism and feminism would predict.

The one category in which a major difference from the national data sets occurs is in the breakdown of localities of residence, and this largely is a function of the random selection of precincts within each state by the polling firm. Both the national and state data put an absolute majority of the gay and lesbian self-identifiers in central cities of fifty thousand or more, about one-third in the suburbs, and the remaining 15 percent or so in small cities and rural areas. However, the state-level data tend to imply that a far greater number of gay and lesbian respondents live in the largest central cities, those with at least a half-million inhabitants, than do the national data; and no gay or lesbian respondents were found in rural precincts in the state-level data sets, while many more were found in small cities than in the national data sets.

This minor exception aside, and taking into account the respondents who answered both a state and a national poll, from these results we may draw an initial impression that the national data are reliable with respect to measuring the demographics, attitudes, and voting behavior of self-identified lesbians and gay men in November 1990.

Elazar's Typology

The American states, of course, are hardly identical, and as a preface to the examination of the three states, I will look at two additional elements of potential importance to our discussion. First is Elazar's scheme of state "political cultures" (1965, chap. 4). I describe his typology, set forth each state's place within it, and speculate on the effects of state political culture on LGB voting behavior within each state.[1] Next I offer a brief description of the political situation in each of the three states in 1990, distilled from Barone and Ujifusa (1991) and from contemporaneous news accounts.

The Elazar typology, thirty years old at this writing, is used here not to give a definitive cast to the politics of any of the three states, but to provide a general context for the political mores and political choices within each state. With respect to LGB voters, Elazar's typology allows us to speculate, first, on the degree to which political cohesiveness is likely to be achieved within the group; and second, on the extent to which the group is likely to vote together with other "progressive" groups, such as African Americans and feminist women, as hypothesized by Adam (1987), or on the contrary is likely to view LGB causes as separate and distinct from other groups' claims for social justice.

Elazar envisions three archetypal political cultures, deriving from a notion that two conflicting ideas of American democracy hold forth in the collective consciousness: America as "many" and America as "one." The *individualistic* culture represents the former of these ideas: that democracy is a marketplace in which political relationships are defined by bargaining among self-interested groups and individuals. Thus, competition among groups and the very notion of interest group politics are considered normal and healthy, and political structures are relatively permeable and close to the citizen.

The *moralistic*[2] culture represents the opposite tendency, according to Elazar: society is conceived as a whole, a "commonwealth," not as a collection of individuals and groups, and the purpose of political activity is to achieve the common good; interest group politics is viewed with disdain. Interestingly, states strongly influenced by the Progressive movement of the early twentieth century tend to fall into the "moralistic" classification; such states tend to use "direct democracy" measures such as the initiative, referendum, and recall as a palliative against the influence of powerful groups and persons on the representative instruments of government.

A third postulated culture, the *traditionalistic,* falls in the middle (or outside) of this conflict; it holds that the fundamental purpose of government is to preserve existing social arrangements, and government tends to be run by and for the benefit of a long-standing elite or squirearchy. Traditionalistic cultures tend to be concentrated heavily in the Southern states, in which, as noted by Key (1949) and Black and Black (1987), the principal political divisions relate to race and to class divisions among whites. The expectation has been that citizen participation would largely be limited to voting, and until the 1960s various legal and extralegal means were used to discourage (or prevent) both black and working-class white citizens even from voting.

A relatively small number of states fall exclusively within one of these three categories, according to Elazar; often there is a dominant culture that is infused with strong tendencies from a second.

Massachusetts was classed as an "individualistic" state by Elazar, one in which government is viewed as an open marketplace for various social interests. Further, the state retains many colonial-era political institutions such as large legislative bodies, numerous elective executive posts, and the annual direct democracy exercise of town meetings. We can therefore expect that bisexuals, lesbians, and gay men would be in a strong position to organize and to exercise influence on government in Massachusetts relative to some other states. We also may speculate, however, that gay voters would be likely to break with nongay African Americans and feminists in the event that their interests were seen to conflict.

California, with a strong Progressive influence on its political structure and heavy in-migration both from within and without the country, was classed by Elazar as having an inherently conflicting political culture in which "moralistic" tendencies dominate, but are undergirded with a strong secondary "individualistic" element. The state has numerous elective offices, but for most voters these officials are quite distant from them.[3] The "moralistic" tendency and the relative lack of direct access to officials make politics a matter of mass organization and appeals. Politics, including initiative and referendum campaigns, are conducted through direct mail and the mass media in a state in which political borders are oddly delineated and poorly understood, and in which very large numbers of voters must be reached. In this environment, LGBs would seem most likely to work in coalition with feminists and racial minorities and to view their interests as tied up with those of fellow coalition members; therefore, distinctiveness from other coalition members would be least likely to appear.

Texas was classed by Elazar as predominantly "traditionalistic," centered around maintenance of the status quo, but with a strong streak of "individualism" as well. The heavy rate of migration to Texas in the past thirty years, both from within the United States and from Mexico and Central America, and the

voting rights revolution together have accentuated the rise of the "individualistic" element in Texas politics. However, the voting base of the "Tory Democrats," the "traditionalists" who ran the state for a century and remain influential today, is and has been small-town and rural social conservatives who are
extremely intolerant of homosexuality. The Tory Democrats, in coalition with
economically conservative urban Republicans, have tended to dominate the
state's politics as against blacks, Latinos, feminists, trade unionists, and urban
white liberals. Two effects can be predicted: feminists and racial minorities
making demands on this largely resistant and impervious system may look
askance at the inclusion of LGB concerns in their agenda; and white gay men
especially may divorce their liberalism on gay rights from a more general Texan
conservatism and view minority and women's concerns as no concern of theirs.
Thus, the prospect that LGB voters could organize either a cohesive vote
among themselves or a coalition with non-LGB minority groups in Texas
politics, given the state's political and social culture, would appear to be the
most problematic of any of these three states.

The Political Situation in the States, November 1990

California

As noted above, California is a "long ballot" state in which a great variety of
state and county-level officials are elected directly. The state also has one of the
most liberal ballot access laws for initiative and referendum measures, and
the measures on the ballot at any particular election to a great extent mold the
debate among the major contenders for statewide office. As it happened, two
significant proposals were placed on the ballot at this election.

One was a comprehensive environmentalist initiative, nicknamed "Big
Green," which would greatly restrict nuclear power, offshore oil drilling, and
pesticide use, mandate recycling of many products, increase auto emission
standards (already the most stringent in the nation), and push the use of mass
transit and "clean" forms of energy. Business concerns and many government
officials feared "Big Green" would vastly increase the costs of products and of
government, particularly at a time when California's economy was sliding into
recession, with its computer and aerospace industries particularly hard hit.

The other was a proposal to limit total years of service in the California
legislature to six years in the state assembly and eight years in the state senate;
the legislature, hoping to head off passage of this draconian measure, had
responded by proposing a limit of twelve years' service in each house and

public financing of state legislative elections. Although this was a response to voter concerns about state legislative elections, it reflected as well the difficulties of the state's most powerful member of Congress, Senate Assistant Majority Leader Alan Cranston, a left-wing Democrat and onetime presidential candidate, who had been cited by a committee of his colleagues for his leading role in the "Keating Five" scandal.

The state had been booming economically in the 1980s on the back of its computer-related industries, and had grown sufficiently on the strength of internal and foreign immigration to acquire an additional seven seats (for a total of fifty-two) in the House of Representatives in the 1990 census. By the time of the election, however, California had suffered a slump in the computer industry, adding to the woes of its ailing aerospace industry, and the ill effects of a drought that began in the mid-1980s.

Republican Governor George Deukmejian was retiring after two four-year terms, and the contest of greatest interest in California in 1990 was the one to choose his successor. Cranston's Senate colleague, Pete Wilson, a moderate conservative and a former mayor of San Diego, was chosen as the Republican nominee. His Democratic opponent was Dianne Feinstein, who had recently stepped down after eleven years as mayor of San Francisco.

Of interest to us is that Feinstein succeeded to the mayoralty upon the assassination in November 1978 of the then mayor, George Moscone, and of City Supervisor Harvey Milk, the best-known openly gay elected official in the country at the time (Shilts 1982; Epstein 1986). Although identified with downtown business interests during her service in San Francisco, she built strong ties to the LGB community in the city.[4] Wilson, after his nomination, actively sought to make inroads among economically conservative LGB voters.

In the event, Wilson was elected by a two-point margin, although the Democrats maintained their majorities in both houses of the legislature. At the same time, the legislature's compromise term-limit proposal was defeated soundly, and the more stringent voter initiative enacting six-to eight-year term limits was passed in its stead. "Big Green" was defeated by a margin of four to three.

Massachusetts

Massachusetts, in contrast to California, maintains colonial-era political institutions, such as the elected Governor's Council, and is a state in which local autonomy remains strongly respected, exercised through annual town meetings and local selectmen. Also, unlike many Eastern states, Massachusetts voters have some access to the initiative and referendum; placing initiative measures on the statewide ballot is rather more difficult than in California, but not impossible. Since the 1950s the state has been dominated by the Democratic Party, although moderate-to-liberal Republicans[5] occasionally win high-visibility offices.

If California was jittery about the state of the economy, the voters of Massachusetts were in a rage. Two years before, as the Democratic nominee for president, their governor, Michael Dukakis, boasted of a "Massachusetts miracle" he said he had wrought in a state dependent on smokestack industry and imported oil by cutting the state's burdensome tax rates (which had earned it the sobriquet "Taxachusetts"), bringing in high-tech industry, and working in partnership with business and labor to make the state more competitive. In the two years since Dukakis's defeat, the "Massachusetts miracle," to the extent it really had existed, had fallen apart; unemployment was high, and the state's budget was seemingly incapable of being balanced (as required by law) because of squabbling and showdowns between Dukakis and his own party's legislature. Anger with Dukakis and the Democrats was so high that only a third of Massachusetts voters, who still voted Democratic for the most part, would identify as Democrats in November 1990. His approval rating in the teens, Dukakis bowed to the inevitable and chose not to seek a fourth term as governor.

The expected Democratic nominee to succeed Dukakis was Francis Bellotti, the state's former attorney general, something of an "old pol" in line with the "Tip O'Neill liberal" tradition in the state party. However, Bellotti was upset in a ripsnorting Democratic primary by John Silber, a blunt-speaking conservative well known for his tenure as president of Boston University, where he made various improvements in the university's stature while picking fights with the faculty and with feminist, minority, and liberal students, including his school's LGB community.[6] Silber's penchant for saying what seemed exactly the wrong thing at the wrong time, and doing it on purpose, led *Newsweek* to dub him "Archie Bunker with a Ph.D."[7] His attacks on welfare, big government, and social experimentation nonetheless struck a responsive chord with the same older white ethnic voters who put conservative Democrat Ed King in the governor's office (dumping Dukakis after his first term) in 1978. Two other liberal state officeholders, including Attorney General James Shannon, also were defeated for renomination. Barone and Ujifusa (1991, 566) commented, "Never in modern American history have the leadership and policies and philosophy of a presidential nominee been so thoroughly repudiated by voters of his own state as Michael Dukakis's were in Massachusetts in September 1990."

The Republicans, meanwhile, nominated William Weld, a former U.S. assistant attorney general in the Reagan administration who resigned in protest over the alleged ethical and managerial lapses of his boss, then Attorney General Edwin Meese. Weld, an unabashed liberal on social issues and equally unabashed conservative on government spending and taxes, defeated a more conventional conservative, state lawmaker Steven Pierce, in the GOP primary.

Liberal and moderate Democrats who had supported Bellotti now found themselves in the uncomfortable position of having to vote for either Silber, who strongly offended their sensibilities, or Weld, a fiscal right-winger and Republican. It was reputedly defections among liberal and moderate Democrats that proved essential to Weld's narrow victory over Silber. Anger at the state Democratic Party and the Dukakis administration spilled over into other contests: a substantial Republican minority was elected for the first time in recent years to the state legislature, a Republican was elected state treasurer, and even U.S. Senator John Kerry, facing nominal opposition, won reelection by only a thirteen-point margin.

Texas

The nation's second-largest and (at the time) third most populous state had an electoral system harking back to the Jacksonian era, with numerous directly elected statewide executive and regulatory officials, judges (including Supreme Court justices) chosen in high-spending partisan elections, and a relatively weak governor's office.[8] Once dominated by conservative "Tory Democrats," it had come to be one of the Southern states in which the Republican Party had made the most significant inroads at all levels, especially in the suburbs and the enclaves of the wealthy and the upper middle class in the major cities of Houston, Dallas, and San Antonio. Rural Anglo (non-Latino white) Texans who formed the base of support for Tory Democrats remained deeply conservative and often split their tickets, supporting old-style Democrats but abandoning liberal and (sometimes) moderate Democrats of the national variety for Republican nominees.

In 1990 the state's first Republican governor since Reconstruction, Bill Clements, was stepping down. Clements, a self-made millionaire and former Nixon administration official, had narrowly defeated a populist Democrat for the governorship in 1978, then lost in 1982 to moderate Tory Democrat Mark White, who in turn was defeated by Clements in the bad economy of 1986. Texas since 1985 had been mired in twin ruts: the "oil bust" of the mid-1980s and the collapse of the savings and loan industry, which had financed significant overbuilding during the "oil boom" of the early 1980s. Clements's retirement, and that of longtime Democratic Lieutenant Governor Bill Hobby, set off an office-clearing in Texas state politics, as numerous officials sought to move up the state's political ladder.

White sought a comeback in 1990, but placed third in the primary behind two more liberal Democrats, State Treasurer Ann Richards and Attorney General Jim Mattox. The campaign was notable for its unusually personal slurs by, and against, all three principal candidates; at one point Mattox charged (without proof) that Richards, a recovering alcoholic, was a cocaine addict, whereas Richards accused Mattox and White of personal dishonesty.

Richards won the runoff, but was considered badly weakened against the Republican nominee, Clayton Williams, like Clements a self-made millionaire with a certain brusque charm who campaigned in a Stetson hat. He had got into the race, he said, because of his son's onetime drug problem, and he won votes with his advocacy of boot camps for first-time drug offenders. Williams, however, began shooting himself in the foot with intemperate remarks, one of which made the national press: speaking of rape, he said, "If it's inevitable, you've just got to lie back and enjoy it." Williams also was criticized within the state for ungentlemanly conduct when he refused to shake Richards's hand at a television debate late in the campaign. Richards, meanwhile, had received attention as a hardball campaigner willing to throw mud as needed, which was criticized in some Texas quarters as unladylike.

Of importance to this study, Williams made an issue of Richards's support from LGB community organizations and ran as an absolute opponent of both homosexuality and civil rights protection based on sexual orientation. Richards's principal base of support was among feminists, and she courted LGB Texans as had no gubernatorial candidate before.

Richards ultimately won the contest between "Claytie and the Lady" by a narrow margin, becoming the first woman to be elected governor of a large state in her own right.[9] Most of her Democratic ticket-mates also were elected or reelected, although left-wing populist Jim Hightower lost his post as agriculture commissioner and a Republican won the post of state treasurer. Texans also reelected conservative Republican Senator Phil Gramm, principal author of the Gramm-Rudman-Hollings deficit reduction law in 1986 and (as a renegade Democratic congressman) of the Gramm-Latta budget cut packages embraced by President Reagan early in his term.

Hypotheses 7 and 8: Results in Specific Contests and Symbolic versus Substantive Voting

Lesbian and gay voting will remain highly distinctive in particular individual contests, not merely in aggregated national partisan results for governorships and seats in Congress, and will be particularly distinctive in high-salience contests.

Lesbian and gay voters will seek both substantive and symbolic gains. Therefore, in a high-salience contest between a "progay" and an "antigay" candidate, they will vote for the "progay" candidate; and in a contest in which there is little difference between the candidates on LGB issues, substantive issue differences will be of greater concern.

Initial Comparative Analyses

California. Table 4.3 compares self-identified lesbian and gay respondents with the rest of the sample; once again, numerous differences are statistically significant. In each instance, the comparative findings on the national level are confirmed on the state level, with one notable exception: there is no statistically significant difference between the size of localities in which the lesbian and gay respondents reside and those in which the rest of the sample reside. Otherwise, like the national sample, California gay and lesbian self-identifiers, compared to their nongay cohorts, were substantially younger, more educated, more liberal, feminist, pro-choice, and environmentalist, more likely to have been raised in non-Christian homes, and disproportionately male.

It is in voting behavior, however, that the most notable divergences occur. There is a sixteen-point gap in Democratic Party identification, and a seventeen-point gap in liberalism, between the lesbian/gay and nongay samples. One may note as well that close to 10 percent of the gay sample identify with third parties. Finally, as stated above, the GOP gubernatorial candidate actively sought LGB voters. Given these facts, the greatest surprise may be the solid support of Dianne Feinstein by more than three-quarters of the gay and lesbian contingent; there is a thirty-point gap between her gay and nongay support. Notable as well is the fact that, unlike in the national data on the U.S. House races, the left-wing vote did not splinter toward minor candidates. Also, despite the disproportion of males in the gay sample, four lesbian and gay male voters in nine said that the sex of the candidate was important in making their voting decision, and the huge majority of these voted for Feinstein.

The vote on "Big Green" by self-identified lesbians and gay men was more along the lines expected. Although pluralities of both groups named the environ-

ment as the most important issue in the campaign for governor, almost half of
the gay/lesbian self-identifiers did so, as against two in seven nongay respondents—a nineteen-point gap. The gap between the groups on "Big Green" was
twenty-one points.[10]

Massachusetts. The first notable difference between the self-identified gay and
lesbian voters of Massachusetts (table 4.4) and those nationally and in most other
states is that there is no gender gap in self-identification; women make up a
majority of the small number of self-identifiers (18 women of 33). The second is
their partisanship; despite the extremely high share of avowed liberals in the
gay/lesbian sample, there is no difference between the gay/lesbian and nongay
Bay Staters in party affiliation. This may reflect an equal degree of voter disaffection, among straight and gay alike, with the Democratic administration and
legislature on economic issues in a basically liberal state; Dukakis's performance
gets a favorable rating from only one in eight gay and lesbian respondents.[11]

Of paramount interest are the voting behavior results. Lesbian and gay voters
would be expected to split their votes in the gubernatorial race, as did other
predominately liberal groups (see discussion of table 4.7 later in this chapter),
given the fact that nonpartisan liberal organizations in Massachusetts (including
LGB political clubs) were nearly unanimous in their refusal to endorse John
Silber. Overall, 58 percent of nongay liberals voted for Silber—as did 42 percent
of nongay conservatives. The ideological confusion of this contest is attested to
in the fact that a consistent one-third of Democrats, across the ideological
spectrum, defected to Weld, *and* one-quarter of Republicans, again from across
the spectrum, defected to Silber. Liberal independents split down the middle,
giving a two-point edge to Weld.

Instead of reflecting this confusion, however, the lesbian and gay voters
rebelled utterly against the Democratic nominee, giving more than three-fourths
of their votes to the Republican and fewer than one in six to the Democrat. At
the same time, their disaffection with the Dukakis administration and the
Democratic Party did not diminish their support for Democratic Senator Kerry,
who took three-quarters of gay/lesbian self-identifiers.

It is interesting to note the self-reporting of voting in the gubernatorial
primaries in September.[12] First, nearly all the gay/lesbian respondents claim to
have voted in one or the other primary. Second, their choices differed significantly
from those of the rest of the voting population, with Bellotti carrying by eleven
votes to three in the Democratic race and Weld by twelve votes to two on the
Republican side. An absolute majority of gay/lesbian liberals reported voting for
Bellotti, and an absolute majority of gay/lesbian moderates said they had voted

for Weld in the primary. A breakdown of general election vote by primary support shows that all but two of the gay and lesbian Bellotti supporters in the sample defected to Weld.

The disaster for Silber among self-identified lesbian and gay voters crossed party lines: only three of ten lesbian and gay Democrats voted for their party's nominee, as did only 17 percent of gays and lesbians who voted for Senator Kerry. Indeed, of the 26 gay and lesbian respondents who voted in both contests, 15 (58 percent) voted for both Kerry the Democrat and Weld the Republican. Further, a breakdown of the general election by ideology showed no effect of this variable on levels of support for Weld among lesbians and gay men, with at least three-quarters of liberals, moderates, and conservatives alike supporting the Republican in the general election.

These differences may be laid at the feet of personal assessments of Silber. The two factors in voters' decisions on which significant differences between gay and nongay voters were found were the belief that the opposing candidate was too extreme and simple dislike of the opponent. Nearly three in ten gay and lesbian voters checked each of these boxes. Of those who did so, all who said the opponent was too extreme, and all but one of those who said they disliked the opponent, voted for Weld.

Texas. As seen in table 4.5, the demographic breakdown between gay and lesbian Texas voters and the rest of the Lone Star State electorate in most cases reflects that found at the national level and in California. Men outnumber women among self-identifiers by roughly two to one, and the population is much younger, less religious, and more urban than their nongay counterparts; in this last case it is of interest that a large disproportion of self-identifiers were found not in the largest cities, but in the moderately large cities, and that significantly fewer self-identifiers were found not just in the smaller towns, but in the middle-sized cities.

The most notable divergences from expectations are the absence of any statistically significant differences in education levels, although somewhat more gay/lesbian Texans report having college educations and postgraduate work, and the absence of any notable differences in party identification, although somewhat fewer self-identifiers affiliated with the Republicans. A significantly smaller number of blacks identified as gay or lesbian (two blacks among fifty self-identifiers), compared to the other racial categories. In addition, although the differences in ideology and feminism are significant indeed, one should note the much larger share of self-identified gay conservatives in Texas than has been seen heretofore. One notes as well President Bush's positive approval rating among

Texas gays, and the fact that a plurality of gay respondents in the president's adopted home state reported voting for him over Michael Dukakis in 1988. (These facts will be assessed later in the chapter.)

The returns, and the reasons cited for the voters' decisions, are intriguing. As in California and Massachusetts, more than three out of four self-identified gay and lesbian voters cast ballots for the gubernatorial candidate perceived as being more "progay." At the same time, this decision appeared not to have been easy for many gay and lesbian voters. Unlike in California, where five gay voters in eight had made up their minds more than a month before the election, only three in eight report doing so in Texas, and fully a third of gay/lesbian voters said they made their decisions within the week before the election—and the majority of these last voted for Williams. It was the earlier deciders who were overwhelmingly in Richards's column.

It is notable that, of the factors cited in making their decision, a significantly larger number of gay and lesbian responses cited "candidate's personal past," an allusion to Richards's admitted recovery from alcoholism, and the need for a "political outsider"; both of these are concerns that would benefit Williams. These were among the factors cited by the late deciders. Another was the negativism of the campaign; those who thought Richards was the dirtier campaigner decided to go with Williams at the end. Those who did opt for Richards at the end did so based on her experience in government, the perception that Williams's campaign threw more mud, and, most important, the belief that Williams was "out of touch." Most interesting is the role of the sex of the candidates. A huge majority of the late deciders who cited this as a concern voted for Williams, whereas a great majority on the earlier deciders who cited this opted for Richards. It appears that some small but statistically significant number of gay men in Texas in 1990 in the end could not bring themselves to vote for a woman.[13]

In the other contests, Republicans did better among lesbian and gay voters. Senator Gramm, facing a nominal challenge from Democratic state lawmaker Ben Parmer, got three gay and lesbian votes in eight; and the vote for the GOP candidates for lieutenant governor and attorney general did not differ significantly, and in the former case did not differ much apparently, from the vote cast by the rest of the electorate.

To sum up, we find in California the only instance of partisanship being a consistent predictor of voting behavior in a gubernatorial contest: Democrats and independents voted heavily for Dianne Feinstein, whereas gay/lesbian Republicans voted just as heavily for Pete Wilson. This finding supports

Hypothesis 8, in that substantive differences determined vote choice in a high-salience contest in which the stands of the candidates on gay issues were not strongly polarized. Gay Republicans in California were self-described moderates who strongly approved of George Bush's performance, were more optimistic than other Californians about the state of the economy, were significantly less concerned about abortion rights and environmental issues than were the others, and appeared to be more concerned about state taxes. In addition, they accepted Wilson's argument that he would be a "strong leader" compared to Feinstein. The similarity of gay Democrats and independents in issue concerns and issue stands made their similarly high levels of support for Feinstein logical.

In Massachusetts and Texas, large majorities of lesbians and gay men, regardless of party affiliation or ideological or issue concerns, voted for the more "progay" candidate in gubernatorial contests in which the candidates' stands on gay rights matters were well known and diverged greatly. This especially is notable in the case of Texas, in which an uncommonly large share of lesbians and gay men described themselves as Republicans, conservatives, and/or George Bush supporters, and therefore naturally inclined to support Clayton Williams had he not run against them.

In each of the three states examined, the shares of the vote given by self-identified gay and lesbian voters to the more "progay" gubernatorial candidates were eerily close to identical: 77, 77, and 78 percent, respectively. The most significant test of cohesion among gay and lesbian voters was in Massachusetts, where the candidate endorsed by the LGB leadership was the Republican. In that instance, the rank-and-file voters split their tickets liberally, giving similar shares of the vote to the "progay" GOP candidate for governor and the "progay" Democratic incumbent U.S. senator. This appears to indicate that self-identified lesbian and gay voters, at least in states with political cultures encouraging political entrepreneurship by organized groups, are not firmly tied to either party at this point and are "up for grabs."

Does this mean there is a cohesive "gay and lesbian vote," accounting for about three-fourths of the self-identified lesbians and gay men, that can be counted on in every election? Not necessarily. One important factor in the cohesiveness of this vote appears to be the salience of the contest. Texas is instructive on this point. The Richards-Williams race received widespread national publicity, and the office of governor, although in fact relatively weak, is perceived by voters as the center of power in the state. Even in the contest for U.S. senator, a significant share of gay and lesbian voters split their tickets to benefit the very conservative Republican incumbent. The relatively low salience of the contests for lieutenant governor and attorney general is shown in the drop-off in the number of respondents who report voting in these contests. In the race for lieutenant governor, the gap between the gay and nongay electorates was lowered from twenty-eight points (in the governor's race) to ten.

Notably, half of self-identified lesbian and gay Texans claimed they voted for George Bush for president in 1988. It is easy to make too much of this figure, given that this was twenty points below Bush's reported support among the rest of the sample, and given that Texas was the president's adopted home state. This does, however, provide circumstantial evidence of a "cultural" effect of a kind different from that present in, say, California.

Leaving voting behavior aside for the moment, I would like to note the demographic similarities and differences among the three states. California and Texas reflected the national pattern of more self-identification by men than by women. Massachusetts, with its small sample, did not confirm the trend. Racial differences in identification rates appeared significant only among African Americans in Texas. Gay voters (men especially) were more urban, confirming the national findings, in Massachusetts and Texas, but not in California; and in Texas, unlike the other two states, there were not large concentrations of the sample in the very largest cities. The gay sample was significantly more educated in California and astoundingly more educated in Massachusetts, but in Texas education levels did not differ significantly between the lesbian/gay and nongay samples. Only in Texas did the rate of religious attendance differ significantly; but in all three states the pattern of religious upbringing did, with a disproportion of respondents having been raised in non-Christian faiths.

I wish to note that, in each of the states, there was a disproportionately small number of lesbians and gay men who reported having been raised in the state's *predominant religious tradition*. The finding on the national level was that being raised as a Protestant appeared to have a suppressive effect on self-identification, and these findings were confirmed in plurality Protestant California and majority Protestant Texas. However, in majority Catholic Massachusetts, the finding was reversed: it was people raised as Catholics, not those raised as Protestants, who were significantly underrepresented in the gay and lesbian sample, and unlike the findings in the national polls or those of California or Texas, in Massachusetts there is a strong, significant *negative* correlation between a Catholic upbringing and gay/lesbian self-identification (see table 4.8).

The findings of the national survey were confirmed uniformly with respect to three variables: age, each state's sample being uniformly younger than the nongay identifiers; ideology, each state's gay and lesbian voters being far more liberal than their nongay cohorts; and greatly augmented rates of strong feminism. In California, the one state in which the question was asked, the environment was by far the priority issue among lesbian and gay voters in 1990.

However, these trends toward liberalism and feminism were reflected in significantly higher identification with the Democratic Party only in California, in which, I speculated earlier, the political structure and culture would create the strongest tendency for self-identifiers to engage in coalition politics. In both Massachusetts and Texas, self-identified lesbian and gay voters did not much differ from the rest of the voters in naming partisan affiliations. This sheds additional light on the finding in the national data bases that identification with the Democratic Party, although significantly greater on the national level, is not found at the levels expected given the relative liberalism and feminism of the gay and lesbian self-identifiers.

Divisions within the Community

Table 4.6 shows the statistically significant and near-significant differences among self-identified lesbians and gay men in the three states on issue attitudes and priorities and in voting behavior based on the sex, feminism, and party affiliation of the respondents. Displayed in comparative fashion, these results are most notable for their apparent inconsistency: what is an important difference in one state is of no matter at all in another.

Among the apparently consistent findings is that ideology correlated with party affiliation—although not in the same way it did among nongay identifiers. Democrats and independents were very similar in their strong liberalism, while most Republicans identified themselves as moderates rather than conservatives. Also relatively consistent is the finding that lesbians and Democrats gave more pessimistic answers in appraising the economic situation than did gay men, independents, and Republicans. Although not found across the board, there appeared to be a tendency among gay and lesbian Republicans to place more emphasis on taxes as an issue, whereas lesbians appeared to be more concerned with abortion and somewhat more concerned with crime-related issues than were gay men, and feminists may have been somewhat more concerned with the environment than were nonfeminists. Abortion attitudes, oddly, did not appear to correlate with feminism, but this may well be a result of the small sample sizes with which we must work.

Interestingly, in the two states where a woman faced a man in a gubernatorial contest, the answer to the feminism identifier gave significant differences, but these cut different ways. In California, feminist lesbians were far more inclined to call the candidate's sex an important factor in their vote choice, and these backed Feinstein unanimously. In Texas, however, only gay men named it as the most important factor, and all voted for the male candidate; a majority of feminist lesbians, and about a quarter of the gay men, but *none* of the nonfeminist lesbians, said the candidate's sex was an important factor.

However, there were no significant, or even near-significant, differences in vote choice based on either sex or feminism in any of the seven contests examined. What is especially worthy of note is that, in two of the three governor's races and the contest for Texas attorney general, even party affiliation made no difference among self-identified lesbians and gay men, either statistically or apparently. This finding, then, does not appear to be attributable to the small number of cases.

The Effects of Political Culture on Coalition-Building

One question raised earlier in the chapter that has yet to be considered is the extent to which the hypothesized political cultures of each of the three states would work to cement or inhibit electoral coalitions among African Americans, Latinos, feminists, and self-identified gay men and lesbians. I speculated that in California gay and lesbian voting would closely reflect that of feminists and these minority groups, whereas in Massachusetts and Texas they might likely diverge in the voting booth. In table 4.7, I compare vote choice by gay and nongay voters by race and by feminism to test whether these speculations are borne out.

In California, the vote breakdown of the races by sexual self-identification is almost identical—except among white gays and lesbians, who are nearly twice as likely to be Feinstein voters as are nongay European-Americans. The same result holds true when feminists and nonfeminists are compared: gay and lesbian feminists differ hardly a jot from nongay feminists, but again support for the Democrat among gay and lesbian nonfeminists is almost twice that among their nongay cohorts. Although I must caution the reader that the number of black, Hispanic, and Asian gay/lesbian self-identifiers is very small, this offers initial support for the notion that gay men and lesbians in California, at least in this high-salience contest, have successfully coalesced with feminists, Latinos, and African Americans. Data on voting in lower-salience contests, such as those for the state's lieutenant governor and attorney general (such as we have for Texas), will be needed in order to see how well the coalition holds up below the top level where the interest is highest.

In Massachusetts there is only one gay respondent of color, so one can fruitfully compare only the differences among whites and the differences based on feminist identification. One also must take into account the very small number of total cases. Even so, the results appear to show lesbians and gay men going their own way. Even given John Silber's intemperate remarks directed at them, a majority of African Americans and three in seven nongay feminists supported the Democratic nominee. Not so the lesbian and gay respondents: be they feminist or not, their support for Silber was in the teens. Only a third as many white lesbians and gay men voted for Silber as did nongay whites.

In the Kerry-Rappaport Senate contest, there are no apparent differences based on sexual self-identification. In each case, feminist support for Kerry was about thirty points higher than that of nonfeminists, but among feminists and nonfeminists alike, gay/lesbian self-identification made little difference in vote choice.

Again, therefore, my earlier speculation that the political culture of Massachusetts would tend to work against strong electoral coalitions, at least with strong feminists (as we cannot assess race here), appears to be confirmed.

In Texas, the small number of respondents makes fruitful only comparisons among whites and (with great statistical caution) Latinos, as well as among feminists and nonfeminists. Within the racial categories one finds very great differences among whites in the high-salience U.S. Senate and gubernatorial races, bringing their percentages for the Democrats close to those found among nongay feminists and African Americans and in excess of those among nongay Latinos. Augmented support for Ann Richards among the gay/lesbian Latinos approaches statistical significance, but in the Senate contest levels of support are about equal among gay and nongay Hispanics. Strongly distinctive voting also is found between gay and nongay nonfeminists in these contests, whereas among feminists of both sexualities support for the Democrats is similar.

This does not carry over as strongly into the two lower-salience contests for lieutenant governor and attorney general, in which support levels among white lesbians and gay men for the Democrats fall below those of nongay Latinos and feminists. Although white and nonfeminist gay people apparently remain distinctive from nongay whites and nonfeminists, the level of distinctiveness is not as strong and does not reach statistical significance at .05. There is a curious finding as well that notably fewer lesbian/gay feminists supported Bob Bulloch for lieutenant governor than did nongay feminists.

Be that as it may, it appears that in this least likely of states, gays and lesbians have managed to integrate themselves, at least in the voting booth, into the coalition of feminists and members of racial minorities that put Ann Richards in the governor's office and now forms the base of the progressive wing of the Texas Democratic Party. The preternatural conservatism of some lesbians and gay men continues to manifest itself in numerous contests, but in the highest-salience contest in which a strong bifurcation in the candidates' stands on gay people and their rights was evident, Texas lesbians and gay men stood together with other groups with which some of them had little ideologically in common.

The Sexuality Gap at the State Level

I now look at the state-level contests to determine whether they confirm the findings of the national survey on the effect of lesbian/gay self-identifiers on elections in the three states. As in the preceding chapter, I first examine the effects of the hypothesized demographic correlates of sexual self-identification in each state, then test the effect of self-identification alone on vote choice in each of the seven contests examined in this chapter; once this is established, the demographic correlates are added, then party affiliation,[14] and finally ideology and feminism.

Table 4.8 reports how the demographic indicators used to predict gay and lesbian self-identification on the national level worked in each of the three states. There was a considerable divergence among the three as to which variables were significant predictors, and no single demographic indicator reached statistical significance in all three states. (Age may have done so but for the very small sample size in Massachusetts, where the significance level for this variable was .073.) Why an indicator found significant at the national level should be highly significant in one state and impotent in another is uncertain.

Tables 4.9, 4.10, and 4.11, for California, Massachusetts, and Texas, respectively, show the effect of gay/lesbian self-identification on vote choice in each of the seven contests considered in this chapter.

Notable at once in the data for California (table 4.9), in contrast to the aggregated national data, is that although the strength of gay/lesbian self-identification declines in the model as the additional variables are added, sexual self-identification retains its independent power to explain vote choice in the California governor's race. That is, even after controlling for ideology and feminism, even after controlling for party affiliation, and even after controlling for all demographic correlates of gay/lesbian self-identification, we find that being a self-identifier made a person significantly more likely to vote for Dianne Feinstein. This serves to reinforce the earlier finding that white and nonfeminist gays and lesbians in the Golden State were twice as likely to vote for the Democratic nominee as were their nongay cohorts.

As shown in the findings for Massachusetts in table 4.10, the results in the Senate race are closer to those expected based on the national model; once ideology and feminism are controlled for, the independent effect of sexual self-identification is eliminated. It is interesting to note, however, that the independent effect retains its statistical significance even after party affiliation is added to the mix of variables.[15] No such effect, however, occurs in the governor's race, in which partisan loyalties were strained. The independent effect remains, and the strength of that effect, measured by the Wald statistic, does not significantly diminish even with the addition of numerous control variables, including party, ideology, and feminism (which, we have seen earlier, are of little use in calling this race). Note as well that the predictive power of the national model is at its weakest in the Massachusetts contests.

Table 4.11, which shows the data for Texas, confirms the finding of the California data set with respect to the high-salience contests for senator and governor: even after controlling for all other variables in the national model, including party, ideology, and feminism, we find that sexual self-identification has an independent effect in determining vote choice.[16] (Indeed, curiously, controlling for demographics somewhat increased the potency of the effect of gay/lesbian self-identification!) In the lower-salience contests, however, no such result holds. Indeed, in the lieutenant governor's race, self-identification standing alone has no significant effect on vote choice, and the effect is marginal in the contest for attorney general.

The Retrospective Model

Table 4.12 presents data on the independent effect of sexual self-identification in classic retrospective voting models. As noted in the last chapter, these models have been applied to presidential contests, and small adaptations have been made to fit the nature of state gubernatorial races. The three presidential-model predictors—party affiliation, approval of the president's performance, and perceptions of the condition of the national economy—were included, along with an indicator of the perceived condition of the economy of the particular state. In only one of the three states, Massachusetts, was an indicator of approval of the incumbent governor's performance included in the survey.

The first item of interest to students of retrospective voting will be the fact that, in these gubernatorial races, perceptions of the state's economy were utterly insignificant as a predictor of voting behavior in a gubernatorial race, as were perceptions of the national economy in all states except Texas. However, approval of George Bush's performance as president had a strong effect above and beyond party identification in California and Texas, and a less potent but still significant effect in Massachusetts, in predicting how a person would vote in the governor's contest.

Of direct interest to our discussion, in California and Massachusetts the gay and lesbian self-identifier variable retained strong independent predictive power. In Texas the effect was borderline: using a vote for Ann Richards as the dependent variable, gay/lesbian self-identification is significant at .05, whereas, using a vote for Clayton Williams as the dependent, sexual self-identification only approaches statistical significance in the retrospective model (significant at .07).

In an attempt to determine whether or not these results were peculiar only to gubernatorial contests, I ran the same tests using the vote in the Senate races in Massachusetts and Texas as dependent variables. (In no statewide race other than that for governor were Californians asked how they voted.) The results are displayed in table 4.13. In neither state was the independent effect of sexuality eliminated employing a retrospective model. Put differently, gay and lesbian self-identifiers had an independent effect on the Senate races using this model. The two most important factors in the Texas Senate race were party affiliation and the Bush approval rating. In the Massachusetts Senate race, on the other hand, these factors paled in comparison to the strength of the (overwhelmingly negative) assessment of Michael Dukakis's performance as governor. As in the gubernatorial models, the perceived condition of the national and state economies were insignificant in the Senate contests.

These control tests expand the possible importance of gay and lesbian self-identification as a factor in voting behavior beyond that seen in the national data. Here is strong evidence that, at least in high-salience contests—including all three gubernatorial races examined here—direct, independent effects on voting behavior unaccounted for by party affiliation, issue attitudes, and other demographic controls *can* be accounted for by self-identification as a lesbian or a gay man.

There are three principal lessons we learn from the tests reported in this chapter. First, self-identification (or not) as a gay man or a lesbian in and of itself has a significant independent effect in explaining why people vote as they do in high-salience elections; this was not clear from the examination of the national data, but is now. Second, any political divisions within the community that manifest themselves in less salient elections appear to dissolve in high-salience contests, and make lesbians and gay men as distinctive in their choice of candidates as are feminists, Latinos, and African Americans. Third, and of greatest importance to the practical politician, the gay and lesbian vote is not wedded to any one party and is up for grabs.

Assessing the Hypotheses

These state-level data confirm the initial findings in the national data bases discussed in the preceding chapter, and serve largely to reconfirm the first three hypotheses. Self-identified gay men and lesbians tend to be younger, better educated, more urban, and more liberal than nongay identifiers, and self-identified lesbians are far more inclined to strong feminism than are other women. In most of the twenty-one states, and in the pooled data from those states, openly gay men also notably outnumbered openly gay women. However, as in the national data, the strong liberalism of this group does not translate automatically into strong Democratic partisanship.

Another finding was that the indicators of likelihood to identify as gay or lesbian at the national level do not work uniformly on the state level; in addition, none of the indicators were found to have statistically significant effects on gay/lesbian self-identification in all of the three states examined. This means as well that the three correlate indicators of group consciousness we can measure with the data—youth, advanced education, and strong partisanship—were not found all together in any one state.

The differences from state to state seem almost arbitrary. In Massachusetts, advanced education is the central predictor of self-identification, gender is irrelevant, and age is not statistically significant. In Texas, however, age and sex are among the strongest predictors, and education is not statistically significant. The single strongest predictor in the national study, living in a more urban area, is the single strongest in Texas, but is of no importance in California and Massachusetts. Even the religion variable of importance differs from state to state, with Christian or non-Christian upbringing being significant in California, nearly significant in Massachusetts, and irrelevant in Texas, but religious attendance being important in the last and impotent in the first two. Even party affiliations did not differ between the gay and nongay samples in Massachusetts and Texas.

There are two possible explanations for these variations. One is that the sample sizes were simply too small to produce reliable results. Although this likely is the reason for the failure of the age and religious upbringing variables to reach statistical significance in Massachusetts, with its relatively tiny sample, this explanation is less convincing with respect to Texas and not convincing at all with respect to California; the last had a sample size ($N = 86$) nearly as great as did the VRS or CBS national data sets discussed in chapter 3. The other explanation is that, simply, different factors are important in gay/lesbian self-identification in different places, and one must know the demographic and attitudinal character of a state particularly well in order to predict which of the demographic elements will play a greater or lesser role. I noted earlier that, with regard to the influence of religious upbringing, the state-level data seem to tell us that self-identification is notably suppressed among those persons raised in the predominant religious tradition of the state.

The role of sex, feminism, and voting blocs within the community, addressed in the fourth and fifth hypotheses, is rather more obscure in the state-level data. Only in California was strong partisan voting evident, and in that state no contest below the gubernatorial level was included in the poll; in the other two states, as has been seen, ticket-splintering was rife. (In Texas, only three of the thirteen gay/lesbian Republicans voted a straight ticket for their party.) Since no questions on foreign policy issues—the principal basis of the "gender gap"—were included in the surveys, the one relatively consistent difference based on either sex or feminism was a stronger emphasis on abortion among lesbians (and sometimes lesbian feminists) than was found among gay men.

The Independent Effect of Lesbian/Gay Self-Identification

The tests of Hypotheses 6 and 7 led to the most interesting finding: the unexpected potency of the gay/lesbian indicator in explaining voting behavior in high-salience statewide contests, above and beyond either retrospective predictors of the vote or the augmentation of liberalism and feminism found among self-identified gay and lesbian voters.

One reason for this finding may be that, in the case of the House races studied using the national data, the added indicator of incumbency was available as something of an aggregate variable by which voters in different districts might be compared. Such comparisons were not possible with the data from the statewide races. Be that as it may, in the one state where an indicator of voters' satisfaction with the incumbent governor's performance was included in the model, self-identification retained its independent effect on the contest to elect his successor. In individual state-level contests for governors, and in one of the two Senate races, there indeed was a "sexuality gap."

This brings us to a second, most important point: not only did self-identification have an independent effect on individual voting behavior, but the gubernatorial results lead one inevitably to two conclusions. One confirms Hypothesis 8. The gubernatorial results in Massachusetts and Texas confirm the first half of this hypothesis, that given a choice between clearly "progay" and "antigay" candidates, the community will unite around the "progay" candidate, *regardless of party:* we saw rates of support of 77 and 78 percent, respectively. The Wilson-Feinstein contest in California appears to confirm the second half of Hypothesis 8, that absent such a bifurcation, substantive issue differences would determine the vote. California's mostly "moderate" gay Republicans voted as strongly for Wilson as its gay Democrats did for Feinstein; the independents, in turn, were as liberal as the Democrats and voted accordingly.

The second conclusion is an initial deduction with respect to Hypothesis 9: either some organized effort by gay and lesbian political activists or the public statements on "gay" issues by the candidates in hotly contested races result in markedly unified voting behavior in the aggregate by self-identified lesbians and gay men. Put another way, not only is there a quantifiable "sexuality gap," but there also appears to be a "gay and lesbian vote," which can be mobilized at the very least in the high-profile contests for state chief executives. As shown in the California contest, this does not require that one candidate make statements or put forth proposals that attack or offend the lesbian and gay community, as did Clayton Williams in Texas and John Silber in Massachusetts. It appears to require only that one candidate enunciate views that conform to the substantive aspirations of most lesbian and gay voters.

Political Culture

The speculative assumptions I made early in the chapter based on the normative Elazar scheme of political cultures appeared to be confirmed with respect to California and Massachusetts, but not with respect to Texas. In California, the combination of a predominately "moralistic" (communitarian) political culture, relatively easy access to "direct democracy" tools, and great distance between voters and representatives leads to mass movement politics in which a disinherited group achieves power only through building coalitions with other such groups. In Massachusetts, politicians and power centers are far closer to the public, and an entrepreneurial, "individualistic" political culture reigns, thereby allowing gays and lesbians the opportunity to break into power at numerous points and obviating much of the need for permanent coalitions in electoral politics.

In the Lone Star State, I expected that the impediments to maintaining cohesion within the group and to building coalitions with other dispossessed groups would be greatest, because of Texas's predominately "traditionalistic" culture and the pressure from that culture on feminists and minorities not to admit lesbians and gay men into their coalition. Yet cohesion among the self-identifiers and distinctive voting at levels equivalent to those of nongay Latinos, blacks, and feminists were found in the high-salience contests, just as they were in California. The inclusion of self-identified lesbians and gay men in a "progressive" coalition in Texas therefore appears to be more advanced than would have been predicted by the Elazar model.

A last question we need to consider here is whether, even if there is a gay and lesbian vote, from whatever source derived, that vote makes any difference. In each of the contests under study, it appears that the results would have been the same even had the self-identified gay men and lesbians all stayed home, because of their small percentage of the voting population. At best we can say at this point that a cohesive, mobilized gay and lesbian vote has the potential to swing an evenly divided contest one way or the other.

Now that we have assessed the 1990 general election exit polls, one significant question remains unanswered: Can lesbian and gay activists mobilize the "gay and lesbian vote," independently of other groups and information sources? The existence of the independent effect on vote choice, especially as manifested in the 1990 governor's race in Massachusetts, suggests that perhaps they can. If the voters effectively mobilize themselves after reading the paper, watching television, and talking with their friends, we can expect to see more of what we see in Texas: a strong penchant to vote in close, high-visibility contests for the highest office in the state—and, inferentially, in the nation—but an increasing lack of cohesion and mobilization from that point down the ballot. If, however, these voters are mobilized (at least in large part) by the collective efforts of activists, we may see a gay and lesbian vote capable of delivery to friends of the community *en bloc*. These issues will be examined in depth in the next chapter.

TABLE 4.1.

Unweighted number and percentage of self-identified gay and lesbian voters in twenty-one states, VRS state general election exit polls, November 1990

	Total N	N Gay/ lesbian	% of Total	N men	N Gay men	% All men	N Women	N Lesbians	% All Women
Northeast									
Connecticut	2166	15	.7	1028	8	.8	1106	7	.6
Massachusetts	2302	33	1.4	1102	15	1.4	1173	18	1.5
New Hampshire	1301	14	1.1	647	5	.8	642	9	1.4
New Jersey	1144	9	.8	532	8	1.5	599	1	.1
New York	1889	27	1.4	851	23	2.7	1022	4	.4
Pennsylvania	1763	11	.6	793	9	1.1	940	2	.2
Rhode Island	1595	21	1.3	782	14	1.8	792	7	.9
Northeast total	12160	130	1.1	5735	82	1.4	6274	48	.8
Midwest									
Illinois	3144	23	.7	1515	14	.9	1585	9	.6
Iowa	1781	11	.6	820	5	.6	937	6	.6
Michigan	2244	9	.4	1085	7	.6	1143	2	.2
Minnesota	1844	19	1.0	910	11	1.2	911	8	.9
Nebraska	1354	8	.6	659	5	.8	665	3	.5
Ohio	1994	9	.5	865	9	1.0	1099	0	.0
Midwest total	12361	79	.6	5854	51	.9	6340	28	.4
South									
Florida	1897	24	1.3	840	16	1.9	1014	8	.8
Kentucky	1345	4	.3	638	3	.5	681	1	.1
North Carolina	2228	22	1.0	1029	19	1.8	1147	3	.3
Texas	2832	50	1.8	1329	33	2.5	1443	17	1.2
South total	8302	100	1.2	3836	71	1.9	4285	29	.7
West									
California	3313	86	2.6	1530	50	3.3	1724	33	1.9
Colorado	1557	28	1.8	769	22	2.9	775	6	.8
Hawaii	1900	24	1.3	902	15	1.7	985	9	.9
Oregon	1029	13	1.3	481	3	.6	532	10	1.9
West total	7799	151	1.9	3682	90	2.4	4016	58	1.4
Grand total	40622	460	1.1	19107	294	1.5	20915	163	.8

NOTE: Raw, unweighted total responses to "long form" VRS state questionnaire, distributed to voters leaving randomly selected polling places in twenty-one states and self-administered by respondents. Question read: "Are you any of the following (check as many as apply)"; the ninth response (of nine) was "gay or lesbian." Total N is slightly greater than the sum of N Men and N Women because a small number of respondents did not indicate their sex on the questionnaire. VRS administered a "short form" questionnaire to voters in another twenty-one states that did not include a question about sexual orientation.

TABLE 4.2.

Comparison of pooled data on self-identified lesbians and gay men from twenty-one state exit polls to findings of national exit polls, November 1990

Item	National (%)	States (%)	Item	National (%)	States (%)
Sex (% Male)	58.9	64.3	$15,000–29,999	25.5	27.1
			$30,000–49,999	29.0	31.3
Age			$50,000–99,999	25.5	21.0
18–29	31.3	25.7	$100,000 or more	3.0	6.2
30–39	28.3	31.8			
40–44	16.8	16.4	Married	10.4	8.7
45–49	12.1	10.1	Attend religious services		
50–59	4.3	9.2	at least once a month	24.4	27.4
60 or older	7.2	6.8			
Race			Religion *raised in*		
White	86.8	82.2	Protestant	31.6	33.3
Black	5.7	8.4	Catholic	32.1	35.8
Hispanic/Latino	5.1	8.4	Other Christian	16.1	8.4
Asian	.7	1.8	Jewish	6.3	8.2
Other	1.8	3.3	Other religion	7.4	5.3
			No religion	6.6	8.8
Size/type of locality					
500,000 or more	17.8	46.5	Party affiliation		
250,000–499,000	13.6	5.0	Democratic	47.8	49.0
50,000–249,000	20.5	3.5	Republican	19.0	14.7
Suburbs	31.7	29.5	Independent, other	33.1	36.3
10,000–49,000	2.1	15.5			
Rural	13.8	0	Ideology		
			Liberal	55.5	49.9
Education			Moderate	38.7	35.2
Not high school graduate	2.3	2.9	Conservative	9.3	11.4
High school graduate	8.6	11.0			
Some college	35.7	26.7	Strong feminist	26.0	21.1
College graduate	25.1	27.2			
Postgraduate work	32.2	28.3	Self-reported 1988 presidential vote		
			Bush (R)	33.2	34.6
Household income			Dukakis (D)	60.1	58.1
Less than $15,000	17.0	14.3	Other	6.7	7.2

SOURCES: National data are from one or both 1990 national general election exit polls discussed in chapter 3; these data are weighted. Figures for the states are derived by adding unweighted raw total responses of the self-identified gay men and lesbians in the twenty-one separate state exit polls, as in table 4.1.

NOTE: This table is presented for descriptive comparisons only; it is not possible to test for significant differences between the national and state figures given here, nor would such tests be valid.

TABLE 4.3.
Self-identified gay and lesbian voters compared with other voters, 1990 California general election

Item	Nongay (%)	Gay/ lesbian (%)	Item	Nongay (%)	Gay/ lesbian (%)
Sex (% male)[a]	49.5	63.0	Country's seriously off track	55.2	62.8
Race					
White	82.1	77.9	Strong feminist[c]	9.9	26.8
Black	8.2	10.1			
Hispanic/Latino	4.4	5.4	Abortion should be[a]		
Asian	4.0	5.3	Always legal	54.0	68.6
Other	1.3	1.3	Sometimes legal	34.1	23.7
			Never legal	11.9	7.6
Locality size					
500,000 or more	23.8	30.7	Vote for governor[c]		
Suburbs	70.5	68.5	Dianne Feinstein (D)	47.2	77.2
10,000 to 49,000	5.7	.8	Pete Wilson (R)	49.1	19.3
			Other	3.8	3.5
Education[b]					
No college	19.5	16.2	Initiatives (% "for")		
Undergraduate	59.2	48.1	"Big Green" comprehensive		
Postgraduate	21.2	35.8	environmental law[c]	42.2	62.9
			12-year service for		
Attend religious services			state legislators	43.9	37.5
at least monthly	30.7	27.3	6- to 8-year service limit		
			for state legislators	55.9	44.3
Age[b]					
18–29	14.1	22.7	Bush approval rating[b]	57.6	41.3
30–39	22.3	26.8			
40–44	12.5	14.7	Self-reported 1988 presidential vote[c]		
45–49	10.0	17.6	Bush (R)	57.9	27.3
50–59	17.0	8.9	Dukakis (D)	36.0	60.4
60 or older	24.0	9.2	Other	6.1	12.3
Party[c]			When made decision in governor's race		
Democratic	40.2	55.9	In three days before election	11.6	8.9
Republican	38.9	15.6	In week before election	10.6	13.5
Independent	17.1	19.3	In month before election	25.5	13.9
Other parties	3.8	9.3	Before then	52.3	63.7
Ideology[c]			One or two most important candidate qualities		
Liberal	21.6	38.8	Strong leader	30.9	27.1
Moderate	45.8	51.4	Better manager[a]	32.9	21.2
Conservative	32.6	9.8	More ethical	19.8	26.3
			Performance in debates	2.1	3.9
Compared to two years ago am[c]			Will bring change	13.9	19.3
Better off	33.8	54.8	Sex of candidate[a]	4.1	9.2
About the same	43.7	30.5	Candidate's party	24.6	17.7
Worse off	22.6	14.7	Opponent too negative	10.7	11.2

TABLE 4.3. *(continued)*
Self-identified gay and lesbian voters compared with other voters, 1990 California general election

Item	Nongay (%)	Gay/ lesbian (%)	Item	Nongay (%)	Gay/ lesbian (%)
Candidate's sex important in			Government ethics	22.1	30.9
vote for governor[c]	20.8	44.6	State taxes	14.2	9.6
			Savings and loans	2.5	4.5
One or two top issues in gubernatorial election			State economy	17.5	13.3
Environment[c]	29.7	48.5			
Crime/drugs[a]	27.3	15.1	Religion raised in[b] (data not shown)		
Abortion	19.6	23.6			
Hiring quotas	6.8	5.4			
Offshore drilling	4.9	4.0	Income[b] (data not shown)		

SOURCE: VRS state exit poll.
NOTE: Data are expressed as percentages of weighted responses.
[a] Significance level = .05.
[b] Significance level = .01.
[c] Significance level = .001.

TABLE 4.4.

Self-identified gay and lesbian voters compared with other voters, 1990 Massachusetts general election

Item	Nongay (%)	Gay/ lesbian (%)	Item	Nongay (%)	Gay/ lesbian (%)
Sex (% male)	48.5	47.0	Worse off	36.3	42.2
Race			Country is seriously off track	60.7	61.3
White	94.6	94.7			
Black	2.5	5.3	Abortion should be		
Hispanic/Latino	1.3	0	Always legal	46.6	67.8
Asian	1.0	0	Sometimes legal	39.7	28.3
Other	.6	0	Never legal	13.6	3.9
Locality size[a]			Strong feminist[c]	11.0	42.8
500,000 or more	31.7	52.6			
50,000 to 249,000	33.4	28.6	Vote for governor[c]		
Suburbs	18.5	0	John Silber (D)	47.6	15.8
10,000 to 49,000	16.5	18.8	William Weld (R)	50.0	77.1
			Other	2.4	7.2
Education[c]					
No college	28.1	6.9	Vote for U.S. Senate		
Undergraduate	52.1	33.9	John Kerry (D)	55.6	73.9
Postgraduate	19.8	59.2	James Rappaport (R)	43.8	26.1
			Other	.7	0
Attend religious services					
at least monthly	33.6	40.9	"Yes" vote on state tax		
			rollback initiative	39.7	32.9
Age[a]					
18–29	20.8	21.8	Bush approval rating[b]	64.1	40.3
30–39	23.6	43.3			
40–44	12.3	20.5	Self-reported 1988 presidential vote		
45–49	9.6	2.9	Bush (R)	57.8	41.1
50–59	10.9	7.8	Dukakis (D)	37.6	50.7
60 or older	22.8	3.7	Other	4.6	8.1
Party			Dukakis approval rating	14.9	12.5
Democratic	32.8	31.9			
Republican	15.6	13.3	Self-reported 1990 gubernatorial primary vote		
Independent, other	51.6	54.8	John Silber (D)	26.0	10.7
			Francis Bellotti (D)	18.5	34.2
Ideology[c]			William Weld (R)	19.3	36.3
Liberal	24.1	61.0	Steven Pierce (R)	9.6	5.2
Moderate	50.7	33.6	Other	3.4	9.1
Conservative	25.2	5.4	Did not vote in primary	23.2	4.5
Compared to two years ago am			One or two most important candidate qualities		
Better off	18.4	22.8	Experience	9.9	6.3
About the same	45.3	35.0	Honesty	27.6	27.9

TABLE 4.4. *(continued)*
Self-identified gay and lesbian voters compared with other voters, 1990 Massachusetts general election

Item	Nongay (%)	Gay/ lesbian (%)	Item	Nongay (%)	Gay/ lesbian (%)
Strong leader	22.2	19.2	Crime/drugs	10.8	0
Better manager	16.3	21.3	State services	17.9	29.6
Outsider	4.8	10.3	Abortion[b]	9.3	22.4
Will bring change	26.1	13.2	State taxes	25.3	18.1
Opponent is too extreme[b]	11.4	29.4	State economy	41.0	47.6
Opponent was too negative	5.7	3.1			
Do not like opponent[b]	12.1	29.1	Preferred solution to state budget crises		
			Raises taxes	52.5	70.3
One or two top issues in gubernatorial election			Cut services	47.5	29.7
Environment	8.8	18.0			
Education	23.1	15.0	Religion raised in[a] (data not shown)		

SOURCE: VRS state exit poll.
NOTE: Data are expressed as percentages of weighted responses.
[a] Significance level = .05.
[b] Significance level = .01.
[c] Significance level = .001.

TABLE 4.5.

Self-identified gay and lesbian voters compared with other voters, 1990 Texas general election

Item	Nongay (%)	Gay/lesbian (%)	Item	Nongay (%)	Gay/lesbian (%)
Sex (% male)[a]	49.5	65.5	Compared to two years ago am		
			Better off	32.3	45.9
Race[c]			About the same	40.9	31.3
White	75.8	76.5	Worse off	26.7	22.8
Black	11.8	3.7			
Hispanic/Latino	11.2	13.1	Country is seriously off track	54.3	64.8
Asian	.7	1.7			
Other	.6	4.9	Abortion should be[c]		
			Always legal	32.2	55.8
Locality size[c]			Sometimes legal	52.4	26.6
500,000 or more	9.4	10.6	Never legal	15.9	17.6
250,000 to 499,000	17.5	43.4			
50,000 to 249,000	32.1	13.0	Strong feminist[c]	6.3	20.9
Suburbs	21.2	24.9			
10,000 to 49,000	19.8	8.2	Vote for governor[c]		
			Ann Richards (D)	50.0	78.0
Education			Clayton Williams (R)	46.4	20.7
No college	27.8	16.0	Other	3.7	1.3
Undergraduate	55.2	59.7			
Postgraduate	17.0	24.3	Vote for U.S. Senate[c]		
			Ben Parmer (D)	36.4	61.6
Attend religious services			Phil Gramm (R)	62.0	38.4
at least monthly[a]	49.2	34.0			
			Vote for lieutenant governor		
Age[c]			Bob Bulloch (D)	55.1	64.9
18–29	17.7	36.3	Rob Mosbacher (R)	42.2	35.1
30–39	25.9	39.7			
40–44	13.0	9.6	Vote for attorney general		
45–49	9.9	6.3	Dan Morales (D)	55.1	71.0
50–59	14.5	5.9	J. E. "Buster" Brown (R)	43.3	29.0
60 or older	18.9	2.2			
			Bush approval rating	63.9	55.8
Party					
Democratic	39.1	40.2	Self-reported 1988 presidential vote[b]		
Republican	34.8	25.5	Bush (R)	63.5	45.2
Independent, other	26.1	34.3	Dukakis (D)	32.7	42.5
			Other	3.9	12.2
Ideology[c]					
Liberal	14.5	37.5	When made decision in governor's race		
Moderate	43.6	40.3	In three days before election	17.0	18.3
Conservative	42.0	22.2	In week before election	10.8	14.0
			In month before election	17.6	29.5
			Before then	54.6	38.1

TABLE 4.5. *(continued)*
Self-identified gay and lesbian voters compared with other voters, 1990 Texas general election

Item	Nongay (%)	Gay/ lesbian (%)	Item	Nongay (%)	Gay/ lesbian (%)
One or two most important candidate qualities			One or two top issues in gubernatorial election		
Experience[c]	28.7	49.5	Education	30.4	37.4
Toughness	24.7	24.2	Ethics[a]	22.4	36.7
Better manager	29.4	24.1	Gun control	13.5	4.9
Opponent out of touch[a]	9.8	19.1	Abortion	18.6	24.5
Candidate's past[a]	5.3	11.4	Savings and loans	4.2	2.8
Political outsider[a]	4.1	11.2	Insurance reform	9.3	5.6
Sex of candidate	1.8	0	Crime/drugs	19.1	20.9
Opponent is too extreme	9.5	3.2	State taxes	11.4	14.0
Opponent was too negative	14.3	13.3	State economy	15.7	19.2
			Religion raised in;[c] Texas economy;[c] Savings and		
Candidate's sex important in			loans important in vote for governor[b] (data not		
vote for governor[b]	19.1	35.6	shown)		

SOURCE: VRS state exit poll.
NOTE: Data are expressed as percentages of weighted responses.
[a] Significance level = .05.
[b] Significance level = .01.
[c] Significance level = .001.

TABLE 4.6.

Significant differences in attitudes and voting behavior in three states among self-identified lesbians and gay men, based on sex, strong feminism, and party affiliation, November 1990 general election

	California			Massachusetts			Texas		
	Sex	Feminism	Party	Sex	Feminism	Party	Sex	Feminism	Party
One of top two issues									
Abortion	.05	.05	.05	.05	n.s.	n.s.	n.s.	n.s.	.05
State taxes	n.s.	(.10)	(.10)	.05	n.s.	.05	n.s.	n.s.	n.s.
State economy	(.10)	n.s.	n.s.	.05	(.10)	n.s.	n.s.	n.s.	n.s.
Environment	n.s.	n.s.	.01	n.s.	.05	n.s.		(not asked)	
Crime/drugs	.05	n.s.	n.s.		(no G/L "yes")		n.s.	n.s.	n.s.
Offshore drilling	n.s.	(.10)	n.s.		(not asked)			(not asked)	
Ethics	n.s.	.01	n.s.		(not asked)		n.s.	n.s.	(.10)
Gun control		(not asked)			(not asked)		.05	.05	n.s.
One of top two factors in vote									
Want a strong leader	n.s.	n.s.	.01	n.s.	n.s.	n.s.		(not asked)	
Want an outsider		(not asked)		n.s.	n.s.	.001	n.s.	n.s.	(.10)
Opponent too extreme		(not asked)		n.s.	(.10)	n.s.	n.s.	n.s.	n.s.
Candidate's personal past		(not asked)			(not asked)		(.10)	n.s.	n.s.
Economy excellent or good									
U.S. economy	.05	n.s.	.05	n.s.	n.s.	n.s.	.01	.05	.05
State's economy	(.10)	n.s.	.05	n.s.	n.s.	n.s.	n.s.	n.s.	n.s.
Am worse off than in 1988	.05	n.s.	n.s.	n.s.	n.s.	n.s.	n.s.	n.s.	n.s.

TABLE 4.6. (continued)

Significant differences in attitudes and voting behavior in three states among self-identified lesbians and gay men, based on sex, strong feminism, and party affiliation, November 1990 general election

	California			Massachusetts			Texas		
	Sex	Feminism	Party	Sex	Feminism	Party	Sex	Feminism	Party
Bush approval rating	n.s.	n.s.	.01	n.s.	(.10)	(.10)	n.s.	n.s.	n.s.
Voted for Bush, 1988	n.s.	(.10)	(.10)	n.s.	n.s.	.01	n.s.	n.s.	n.s.
Ideology	n.s.	n.s.	(.10)	n.s.	n.s.	.05	(.10)	(.10)	.05
Abortion always legal	n.s.	n.s.	n.s.	(.10)	n.s.	.01	n.s.	n.s.	n.s.
Sex of gubernatorial candidates important	n.s.	(.10)	n.s.		(not asked)		n.s.	.05	(.10)
Votes on initiative measures									
6- to 8-year term limit	n.s.	(.10)	n.s.						
Tax rollback				n.s.	.05	.001			
Voted for Democrat for									
Governor	n.s.	n.s.	.001	n.s.	n.s.	n.s.	n.s.	n.s.	n.s.
U.S. Senate		(no Senate race)		n.s.	n.s.	.05	n.s.	n.s.	.001
Lieutenant governor		(not asked)			(tied to Governor)		n.s.	n.s.	.05
Attorney general		(not asked)			(not asked)		n.s.	n.s.	n.s.

SOURCES: VRS state exit polls.

NOTE: Results are expressed as significance levels of .05, .01, or .001. Relationships nearing statistical significance, at .10, are marked (.10). Relationships not significant at .10 or lower are marked "n.s."

TABLE 4.7.

Vote choice comparison of gay and lesbian self-identifiers with nonidentifiers, after race and self-identification as a strong feminist are controlled for, in three states, November 1990

	Nongay (%)	Gay/ lesbian (%)	Gay/ lesbian N		Nongay (%)	Gay/ lesbian (%)	Gay/ lesbian N
California governor				Strong feminist			
(voted for Dianne Feinstein)				No[b]	34.5	58.1	39
Race				Yes	64.7	73.5	12
White[c]	42.9	78.4	61				
Black	83.3	80.4	8	Texas governor			
Latino	65.0	78.4	4	(voted for Ann Richards)			
Asian	42.4	42.7	4	Race			
Other	36.0	100.0	1	White[c]	40.2	72.8	41
				Black	89.4	100.0	2
Strong feminist				Latino[d]	70.3	100.0	7
No[c]	43.7	78.5	57	Asian	54.4	100.0	1
Yes	77.9	73.9	21	Other	73.1	74.2	3
Massachusetts U.S. senator				Strong feminist			
(voted for John Kerry)				No[c]	47.7	74.9	43
Race				Yes	83.8	89.6	12
White[d]	54.7	72.4	27				
Black	73.1	100.0	1	Texas lieutenant governor			
				(voted for Bob Bulloch)			
Strong feminist				Race (no black gay/lesbian respondents)			
No	52.2	60.4	16	White[d]	47.7	63.4	37
Yes	82.4	91.9	12	Latino	73.0	65.0	2
				Asian	64.5	100.0	1
Massachusetts governor				Other	71.0	74.2	3
(voted for John Silber)							
Race				Strong feminist:			
White[b]	47.3	16.6	27	No[d]	53.9	68.6	34
Black	56.0	0	1	Yes[d]	76.2	50.4	9
Strong feminist				Texas attorney general			
No[b]	48.1	13.6	16	(voted for Dan Morales)			
Yes[d]	43.5	18.7	12	Race (no black gay/lesbian respondents)			
				White[b]	45.7	67.7	37
Texas U.S. senator				Latino	83.8	100.0	3
(voted for Ben Parmer)				Asian	58.8	100.0	1
Race				Other	49.5	74.2	3
White[c]	27.9	62.6	40				
Black[a]	74.7	0	2	Strong feminist			
Latino	52.0	59.2	6	No[d]	53.5	70.3	34
Asian	45.4	100.0	1	Yes	81.7	73.7	9
Other	60.5	74.2	3				

SOURCE: VRS state exit polls.

[a] Significance level = .05.
[b] Significance level = .01.
[c] Significance level = .001.
[d] Neared significance (.051 to .099).

TABLE 4.8.

Logistic regression of three state surveys of factors correlating with gay or lesbian self-identification, 1990 national general election exit polls

Variable	California				Massachusetts				Texas			
	B	S.E.	Wald	Significance	B	S.E.	Wald	Significance	B	S.E.	Wald	Significance
Age	−.1940	.0724	7.1880	.0073	−.2455	.1366	3.2306	.0723	−.3915	.1160	11.3948	.0007
Education	.3280	.1293	6.4372	.0112	.9039	.2516	12.9060	.0003	.2190	.1619	1.8303	.1761
Sex	−.5261	.2506	4.4055	.0358	.0588	.4049	.0211	.8845	−.5867	.3205	3.3508	.0672
Race	.0794	.3005	.0698	.7916	−.2510	.9108	.0759	.7829	.0074	.3929	.0004	.9850
Income	−.1869	.1151	2.6371	.1044	−.5846	.2147	7.4173	.0065	−.5044	.1656	9.2794	.0023
Size of locality												
500,000 or more	2.0345	1.2812	2.5216	.1123	.9013	.5389	2.7970	.0944	1.2876	.8446	2.3242	.1274
250,000–499,000		(no cases)				(no cases)			1.9953	.7531	7.0204	.0081
50,000–249,000		(no cases)			.5303	.5900	.8079	.3687	−.3261	.8507	.1469	.7015
Suburbs	1.8750	1.2690	2.1830	.1395		(no cases)			1.1198	.7676	2.1283	.1446
Religious upbringing												
Catholic	.5760	.3011	3.6602	.0557	−1.0215	.4949	4.2605	.0390	.7876	.3526	4.9882	.0255
Other Christian	−.2889	.5282	.2991	.5844	−.2975	1.1006	.0731	.7869	−.7518	.6414	1.3740	.2411
Jewish	.3900	.5684	.4707	.4927	.5392	.5671	.9042	.3417	.3925	.8626	.2070	.6491
Other religion	.6210	.6187	1.0073	.3156	−.0774	1.2327	.0039	.9499	−.3415	.8908	.1470	.7014
No religion	.9720	.3790	6.5779	.0103	−.5735	1.1185	.2629	.6081	1.3438	.5605	5.7472	.0165
Religious attendance	−.0053	.2714	.0004	.9844	.4323	.4240	1.0395	.3079	−.8180	.3448	5.6292	.0177
Constant	−5.1038	1.4295	12.7473	.0004	−5.7662	1.4015	16.9271	.0000	−2.3860	1.0794	4.8860	.0271
(N)		(2,891)				(1,987)				(2,466)		

NOTE: Baseline measure for size of locality was residence in a town of 10,000 to 49,999 (no "rural" precincts were selected in any of the three states); baseline measure for religious upbringing was Protestant.

TABLE 4.9.

Effect of gay or lesbian self-identification on voting behavior in 1990 gubernatorial contest in California, alone and when controlled, in succession, for demographic variables, party affiliation, and ideology and feminism

	Explanatory measures				Predictive measures	
	B	S.E.	Wald	Significance	Mean	% Correct
Governor (N = 2,783)						
					47.88	
Voted for Democrat (Dianne Feinstein)						
Self-identification alone	1.4462	.2913	24.6499	.0000		53.72
Add demographics	1.5040	.3054	24.2502	.0000		64.61
Add party identification	1.1979	.3563	11.3004	.0008		79.03
Add ideology, feminism	1.0242	.3675	7.7684	.0053		79.91
					48.36	
Voted for Republican (Pete Wilson)						
Self-identification alone	−1.4182	.3018	22.0816	.0000		51.45
Add demographics	−1.4380	.3143	20.9358	.0000		63.77
Add party identification	−1.0823	.3622	8.9271	.0028		79.14
Add ideology, feminism	−.9365	.3695	6.4239	.0113		79.74

SOURCE: VRS California state exit poll.

TABLE 4.10.

Effect of gay or lesbian self-identification on voting behavior in 1990 gubernatorial and U.S. Senate contests in Massachusetts, alone and when controlled, in succession, for demographic variables, party affiliation, and ideology and feminism

	Explanatory measures				Predictive measures	
	B	S.E.	Wald	Significance	Mean	% Correct
U.S. senator (N = 1,903)						
Voted for Democrat (John Kerry)					55.80	
Self-identification alone	1.2764	.5180	6.0711	.0137		56.30
Add demographics	.9919	.5287	3.5189	.0607		60.53
Add party identification	1.1956	.5754	4.3179	.0377		69.42
Add ideology, feminism	.8477	.6098	1.9322	.1645		69.70
Voted for Republican (James Rappaport)					43.54	
Self-identification alone	−1.2530	.5180	5.8505	.0156		56.88
Add demographics	−.9654	.5290	3.3312	.0680		61.64
Add party identification	−1.1723	.5768	4.1298	.0421		69.47
Add ideology, feminism	−.8240	.6120	1.8126	.1782		69.70
Governor (N = 1,908)						
Voted for Democrat (John Silber)					47.19	
Self-identification alone	−1.7125	.5673	9.1104	.0025		52.29
Add demographics	−1.5501	.5738	7.2965	.0069		57.33
Add party identification	−1.6716	.5867	8.1168	.0044		63.21
Add ideology, feminism	−1.6106	.5907	7.4352	.0064		63.78
Voted for Republican (William Weld)					50.34	
Self-identification alone	1.2710	.4777	7.0806	.0078		51.08
Add demographics	1.1711	.4846	5.8394	.0157		57.25
Add party identification	1.3020	.5039	6.6756	.0098		63.10
Add ideology, feminism	1.2690	.5081	6.2364	.0125		64.24

SOURCE: VRS state exit poll.

TABLE 4.11.
Effect of gay or lesbian self-identification on voting behavior in 1990 statewide contests in Texas, alone and when controlled, in succession, for demographic variables, party affiliation, and ideology and feminism

	Explanatory measures				Predictive measures	
	B	S.E.	Wald	Significance	Mean	% Correct
U.S. senator (N = 2,344)						
Voted for Democrat (Ben Parmer)					36.84	
Self-identification alone	1.1817	.3116	14.3817	.0001		63.96
Add demographics	1.5076	.3331	20.4851	.0000		70.24
Add party identification	1.5922	.3928	16.4328	.0001		78.30
Add ideology, feminism	1.3510	.3995	11.4348	.0007		80.09
Voted for Republican (Phil Gramm)					61.57	
Self-identification alone	−1.1103	.3115	12.7102	.0004		62.33
Add demographics	−1.1961	.3314	13.0298	.0003		70.12
Add party identification	−1.2951	.3855	11.2884	.0008		77.69
Add ideology, feminism	−1.0327	.3915	6.9586	.0083		78.72
Governor (N = 2,367)						
Voted for Democrat (Ann Richards)					50.51	
Self-identification alone	1.1372	.3345	11.5556	.0007		50.76
Add demographics	1.4391	.3586	16.1029	.0001		66.99
Add party identification	1.2810	.3983	10.3435	.0013		77.87
Add ideology, feminism	.9582	.4103	5.4530	.0195		79.27
Voted for Republican (Clayton Williams)					45.88	
Self-identification alone	−1.0563	.3416	9.5620	.0020		54.72
Add demographics	−1.0780	.3651	8.7171	.0032		67.59
Add party identification	−.8843	.3994	4.9037	.0268		77.09
Add ideology, feminism	−.5442	.4110	1.7531	.1855		77.99

TABLE 4.11. (*continued*)

Effect of gay or lesbian self-identification on voting behavior in 1990 statewide contests in Texas, alone and when controlled, in succession, for demographic variables, party affiliation, and ideology and feminism

	Explanatory measures				Predictive measures	
	B	S.E.	Wald	Significance	Mean	% Correct
Lieutenant governor (N = 1,900)						
Voted for Democrat (Bob Bulloch)					55.36	
Self-identification alone	.3674	.3351	1.2016	.2730		55.00
Add demographics	.6598	.3576	3.4036	.0651		64.46
Add party identification	.3437	.3939	.7613	.3829		75.02
Add ideology, feminism	.2026	.4002	.2563	.6127		74.95
Voted for Republican (Rob Mosbacher)					42.04	
Self-identification alone	−.2565	.3352	.5856	.4441		57.67
Add demographics	−.3830	.3604	1.1290	.2880		66.36
Add party identification	−.0945	.3980	.0564	.8123		75.32
Add ideology, feminism	.1373	.4037	.1156	.7338		75.62
Attorney general (N = 1,873)						
Voted for Democrat (Dan Morales)					55.48	
Self-identification alone	.7062	.3508	4.0520	.0441		54.86
Add demographics	1.0742	.3736	8.2664	.0040		65.85
Add party identification	.9006	.4221	4.5525	.0329		76.86
Add ideology, feminism	.6324	.4319	2.1436	.1432		78.28
Voted for Republican (Buster Brown)					42.98	
Self-identification alone	−.6518	.3508	3.4506	.0632		56.18
Add demographics	−.8558	.3729	5.2679	.0217		66.95
Add party identification	−.7249	.4224	2.9453	.0861		77.23
Add ideology, feminism	−.4069	.4328	.8839	.3471		79.13

SOURCE: VRS state exit poll.

TABLE 4.12.
Logistic regression of retrospective voting model and gay or lesbian self-identification as factors in the vote for Democratic nominees for governor in three states, 1990

Variable	California				Massachusetts				Texas			
	B	S.E.	Wald	Significance	B	S.E.	Wald	Significance	B	S.E.	Wald	Significance
Party affiliation												
Democratic	1.5006	.1350	123.4895	.0000	.7863	.1211	42.1739	.0000	1.6842	.1550	118.0079	.0000
Republican	-1.5010	.1484	102.3163	.0000	-.8140	.1671	23.7225	.0000	-1.0942	.1529	51.2320	.0000
Approval of												
Bush	-1.3339	.1201	123.3378	.0000	-.3312	.1200	7.6140	.0058	-1.7564	.1449	147.0139	.0000
Governor	(no indicator)				-.3964	.0781	25.7896	.0000	(no indicator)			
Economic evaluations												
National	.0738	.1030	.5132	.4737	.0400	.0917	.1902	.6628	-.2489	.1170	4.5286	.0333
State	.0722	.0941	.5877	.4433	.1023	.1042	.9641	.3263	-.0033	.1124	.0009	.9762
Gay/lesbian	1.2225	.4072	9.0150	.0027	-2.0110	.6866	8.5791	.0034	.8516	.4209	4.0942	.0430
Constant	-2.5572	.3096	68.2349	.0000	.0972	.4476	.0471	.8281	-1.7348	.3391	26.1708	.0000
% correct (N)	80.91 (2,442)				66.45 (1,633)				80.08 (2,010)			

TABLE 4.13.

Logistic regression of retrospective voting model and gay or lesbian self-identification as factors in the vote for Democratic nominees for U.S. Senate, Massachusetts and Texas, 1990

Variable	Massachusetts				Texas			
	B	S.E.	Wald	Significance	B	S.E.	Wald	Significance
Party affiliation								
Democratic	.9715	.1377	49.7728	.0000	1.5430	.1462	111.3672	.0000
Republican	−1.0567	.1737	37.0087	.0000	−1.5501	.2040	57.7512	.0000
Approval of								
Bush	−.6830	.1322	26.7139	.0000	−1.5920	.1350	139.1012	.0000
Governor	1.0017	.0926	116.9022	.0000	(no indicator)			
Economic evaluations								
National	.1179	.0995	1.4037	.2361	.0994	.1228	.6550	.4183
State	−.0402	.1160	.1201	.7289	.0115	.1181	.0095	.9222
Gay/lesbian	1.4023	.6268	5.0055	.0253	1.2273	.4291	8.1831	.0042
Constant	2.3646	.5113	21.3867	.0000	−3.3971	.3656	86.3189	.0000
% correct (N):	70.92		(1,617)		80.03		(1,984)	

 FIVE

Can the Activists Turn Out the Vote?
The Case of Deborah Glick

In the exit polls discussed in the last two chapters, indeed in most political surveys, voters are asked about their demographic characteristics and certain of their political attitudes and affiliations. It is a rare survey, however, that asks about specific influences on vote choice and voter mobilization that derive directly from the voter's own neighborhood. Such influences include contacts by specific candidates' organizations, activity by certain neighborhood political groups not affiliated with the candidate, and endorsements, especially those of general circulation newspapers. For our ends, we are interested specifically in the effect of endorsements and electoral activity by political activists within the LGB community—particularly when those activists are divided.

It is our good fortune that a poll exists that asks nearly all the questions we seek to answer in a district with a large LGB population, and in a contest that meets our specifications. This survey, as noted briefly earlier, is an exit poll conducted in a 1990 Democratic primary contest for an open seat in the New York State Assembly, the lower house of the state's legislature, from a district in lower Manhattan, in which an open lesbian and an openly gay man were among the five candidates.

As discussed within, this poll, called here the "Glick poll" after the winner of the primary contest in question, goes beyond the usual exit poll format employed at the national and state level. Among other innovations, this poll asks the respondents which local newspaper, magazine, and political club endorsements mattered in deciding for whom to vote, which candidate organizations had reached them personally in the last days before the primary, *two* questions indicating sexual self-identification, and a factual question bearing on name recognition about the sexual orientation of each of the candidates.

The Political Landscape

New York City has effectively been dominated by the Democratic Party for the past century. Despite the success of liberal and moderate Republicans in occasionally capturing citywide office (the mayor at this writing is a Republican, Rudolph Giuliani) and the odd seat in Congress or the City Council, the city is under single-party domination except for the borough of Staten Island and scattered neighborhoods in Queens.

Most elections—save those for the mayoralty—have been largely noncompetitive even within the party (Brecher et al. 1993). This is partly a result of the strength of the city's "regular" party organizations, which since the rapid decline of the influence of the Society of St. Tammany in the 1960s have broken into separate borough organizations. The most significant dissipation of the old organization's influence has been in Manhattan, in which a number of "reform" Democratic clubs arose in the 1960s. These clubs were characterized by a desire to reorient the city party from its traditional role as a dispenser of patronage to an instrument for enacting liberal public policy (Brecher et al. 1993). The reformers eventually achieved control of the Manhattan organization and, effectively, became the organization. Individual clubs, however, still exercise influence in intraparty affairs, and in primary elections for open seats.

The fundamental political division in the city of late had been between supporters and opponents of the city's former mayor, Edward Koch, who in September 1989 had been defeated for nomination to a fourth term by Manhattan Borough President David Dinkins. A Manhattan reform liberal himself, Koch had been criticized fiercely by many liberals, particularly in Manhattan, who charged that he played politics with the city's racial, ethnic, and religious divisions and catered to the prejudices of white ethnics in the "outer boroughs," had done too little about the problems of poverty, homelessness, and AIDS, and had allowed corruption to flourish in city government.

The Sixty-first State Assembly District, which we shall examine here, was a slice of lower Manhattan centered around Greenwich Village, a longtime colony of artists, musicians, and "bohemians" that today is the center of perhaps the largest "gay ghetto" in the eastern United States. The Village also was the site of the Stonewall riots of June 1969, which commonly are cited as the beginning of the Gay Liberation movement.[1] Surrounding neighborhoods, including SoHo, TriBeCa, and the East Village also were included in the district, which had a total population of approximately 120,000. Like most of Manhattan, the district was overwhelmingly liberal and Democratic in national and state elections, and victory in the district's Democratic primary was tantamount to election. The district was overwhelmingly white, a significant share of its residents were of Jewish ancestry, and a phenomenal share had had some sort of postgraduate education. The district is home to a weekly "neighborhood" tabloid newspaper of international repute and circulation, the *Village Voice.*

Although Mayor Koch came out of the Manhattan reform Democrats' movement that had sunk Tammany Hall in the 1960s, and had actively sought and signed a citywide gay rights law in 1986, the Sixty-first District had voted heavily against him in 1989 for many of the reasons discussed above.

Several "independent" Democratic clubs vie for influence in primary elections in the district. Given New York's history of strong private organizations influencing the Democratic Party (Tammany Hall being only the most notable and successful example), the Democrats' one-party dominance of most of the city, and the practical impossibility of using broadcast advertising in most local contests (it costs far too much and covers too wide an area to be practical), the Democratic political clubs and their endorsements provide the humanpower the candidates need and the voting cues some residents want (Brecher et al. 1993).

Greenwich Village and neighboring East Village were home to three principal competing "mainstream" clubs: the pro-Koch Village Reform Democratic Club (VRDC), the anti-Koch Village Independent Democrats (VID) and, outside of the divisions over Koch, the Downtown Independent Democrats (DID).[2]

In addition, two competing clubs focused specifically on the sexual-minority community. The older and larger of the two, the Gay and Lesbian Independent Democrats (GLID), was founded in 1974 as an outgrowth of the campaign of the first openly gay candidate for office in New York, Jim Owles.[3] By the early 1990s the club had a paid membership of two hundred and a mailing list of four hundred, composed almost entirely of residents of Manhattan; about forty-five members were active.[4]

The formal division of LGB Democratic Party activists into two camps occurred in 1986 (the year of the passage of the city gay rights law), over the election of Koch opponent Deborah Glick as GLID's president and the harsh criticism of pro-Koch members of the club for cooperating with the administration in order to keep patronage positions. Many of the pro-Koch members split from GLID and formed the competing, pro-Koch Stonewall Democratic Club.[5]

Among the influential publications in the district, the *Village Voice* has already been mentioned. The daily newspaper of choice was the *New York Times,* the city's only broadsheet, in strong preference to New York's three daily tabloids. Two weekly New York publications directed toward the LGB community also were circulated, the tabloid *New York Native* and *Outweek* magazine. The former was highly controversial owing to its editor's strong doubts, set forth frequently in the pages of the *Native,* that a single virus alone—without regard to "lifestyle" factors such as drug use and frequent sex with multiple partners—was the cause of AIDS. *Outweek* was widely criticized for its practice of "outing" closeted celebrities.[6]

The 1990 Assembly Race

In 1990, longtime State Assemblyman William Passannante chose to retire, setting off a wide-open contest to succeed him. Given the absence of significant statewide or congressional primary contests,[7] the only serious competitors for the voters' attention in the 11 September Democratic primary were a contest for Manhattan surrogate judge and the contest to replace Passannante in the assembly. Five candidates filed.

Elizabeth Shollenberger, a lawyer, was a moderate liberal who stressed crime fighting and was closest of the candidates to the Koch faction. The principal anti-Koch candidate was Deborah Glick, the open lesbian whose election to head GLID had resulted in the defection of the pro-Koch LGB Democrats from the club. The other three contenders were Kathryn Freed, an attorney and former legislative aide; Tony Hoffmann, a schoolteacher with ties to the VID; and Robert Rygor, an openly gay former state tax official. Shollenberger, Hoffmann, and Freed all were, at the time of the primary, elected party leaders in portions of the Sixty-first District.[8]

All five candidates were to one or another extent liberals and reformers, and issue differences were not stressed in the campaign; Shollenberger particularly emphasized combating crime, and Freed the need for affordable housing, but beyond this issues played a secondary role.[9] The campaign rather was notable, as stated obliquely in the *Times* editorial below, for the personal attacks of the two leading candidates against each other. Shollenberger charged that Glick was a "one-issue candidate" and "too radical" to be effective in Albany. Glick, in turn, attacked Shollenberger for being too negative and for making veiled appeals to homophobia.[10] Considerable attention was focused on the race by the national LGB community because it was the first in New York in which an open LGB candidate had a serious chance of winning a state legislative seat.[11]

Glick won the endorsement of *Outweek* as well as the expected endorsement from GLID. Beyond the LGB community, she was endorsed by the *Village Voice.*

However, the strain between the pro-Koch and anti-Koch Democratic activists in the LGB community was evident when the Stonewall club endorsed the heterosexual Shollenberger over the openly lesbian candidate. Shollenberger picked up additional endorsements from the pro-Koch VRDC and the *New York Post*. Freed was given the blessing of *New York Newsday* and the DID, and Hoffmann won that of the VID.[12]

A crucial endorsement was left outstanding one week before the election: that of the *New York Times*. After editors interviewed each of the five contenders, the newspaper disclosed its decision five days before the vote. Its choice was not made with enthusiasm:

Each of the five candidates has serious drawbacks.

[Rygor] . . . demonstrates little substance. [Hoffmann and Freed] . . . are caring and hard-working, but do not come across as strong leaders. [Shollenberger] . . . has done the most for her community and offers sensible moderation. But her negative campaigning and past use of harsh political tactics are distressing.

Deborah Glick, a political activist who hopes to be the first openly homosexual state legislator, is short on professional and community credentials but has impressive political skills that might make her an effective lawmaker. In a close call, we endorse Ms. Glick, hoping she knows that to be a one-issue legislator invites being a one-term legislator.[13]

Although the *Times* had endorsed an openly gay candidate for City Council the year before,[14] its endorsement of Glick was considered something of a coup by LGB activists, many of whom had attacked the *Times* during the 1980s for its allegedly poor coverage of LGB issues and AIDS, and for the paper's insistence on exclusively using the word "homosexual" instead of "gay" or "lesbian" until 1986.

On 11 September, Deborah Glick won the primary with 43 percent of the vote.[15] Shollenberger placed second. Anecdotally, Glick's victory was attributed to two factors: her LGB base, and the *New York Times* endorsement.

The Glick Poll

Because a victory by Glick would be a milestone in the development of the LGB movement in New York, and because the "gay vote" was widely cited as being Glick's essential base of support, political scientists Robert W. Bailey of Columbia University and Kenneth S. Sherrill of Hunter College, and pollster Murray S. Edelman of VRS, together with a rotating circle of individuals including John Leitner and Edward Baca, devised an exit poll on the Sixty-first

District primary, with the specific aims of determining how large the self-identified gay and lesbian community was in the district, the extent to which it supported Glick, and the extent to which other demographic factors, issue stands, and intervening variables (such as endorsements and campaign activity) may have affected the outcome.

The same polling methodology used by VRS in its national and state exit polls was employed. Eleven precincts (called "election districts" in New York) in the district were selected at random. Every Nth voter leaving the polling place was handed a survey form, a single sheet of paper printed on both sides, labeled a "secret ballot." Answers were indicated by checking boxes; no open-ended responses were permitted. The respondent completed the form, then folded it and placed it in a box. No questions were asked directly by the worker handing out the forms, and respondents were instructed not to write their names on the forms. A total of 516 respondents completed the survey. Cases were weighted after the election to reflect the official returns.

Demographic questions included sex, race, education level, income, age, "religious background," frequency of religious attendance, and a "grab bag" similar to that on the VRS surveys. In the "grab bag" were boxes in which the respondent could indicate that he or she was married, a member of an unmarried couple, retired, unemployed, a union member, a teacher, a student, an Italian, a resident of a rent-controlled apartment, or (the fourth item of ten in the "grab bag") gay or lesbian. A second indicator of sexual self-identification was included as the last question on the survey, reading "Which of these best describes your sexual orientation?" and offering five responses, from "exclusively heterosexual" to "exclusively homosexual," condensed from the seven points on the Kinsey scale.

Respondents were asked to choose, from a list of twelve, one or two issues that were most important in casting their State Assembly votes. Among the issues listed were gay/lesbian rights, AIDS, abortion, and crime and violence. Additional factors in the vote were split into two categories of nine questions apiece, asking in one set which qualities were important to the voter in the candidate she or he supported, and in the other asking whether the voter did *not* support a candidate for a particular reason. In each of these two categories, possible responses included the gender and the sexual orientation of the candidates. Questions also were asked about whether the respondent would be willing to pay higher taxes for more police patrols, and whether she or he thought "activist groups such as ACT-UP" had hurt or helped the cause of gay rights.

The only primary contest other than the assembly race asked about on the survey was the contest for surrogate judge, which we shall leave aside. Two indicators of past voting behavior were included: how the respondent had voted (if at all) in the 1989 Democratic primary for mayor between Koch and Dinkins, and the 1989 general election for mayor between Dinkins and Republican nominee Rudolph Giuliani. Respondents also were asked which contest was the most important in bringing them out to vote: that for surrogate judge, that for state assembly, or that for state comptroller.

At this point we can see that the Glick poll asked several questions in the common categories that rarely if ever were asked on a previous political survey: two separate sexual self-identification questions, an indicator that one belongs to an unmarried couple, and questions specifically relating to attitudes on LGB issues and LGB activists and politicians.

Three additional questions further set the survey apart from those preceding it. The most important for our purposes listed thirteen actual or purported endorsing organizations or publications and asked the respondent if any of these were important in convincing her or him to vote for her or his candidate in the assembly race. Respondents were limited to a maximum of two choices. Each of the four daily newspapers, the three weeklies, and the five Democratic clubs discussed previously were included on the list, as was candidate Robert Rygor's "New Frontier Democrats." Another question asked the respondent to check the names of all candidates whose campaigns had contacted her or him by phone or in person "in the last few days." A third—the one question on the survey with objectively "correct" answers—asked the respondent to check the names of all candidates who were gay or lesbian.

Analysis

Those respondents who did not indicate a preference in the assembly race were excluded from the analysis, leaving 339 weighted cases. The form of analysis was much the same as with the VRS national and state exit polls.

First, a comparative breakdown was produced between the self-identified lesbians and gay men and the rest of the sample. This differed from the preceding analyses in one notable respect: an initial comparison was made between those who checked the "gay/lesbian" self-identifier item in the "grab bag" section and the separate self-reporting of "sexual orientation" on the five-point scale to determine whether any discrepancies existed. The comparative breakdown involved simple crosstabulations of the weighted data. Demographic variables were examined, then attitudinal ones, then voting behavior and factors thought to contribute to vote choice. A similar comparative breakdown then was done to determine differences, if any, between self-identified gay men and lesbians. (Regrettably, no indicator of feminism appeared in the survey.)

I then proceeded to several logistic regression analyses. The first sought to test the effect of the demographic factors identified in preceding chapters on gay/lesbian self-identification. The factors of size of locality and region, obviously, were not included, as they were identical for all respondents, but the other demographic correlates of self-identification (see table 3.7 in chapter 3) were available to be tested.

Testing for the factors that might influence primary voting leads us away from the models used previously to test the effect of gay/lesbian self-identification on voting behavior in general elections. All respondents and candidates are Democrats, and primary elections do not respond to the same forces that drive general elections; they are more easily compared to nonpartisan elections, for which no reliable models of voting behavior have been developed. Further, we have no indicators of ideology or feminism in the poll.

Therefore, I take the anecdotal explanation for Glick's victory as the starting point, and hypothesize that strong support from the lesbian and gay community and support from nongays influenced by the endorsement of Glick in the *New York Times* were the essential blocks upon which her victory was built. The strong lesbian and gay support would be manifested in several ways. The issue concerns of the gay/lesbian sample as a whole would center strongly around gay and lesbian rights, and possibly around crime and violence; AIDS also would be a primary concern among gay men, whereas legal abortion would register high as a concern among lesbians. Because of the publicity in the LGB community surrounding the contest, and because of Glick's past high position in GLID, the gay/lesbian sample should know almost without exception that Glick is a lesbian and may be more likely to have been contacted by Glick campaign workers in the days leading up to the primary. The gay/lesbian sample should cite the endorsements of LGB-oriented political clubs and publications as important in their vote choice. Finally, because of the pro- and anti-Koch conflict, we may expect that lesbians and gay men who supported Koch in 1989 would be far less likely to vote for Glick than would Dinkins supporters, and that the pro-Koch gay and lesbian voters most likely would split to Liz Shollenberger, endorsee of the pro-Koch Stonewall club.

An initial set of crosstabulations will test this theory. Then, should there be other variables on which the gay and nongay samples differ significantly in the crosstabular analysis, and which have a sound theoretical basis for inclusion, these will be included in an initial logistic regression model. From this, a refined logit model will remove those variables from the initial one that give no additive explanatory power.

Comparative Analysis

Demographics

Table 5.1 displays the demographic breakdown of the assembly voters' sample, giving the simple frequency distribution, then the comparison between the gay and nongay samples.

The Democratic primary voters of the Sixty-first District in 1990 were highly atypical of the country, or even of the rest of New York City, in several important respects. An absolute majority of the primary voters had attended at least some graduate or professional school, and seven out of eight held at least a bachelor's degree. One-third of the respondents reported making at least $75,000 a year. A relatively small percentage were legally married, fewer than a third (and fewer than two-fifths of the nongay respondents), while a considerable share were living together as couples outside of marriage. A rather small share were under the age of thirty as well, which may be a factor of the cost of living (three in seven respondents live in rent-controlled or rent-stabilized apartments), or simply of the tendency of younger people to turn out to vote, especially in primary and nonpartisan elections, at a much lower rate (Wolfinger and Rosenstone 1980). Forty-five percent of the respondents were of Jewish background, outnumbering self-described Protestants and Catholics combined. Whatever the religious background, however, religion played a minimal role in the lives of the respondents: only one in six attended religious services even once a month, and four in nine said they never darkened the door of a synagogue or church.

The district also was distinguished by its very high percentage of self-identified lesbians and gay men, who accounted for 22 percent of those who voted in the assembly primary. The separate question asking the respondents their sexual orientation on a five-point scale yielded minimally higher percentages: 24 percent were exclusively or predominately homosexual, and another 6 percent called themselves either bisexual or "mostly" heterosexual. When crosstabulated with the self-identifier question in the "grab bag," it was found that all but four of the seventy-four gay/lesbian self-identifiers said they were exclusively or predominately homosexual, whereas three of the remainder called themselves bisexual. (One respondent, out of confusion or whimsy, claimed to be both "exclusively heterosexual" and "gay/lesbian.")

Students of bisexual voting behavior should be aware that, of fourteen self-described bisexuals on the five-point scale, eleven did *not* check the gay/lesbian self-identifier item. Neither, for reasons uncertain, did three of the thirty-two "mostly homosexual" respondents, nor did five of the fifty-seven "exclusively homosexual" respondents. Among these last two categories there were no discernible differences between the gay/lesbian identifiers and nonidentifiers, and it is possible that the respondents simply neglected to answer the question in the "grab bag" section. However, to retain consistency in definition, I shall use the "grab bag" question as the indicator of "sexual orientation," rather than the five-point scale.

The most glaring difference between the self-identifiers and the rest of the respondents was the division by sex. A four-to-three majority of nongay identifiers were women; but three-quarters of the gay/lesbian sample were men. This conforms to our earlier findings that a disproportion of gay men tend to live in large central cities, whereas the largest share of lesbians reside in the suburbs. Race, it should be noted, played no significant role in self-identification in this district in which nineteen of twenty respondents were white.

Although the age differences were not as glaring as some found previously, the gay/lesbian sample was relatively younger than the rest of the respondents, with a minimal share of lesbian and gay respondents who were sixty or older and nearly half being between the ages of eighteen and thirty-nine. In addition, 10 percent of gay/lesbian self-identifiers were students, as against 3 percent of the nongay identifiers. The two groups differed hardly at all in levels of education or income, or in the few occupational indicators, save that a much smaller share (bordering on statistical significance) were retirees, again reflecting age differences.

A very interesting sociological finding is that a large proportion of the gay folk in the sample are coupled. Although none of those in the gay sample are legally married (a finding unlike that in the state-level and national data seen previously), and although big-city gay men especially have been accused as a class of promiscuity, 42 percent of the gay/lesbian self-identifiers report they belong to cohabitant couples, as against 51 percent of the nongay identifiers (39 percent in married couples, 12 percent in unmarried couples).

The previous findings as to the suppression of religiosity in most places among lesbians and gay men are confirmed here, with significantly smaller shares of gay people attending religious services than their heterosexual counterparts, and attending less frequently, even when one controls for the widespread secularism of the nongay respondents.

Attitudes

The Glick poll contained a relatively small battery of issue-related questions. The principal cluster asked respondents to choose no more than two
issues, from a list of twelve, that they considered the most important in casting
their vote in the assembly race. It is in the results reported in table 5.2 that the
great divergence in priorities hypothesized earlier can be seen.

Among the nongay identifiers, crime and violence was named by an absolute
majority, and no other issue came close to this one in the ranking of importance. Following in a virtual three-way tie for the second tier of priorities were
homelessness, tenants' rights, and abortion. In a third tier, named by around
20 percent of nongay respondents, were AIDS, schools, and riverfront development. Five other issues trailed in importance—among these gay and lesbian
rights, which was ranked at the bottom of the list.

There could be no greater difference on this last issue. Gay and lesbian self-
identifiers ranked gay and lesbian rights at the top of their list: 70 percent
named it one of their top two issues of importance. Next was AIDS, with half
the sample indicating it. Following in third, at 43 percent, was crime and
violence. No other issue was remotely close: homelessness followed in fourth
place, named by a quarter of respondents, and abortion trailed in fifth, chosen
by one in five respondents. All other issues trailed in the teens or the single
digits.

The district, in brief, agreed on the importance of crime and violence,
homelessness, and abortion. From there the priorities of the gay and nongay
respondents went their separate ways. In a very real sense, a candidate appealing
to the "gay and lesbian vote" in the district had to address a discrete and
insular constituency.[16]

Voting Behavior and Decision Making

Table 5.3 displays in its first result a forty-three-point sexuality gap between
gay and nongay support for Deborah Glick. The winning candidate's strength
is evidenced in the fact that, even had all the lesbian and gay voters stayed
home, she would have won the five-way primary with about one-third of the
vote. Glick's large margin of victory, however, would not have been achieved
absent the tremendous support she rallied among her base constituency. It is
interesting that in the only other seriously contested race on primary day, the
contest for Manhattan surrogate judge, in which there was little organized
activity by the lesbian and gay community, there was no significant gap

between the gay/lesbian self-identifiers and the rest of the respondents (data not shown).

Nearly all respondents said they had voted both in the 1989 Democratic mayoral primary and in the general election that followed. Again, 77 percent of the gay and lesbian self-identifiers voted for the preferred candidate, David Dinkins,[17] as did a majority of nearly two to one among the nongay identifiers voting in the 1990 primary. In the general election the district went to Dinkins by a very large margin; but the number of disgruntled Koch supporters who voted for Rudolph Giuliani is notable, as is the minuscule increase in Dinkins's margin among these registered gay and lesbian Democrats between the primary and the general election.

One possible reason for Glick's large margin is evidenced in the factors listed as important in a candidate in table 5.3. Asked what attributes they sought in their state assembly member and given a list of nine, from which they could choose up to two, absolute majorities of the nongay respondents named knowing the district and working hard as their top two factors. Among the gay and lesbian respondents, who until this time had had no elected public representatives at any level in New York City, an absolute majority said the most important attribute was that the member be gay or lesbian, compared to 3 percent of nongay identifiers who so responded.[18] Knowing the district ranked fourth in priority among the gay/lesbian respondents. Interestingly, given the predominance of men in the gay sample, a disproportion of gay folk said that having a female assembly member was very important.

Conversely, very few respondents of any sexuality said they had declined to vote for a particular candidate for any of nine reasons stated in the next question. More than two-thirds did not name any. The only two that mattered even to double-digit percentages (in the midteens) were "running a dirty campaign," the principal rap against Shollenberger, and "running a one-issue campaign," the principal rap against Glick. In neither case was there a significant difference between the sexualities. The only such difference was that 6 percent of the gay/lesbian sample (four respondents) said they did not vote for some candidate because that candidate was heterosexual.

It is clear that, to most of the voters casting ballots in the assembly race, it was the single most important contest on the ballot that day. This was especially true for the gay and lesbian respondents, 76 percent of whom indicated this was the contest in which they had the greatest interest.

These levels of interest certainly could be laid in part at the feet of the five assembly campaigns, which among them contacted an absolute majority of the respondents in the "few days" (not specified in the poll) leading up to the primary. Glick's campaign reached a third of the voters in person or by telephone, Shollenberger's a quarter, and Freed's and Hoffmann's in the high teens, with Rygor's far in the rear. In only one case was there a statistically significant difference in contact rates: Glick's campaign reached just under 30 percent of nongay voters, but 42 percent of gay/lesbian self-identifiers.

In a test of the voters' knowledge—and perhaps of the candidates' ability to get themselves recognized by the voters—the survey respondents were asked to check the names of all candidates who they "knew" to be gay or lesbian. Three-fifths of nongay respondents and eight-ninths of gay/lesbian respondents knew that Glick was a lesbian. Rygor was considerably less successful: only two-ninths of his own gay/lesbian constituency and one-eighth of nongay respondents knew of his sexual orientation. Small numbers of respondents, gay and straight alike, incorrectly named Shollenberger, Freed, and Hoffmann.

Gender Differences: Unexpected, Important Findings

Table 5.4 presents the significant and near-significant differences within the lesbian and gay subsample based on sex, and shows the data on the nongay population from the three tables preceding for purposes of comparison. Although gender effects on vote choice were not found and the effects on attitudes were minimal,[19] certain demographic findings are of interest beyond the scope of political analysis.

The national and state-level data bases examined earlier show that men outnumber women among self-identifiers by margins of three to two or more. Even by this standard, the Sixty-first District sample is disproportionately male, comprising fifty-five men and nineteen women. Because a large share of self-identified gay men tend to reside in central cities, it may be postulated that in this central city district, the largest share of the gay men will be immigrants to the district, and the largest share of lesbians will more closely share the characteristics of the nongay residents.

In several respects, the postulate above is borne out in the data. The age breakdown of the self-identified lesbians is virtually identical to that of the nongays and quite divergent from the gay men. Also indicating longer ties to the community are the identical shares of lesbians and nongays among those naming tenants' rights as an important issue and stating that it is important for the candidate they choose to know the district; much smaller shares of gay men named both.

Lesbian self-identifiers did differ in two important respects from their nonlesbian sisters: many more lesbians said the election of a woman was of great importance, and the lesbian sample appears to be somewhat better educated than either gay men or nongay women.

In addition to the results above, two findings that I did not expect, and that do not relate directly to political attitudes or vote choice, must be noted. First, half of the lesbian self-identifiers report that they are *not* exclusively homosexual in orientation—whereas four-fifths of the gay men say that they are!

In previous chapters I sought reasons why women should be less likely to call themselves homosexual than men, and speculated that social factors were principal causes: both norms regarding intimacy among women, which may make it more difficult for a woman to comprehend her feelings for another woman as having a sexual underpinning, and the fact that lesbians are significantly more likely to have custody of children, which the disclosure of their sexuality could affect adversely. It also is possible, of course, that women are less inclined physiologically to be homosexual than are men.

This result raises another possibility: that a disproportion of gay women actually do have sexual feelings for persons of both sexes, and that these women have a significantly greater degree of choice regarding toward whom their affections will be directed, which most men with same-sex attractions do not have. This cannot be determined in any definitive way from a sample of nineteen lesbian primary voters in the vicinity of Greenwich Village. But this observation should be followed up in future research on the nature of homosexuality.

The religion results, which near statistical significance, also give us some further guidance as to the source of religious differences within samples of self-identifiers noted in chapters 3 and 4. I speculated, based on the results of table 5.1, that once again the predominate religious tradition in the district had the effect of suppressing lesbian and gay self-identification among its adherents. But lesbians and nongays indicate that they are Jewish, Christian, or something else at identical rates; once again, the gay-straight differences are actually differences between the gay men and the rest of the sample.

This finding is not replicated in the national and state-level data, and it does not explain away the apparent suppressive effects of dominant religious tradition on self-identification at these levels reported in chapters 3 and 4. But it does show that, among downtown Manhattan Democrats, differences in religious affiliation between the straight and gay populations more likely are the result of gay male immigration. Thus, we must approach the causes of gay-straight religious differences with somewhat more caution.

The Effect of Endorsements

Table 5.5 recapitulates the endorsements of the political clubs in the district and the predominant general interest and LGB-oriented newspapers and magazines that circulate therein. It is well to note the bottom row of figures first, in that they indicate that two-thirds of the respondents reported having been influenced by the endorsement of at least one club or publication. (Again, the respondent could check no more than two.) The figure was slightly higher for lesbian and gay respondents: 77 percent indicated at least one endorsement as important to their vote choice.

Of those who cited an endorsement, about half the respondents in each sexuality category cited that of the *New York Times.* This certainly offers initial corroboration of the anecdotal belief that the *Times's* endorsement may have helped Glick win crucial heterosexual support. Yet it also indicates that, to self-identified gay and lesbian voters, the vote of confidence in Glick from the much-criticized *Times* was of equal importance.

Again, from this point, the influences on the respective categories of voters rather diverged. Among the nongay respondents, four endorsing bodies fell into a second tier, with from 9 to 13 percent of respondents citing them: each of the three general membership Democratic clubs in the district, and the *Village Voice.* Beyond this, the effects of the endorsements of the daily tabloids were utterly unfelt, as were (predictably) the nods given by the LGB-oriented clubs and media.

Among the gay and lesbian respondents, the endorsements of two publications affected the votes of about 20 percent each: the *Village Voice* and the LGB magazine *Outweek.* In fourth place, cited by one gay or lesbian respondent in six (twelve in number), was GLID, the club Glick used to head. Its competitor and archrival, the Stonewall club, was cited by one in ten gay respondents (seven in number); interestingly, eight of the fifteen respondents in the entire survey who cited the Stonewall club as an influence were heterosexual! A larger share of gay men and lesbians, one in seven (ten in number), named the VID endorsement as important. Again, the endorsements of the daily tabloids did not register; neither did those of the VRDC or the DID.[20]

Our initial examination of the data shows a sizable "sexuality gap" in voting behavior. Very little of this is attributable to demographic differences in the samples: no significant differences were found between gay and nongay primary voters except for age, the religion variables, a slight disproportion of students, and (as expected) the marital status variables. The greater share of differences was found in the issue priorities of the gay/lesbian self-identifiers, who put gay and lesbian rights at the top of the list, followed by AIDS; and in the strong desire among much of the sample for a lesbian or gay elected representative.

The initial findings, however, tell us that even with Glick's high name recognition (and "sexuality recognition") in the lesbian and gay community and the strong desire of the gay/lesbian respondents for a gay or lesbian elected official who would work hard on LGB rights and AIDS issues, a significant share of these respondents also looked to "straight" sources for voting cues. Two of five looked to the *New York Times* and one in five looked to the *Village Voice* to confirm their predilections.

The Vote for Glick

Crosstabular Analysis

I now move to the specific factors that may have influenced a vote for or against Deborah Glick within the lesbian and gay community. In the first stage, I again look at simple crosstabulations and tests of statistical significance for several variables hypothesized to be related to support of or opposition to Glick among the seventy-four lesbians and gay men in the sample who voted in the assembly primary.

Table 5.6 presents the findings of these crosstabulations. None of the hypothesized demographic variables had any effect on vote choice, nor, interestingly, did the attitude that AIDS was one of the top two issues, nor was the endorsement of Glick's club, GLID. Instead, the strongest differences were seen between those who said one of the most important qualities of their choice be that s/he was gay or lesbian (94 percent support for Glick) and those who did not (58 percent support), and between those who labeled gay and lesbian rights one of the top two issues (88 percent for Glick) and those who did not (51 percent for Glick).

Conversely, the strongest drag on Glick's support was the perception of a minority in the gay and lesbian community that she was running a single-issue campaign; among the nine respondents who mentioned this, Glick won the support of only three. A second significant drag, which cannot be good news to GLID, was the endorsement of Liz Shollenberger by the Stonewall club and the endorsement of Tony Hoffmann by GLID's anti-Koch cohort organization, the VID. The minority ($N = 15$) who believed that militant activism had not helped the cause of gay and lesbian rights gave only half its votes to Glick, as against five-sixths of those who thought otherwise. A larger number (*N* = 26) who said that knowing the district was important gave a somewhat smaller share of its votes to Glick (60 percent) than did the rest (86 percent). Finally, five of the eleven Koch voters in the sample voted against Glick, whereas four-fifths of the anti-Koch primary voters in 1989 supported her; this result neared statistical significance at .058.

The result that may be of the greatest interest, however, is that two "straight" media outlets exercised a significant influence on voting for or against Glick within the lesbian and gay community. All but three of the twenty-nine respondents who mentioned the *New York Times* as important in making their decision, and all but one of the sixteen who similarly named the *Village Voice* voted for Glick, whereas roughly one-third of those who did not mention these newspaper endorsements voted against her. The same result was obtained for *Outweek,* the gay newsmagazine, as for the *Village Voice,* but because of slight differences in weighting, the *Outweek* result barely missed being statistically significant, at .062. (The *Voice* result was significant at .046.)

This appears to tell us that, even with the desire for gay representation evident in these numbers, the gay and lesbian voters of this highly educated, secular, and, apparently, extremely liberal district still look to nongay sources for cues as to whether the leading gay candidate can win enough straight support to win. I hypothesize therefore that, as do many other voters, a goodly share of gay and lesbian voters want to vote for a potential winner, and do not merely choose the candidate who is most supportive of their goals, but make calculations in multi-candidate races as to whether supporting such a candidate would mean wasting their votes.

To test this hypothesis, I first broke out the endorsements cited by the respondents into five categories: gay media, nongay media, gay clubs, nongay clubs,[21] and those respondents who did not indicate that any of the listed endorsements were important. I then further broke out these categories into two new variables. The first indicated whether the endorsements cited were solely from nongay sources, solely from gay sources, or comprised one from each; the second indicated whether the endorsing media cited were solely publications, solely the political clubs, or comprised one from each. These two variables then were crosstabulated to produce table 5.7, which shows the pattern of endorsements by sexual self-identification.

The most noteworthy result is that, of those gay or lesbian respondents who indicated that at least one endorsement was important, only one in five named solely LGB-oriented publications and/or political clubs, and fully half named only nongay endorsement sources. In contrast, fewer than one in ten nongay identifiers who indicated that at least one endorsement was important named any LGB-oriented endorsement source, and save for one respondent, all named a nongay source as important as well. There was no significant difference between the sexualities in reliance on clubs, publications, both, or neither.

The next important question is whether the pattern of endorsements named had any effect on vote choice in the gay/lesbian sample. An initial crosstabulation showed no significant difference based on endorsement source; that is, those who relied solely on nongay endorsements did not vote significantly differently from those relying on gay sources, mixed sources, or none. Oddly, however, the initial look found a highly significant difference based on endorsement medium: those who named political clubs as their sole endorsement source(s) were far less likely to vote for Glick (40 percent for Glick, versus 85 to 90 percent from the other three categories: publications only, one publication and one club, and no endorsements). A further examination shows that the culprit appears to be the nongay political clubs, none of which endorsed Glick. All but one of the seven gay/lesbian self-identifiers who named nongay clubs as their sole endorsement source voted against Glick (significant at .01), as did three of the five who named one gay and one nongay club (significant at .05).

The crosstabulations indicate that Glick voters were concerned principally with electing a lesbian or gay public representative who would address their specific civil rights concerns, which were not taken by the nongay respondents to be of overriding importance. Even so, they appear to have been deeply concerned that they could not do this alone, and that a successful gay candidate had to have the endorsement of important nongay sources. Even within the lesbian and gay community, endorsements mattered, and particularly the endorsements of the nongay media, which were favorable to Glick, and of the nongay Democratic clubs, which were not. In addition, Stonewall's refusal to endorse Glick apparently registered significantly with a small share of the gay and lesbian voters in the Sixty-first District. On the other hand, the one-fourth of lesbian and gay respondents who did not rely on the word of any of the twelve endorsement media, most of these respondents being lesbians, were overwhelmingly (88 percent) supportive of Glick.

Logistic Regression Analysis

Using the initial hypothesis and the crosstabular findings, I then constructed an initial logistic regression model of the likely sources of Glick's votes. The model was tried first using the entire voting sample ($N = 339$), then (with the sexual self-identification variable removed) with the seventy-four lesbian and gay respondents in isolation.

The results of the all-voter regression, side by side with those of the gay/lesbian-only regression, are shown in table 5.8. I take the all-voter data first.

Surprisingly, after controlling for some related variables, we find that self-identification as gay or lesbian was *not* a significant factor, although it approached significance at .088. Two directly related variables were, however, quite important: the desire for a gay or lesbian legislator, and the naming of gay/lesbian rights as a top issue affecting the vote. By far the most powerful factor influencing the total sample in its decision for or against Deborah Glick was the *New York Times* endorsement, thus confirming the anecdotal speculation. The endorsement of the *Village Voice,* although not as potent as that of the *Times,* also had a significant effect. As predicted, three indicators pulled Glick's vote down: the perception that she was waging a single-issue campaign (which even the *Times* endorsement reinforced), the endorsement of Liz Shollenberger by the LGB-oriented Stonewall club, and opposition to her among Koch supporters. Five other factors did not register at all: the knowledge (or lack thereof) that Glick was a lesbian, being contacted by the Glick campaign in the days preceding the election, the naming of AIDS as a top issue, and the endorsements of *Outweek* and of Glick's own club, GLID.

Looking now at the gay and lesbian voters in isolation, we must proceed with caution, as the very high standard errors associated with the small sample size reduce some potentially important factors to statistical insignificance. The only statistically significant factor, standing alone in this mix, is the desire for a gay or lesbian legislator. Five other indicators, however, approach statistical significance. On the positive side for Glick, the most important again was the *Times* endorsement, trailed by contacts by her campaign organization—the mobilization factor was completely unimportant to the rest of the sample after other variables were controlled for—and the naming of gay/lesbian rights as a top issue. On the negative side for her, the most important, as in the all-voter sample, was the perception of a single-issue campaign, trailed by the Stonewall endorsement. It is interesting that neither the *Village Voice* endorsement nor the Koch vote, named as important by the total sample, was significant among the gay/lesbian sample; nor were the endorsements of *Outweek* or GLID, the knowledge of Glick's sexual orientation, or the naming of AIDS as a top issue.

It is notable, finally, that this initial model did a remarkably good job of predicting individual votes for or against Glick: the model's predictive power was nearly 80 percent among the total sample, and 88 percent among the gay/lesbian sample. This would be quite good in a general election, in which the factor of party could be included as the chief predictive variable. Given that models to date attempting to predict turnout or voting behavior in presidential primaries correctly predict only about 60 percent of the cases, an 80 or 85 percent figure in a five-way primary contest is quite something.

Using these results, I respecified the model to exclude clearly insignificant factors in an attempt to improve its predictive accuracy. The results for these refined models are presented in table 5.9, with those for the total, all-voter sample given at left, then those for the gay and lesbian sample at right.

No surprises were found in respecifying the all-voter model, save perhaps for the fact that, again, sexual self-identification barely escaped statistical significance as an important factor in its own right. Once again, the *Times* endorsement was by far the most important factor in the contest, and the second most important factor in Glick's favor was the desire for a lesbian or gay legislator. Once again, the most significant factors against Glick were the single-issue perception and the opposition of the Stonewall club. The refined model was but a shade less potent than the initial model as a predictor of individual vote choice.

In the gay/lesbian model, three factors were statistically significant in their own right: in Glick's favor were the desire for a gay or lesbian representative and the *Times* endorsement, whereas against Glick stood the single-issue perception. None of the other three factors included in the model—the Stonewall endorsement, contacts by the Glick campaign, and naming gay and lesbian rights as a top issue—reached the level of statistical significance, but they had perceptible explanatory and predictive power among them. Removing these last three items from the model, leaving in only the first three, reduced its predictive power to 84 percent, slightly below the level of the initial model. The refined six-variable model, on the other hand, predicted the votes of a phenomenal 91 percent of lesbian and gay respondents.

I go back now to the hypotheses laid out earlier in this chapter. I predicted that issue concerns, particularly gay and lesbian rights, AIDS, abortion, and crime and violence, would be primary factors in the voting of lesbians and gay men. In fact, only one of these, gay and lesbian rights, had a substantial effect, and that effect was marginal compared to the simple concern, addressed not at all in my initial hypotheses, with electing a lesbian or gay public representative for the first time ever. The gay sample did know almost without exception that Glick was a lesbian, but this knowledge had no separate effect on voting behavior. Rather more gay than nongay voters were contacted by the Glick campaign in the waning days of the contest, and this appears to have had some effect in mobilizing the vote within the gay and lesbian community.

The most interesting findings, perhaps, were the absence of independent effects of Glick's endorsements by LGB publications and by GLID, and indeed the considerable lack of reliance on the LGB endorsement media by the specific voters toward whom the endorsements were directed. Three gay and lesbian voters in eight, and half of those who said they were influenced by any endorsements at all said the endorsements that influenced them were exclusively those of *nongay* publications and/or clubs. The one gay endorsement that appeared to matter, to gay and nongay voters alike, was that of a heterosexual candidate by the Stonewall Democratic Club; it was the one hole in a solid wall of lesbian and gay organizational support.[22]

Most important to Glick by far was the endorsement of the *Times*, backhanded though it was. In addition to swaying undecided heterosexuals, it evidently convinced a number of gay and lesbian voters that Glick had a serious chance of winning.[23] Even in endorsing her, however, the *Times* somewhat condescendingly cautioned her that "being a one-issue legislator invites being a one-term legislator," thereby giving credence to one of the principal accusations against her campaign, raised in particular by Shollenberger. A significant number of voters, again gay and straight alike, voted against Glick because she was perceived, rightly or wrongly, as a Debbie One-Note.

In brief, then, Deborah Glick went to the New York State Assembly because she was an open lesbian activist, in a district in which a substantial, unrepresented minority of lesbians and gay men craved a seat at the table of power, who managed to be taken seriously for her political skills by the heterosexual majority despite worries that her base constituency was her only concern. She also may have been lucky in her opposition; had the *Times* editorial board not balked at what it saw as the stridency and negativism of Liz Shollenberger's campaign, the editorial makes clear, she and not Deborah Glick would have won the endorsement and, it may be argued, the nomination.

What the Glick Poll Teaches Us

It is time now to step back from this particular contest, historic though it is for lesbian and gay New Yorkers, and ask what the Glick poll tells us above and beyond what was learned in the preceding two chapters, and how this new knowledge relates to the hypothesis of a gay and lesbian vote in America.

First, it appears that, as expected, lesbians and gay men in the Glick study were far different in their issue concerns than were the rest of the sample: gay and lesbian rights and AIDS were the major priorities. However, the specific issue concerns, as I have just noted, were secondary to a more basic desire for representation. The sexuality gap has some roots in issue differences, and in contests in which no gay or lesbian candidate is on the ballot these issue differences, stemming from the influences of liberalism and feminism, may indeed be the paramount determinant of the sexuality gap. When a gay or lesbian candidate is running, however, the need to feel included in the process appears to take precedence.

Second, we see that lesbian and gay voters appear to have the same aversion to wasting their votes as do heterosexuals, and look to sources in the majority community for confirmation that "their" candidate has some substantial support among the nongay majority. The endorsement of the area's leading general circulation newspaper was the great factor in providing such assurance; the support of the well-known, widely read, leftist "neighborhood" weekly was not.

From the facts in hand, we can begin to make sense of the factors that lead to cohesive voting by lesbians and gay men. The gay or lesbian voter, having been shut out of the political process until recent years and still treated as an outcast by important people in government, fundamentally wants someone who will listen to her concerns respectfully and sympathetically. The priority of those concerns differs from the priorities of her straight neighbors, but the most important thing is to be heard and treated with respect. A candidate with a long history of such treatment will maintain the support of that gay voter as against one who begins making the appeal only when it appears politically necessary or convenient to do so; witness the case of Dianne Feinstein and Pete Wilson in California.

Best of all for this voter would be to have an openly lesbian, gay, or bisexual elected representative. When an open LGB candidate runs, however, it is important that she pull in sufficient evidence of support from outside the LGB community to prove that she can win, and that she not be pegged as a "gay candidate," appealing only to the homosexual and bisexual minority.

It appears that an LGB candidate's organization can play an important role in mobilizing the voter to go to the polls and vote, provided that the above conditions have been met. If not, then the endorsements of LGB-oriented political groups and publications will not matter, and indeed a split in the ranks, a failure to endorse by a LGB-oriented club or publication, appears to have a significant effect in breaking cohesion. The good news for LGB organizers is that their organizations matter: their unity and their mobilizing power, given sufficient nongay support for the candidate, play an important part in turning "lavender" voters into a cohesive "lavender vote."

One other tendency should be noted: the minority of the lesbian and gay subsample that appeared to be concerned that Glick was too concentrated on LGB rights. About three in ten gay or lesbian Democratic primary voters did *not* list gay and lesbian rights as a major concern, and furthermore, a small number actually refused their votes to the "gay candidate" because they were worried that she was running a one-issue campaign not sufficiently attuned to the needs of their straight friends and neighbors. These manifestations on the surface fit the characteristics of assimilationism. In saying this, I do not mean that all Glick's voters were "cultural pluralists," only that a candidate such as Glick may have had difficulty winning widespread support in her own community were its attitudes predominately assimilationist in character.

The Glick poll also tells us that the central factor in convincing nongay voters to support Glick was the support of the two principal nongay general circulation newspapers, the daily *Times* (by far the more influential) and the weekly *Village Voice.* We do not find the demographic variations that we have seen in partisan elections for governors and members of Congress. Therefore, it is not possible to determine whether such endorsements would have the same effect on coalition building with the heterosexual community outside this highly educated, rather well-off chunk of lower Manhattan.

What is notable is that, even with these endorsements, only a third of nongay voters, albeit a plurality, supported Glick in the primary in such a district. This may be attributable in part to the perception of her as a one-issue wonder and the apparent split among the gay activists evidenced in Stonewall's endorsement of Shollenberger, which as we have noted may have had more to do with internal Democratic club politics than with the relative qualifications of the candidates. However, it evidences a basic difficulty in a lesbian or gay male candidate building coalitions even with highly educated, liberal heterosexuals in a major urban center.

The Glick poll greatly improves our previous understanding of lesbian and gay attitudes and voting behavior. Given an exceedingly well educated constituency sharing most of the same demographic characteristics, the single factor of self-identification as gay or lesbian results in a great gap in issue priorities and in what is most wanted in an elected official. Yet a significant manifestation of heterosexual support is of equal importance to the victory of a lesbian or gay candidate. Nonetheless, a sufficiently organized base of gay and lesbian voters is the foundation upon which that later support must be built. It was Deborah Glick's good fortune and skill to pull in enough support from wary heterosexuals, while holding on to her base of lesbians and gay men with a strong appeal for gay rights and gay representation, in order to win.

So far we have examined races for Congress and for state governorships and, in this chapter, a contest for state legislative office, all of them taking place in an "off year." How will our discoveries so far hold up, however, when subjected to the unique dynamics of a presidential contest that, as noted in the beginning of this work, had the highest salience of any election in U.S. history for lesbian, gay, and bisexual voters? And how will the inclusion of self-identified bisexuals in the sample affect what we have found to date with respect to self-identified lesbians and gay men? The answers to these final questions are found in the next chapter.

TABLE 5.1.

Frequency distribution of demographic indicators, and comparison between self-identified lesbians and gay men and other voters, Democratic primary for New York State Assembly, Sixty-first District, September 1990

Variable	Total (%)	Nongay (%)	Gay/ lesbian (%)	Variable	Total (%)	Nongay (%)	Gay/ lesbian (%)
Sex (% male)[c]	50.0	42.7	74.5	Member of unmarried couple[c]	18.7	12.2	42.0
Age[a]							
18–29	8.4	7.2	12.4	Religious background[b]			
30–39	26.8	24.5	35.2	Jewish	44.6	49.8	27.3
40–49	29.1	28.4	31.5	Protestant	21.8	20.1	27.7
50–59	16.8	17.2	15.2	Catholic	19.1	18.3	22.0
60 and older	18.9	22.6	5.7	Other	7.7	5.9	13.7
				No religion	6.7	5.9	9.3
Race							
White	94.8	94.3	96.3	Religious attendance[a]			
Black	3.2	3.7	1.1	At least once			
Latino	1.6	1.3	2.6	a month	17.1	18.9	10.8
Asian	.5	.6	0	Once or twice			
				a year	38.5	40.6	31.1
Education				Never	44.4	40.4	58.1
High school							
or less	1.9	2.0	1.8	Italian	3.2	3.3	3.2
Some college	12.4	14.5	5.1				
College graduate	30.6	29.7	33.6	Live in rent-controlled/			
Postgraduate work	55.1	53.9	59.4	stabilized			
				apartment	43.3	43.1	43.9
Income							
Less than $15,000	2.6	2.9	1.7	Sexual orientation[c]			
$15,000–24,000	7.0	7.4	5.5	Exclusively			
$25,000–34,000	15.5	15.4	15.7	heterosexual	69.3	89.8	1.2
$35,000–49,000	18.8	15.9	28.9	Mostly			
$50,000–74,000	23.4	26.1	14.1	heterosexual	2.7	4.8	0
$75,000 or above	32.7	32.3	34.1	Bisexual	2.9	2.4	4.6
				Mostly			
Student[a]	4.4	2.9	9.6	homosexual	6.0	1.0	22.7
Teacher	8.5	8.0	10.2	Exclusively			
Union member	13.4	12.9	15.1	homosexual	18.0	1.9	71.6
Unemployed	3.7	3.7	3.5				
Retired	11.3	13.0	5.2	N	339	265	74
Legally married[c]	30.7	39.3	0			(78.1%)	(21.9%)

SOURCE: Columbia University/Hunter College primary election study. Data set was made available through the courtesy of Robert W. Bailey (Columbia University), Kenneth S. Sherrill (Hunter College, CUNY), and Murray S. Edelman (VRS).

NOTE: Data in this and subsequent tables are expressed as weighted percentages of all respondents who voted in the State Assembly primary.

[a] Significance level = .05.
[b] Significance level = .01.
[c] Significance level = .001.

TABLE 5.2.

Frequency distribution of attitudinal indicators, and comparison between self-identified lesbians and gay men and other voters, Democratic primary for New York State Assembly, Sixty-first District, September 1990

Variable	Total (%)	Nongay (%)	Gay/lesbian (%)
One or two most important issues in assembly race			
Riverfront development[a]	14.9	17.1	7.0
Schools[b]	15.6	18.9	3.5
Crime and violence	51.2	53.5	43.1
Homelessness	28.1	29.0	24.6
AIDS[c]	27.0	20.4	50.7
Tenants' rights[b]	24.3	28.2	10.4
Government services	11.0	12.0	7.6
Gay/lesbian rights[c]	21.6	8.1	69.7
State budget crisis[a]	11.7	13.7	4.6
Abortion	26.2	27.9	20.2
Health care	13.9	13.9	14.1
Drugs	12.8	13.4	10.9
No response checked	6.1	6.6	4.1
Have activist groups such as ACT UP helped or hurt the cause of gay rights?[c]			
Helped more	57.4	49.5	79.8
Had no effect	12.5	13.7	9.3
Hurt more	30.1	36.8	10.9
Willing to pay more taxes for more neighborhood police patrols	77.5	78.5	74.3

SOURCE: Columbia University/Hunter College primary election study.
  [a] Significance level = .05.
  [b] Significance level = .01.
  [c] Significance level = .001.

TABLE 5.3.
*Frequency distribution of indicators of voting behavior and hypothesized intervening
variables (except for endorsements), and comparison between self-identified lesbians and gay
men and other voters, Democratic primary for New York State Assembly, Sixty-first
District, September 1990*

Variable	Total (%)	Nongay (%)	Gay/lesbian (%)
Vote in assembly race[c]			
Deborah Glick	43.6	34.2	76.9
Liz Shollenberger	20.4	22.8	12.0
Kathryn Freed	19.2	23.3	4.6
Tony Hoffmann	14.2	16.3	6.5
Robert Rygor	2.6	3.3	0
Vote for mayor, 1989 Democratic primary[a]			
David Dinkins	60.7	56.1	76.5
Edward Koch	27.5	31.1	14.8
Other candidates	8.6	9.6	5.2
Did not vote	3.2	3.1	3.3
Vote for mayor, 1989 general election			
David Dinkins (D)	74.7	72.5	82.5
Rudolph Giuliani (R)	19.1	20.9	12.8
Other candidates	2.8	3.1	1.7
Did not vote	3.3	3.4	3.0
Which contest was most important in bringing you out to vote today?[a]			
Surrogate judge	23.3	26.3	13.2
State assembly	63.6	59.9	76.0
State comptroller	13.1	13.8	10.7
Vote for surrogate judge (no significant differences)			
Candidates respondent believes are gay			
(Glick and Rygor are gay; others are not)			
Deborah Glick[c]	66.0	59.7	88.5
Liz Shollenberger	2.4	1.7	4.7
Kathryn Freed	2.2	2.0	3.2
Tony Hoffmann	1.7	1.5	2.4
Robert Rygor[a]	15.2	13.1	22.8
Factors important in candidate for assembly			
Is gay or lesbian[c]	13.8	3.1	51.8
Is heterosexual	.8	1.0	0
Is a fighter	32.7	31.0	39.0
Is independent of political clubs	17.3	17.0	18.6
Is a hard worker	50.7	53.5	40.8
Knows the district[b]	50.8	55.2	35.5

TABLE 5.3. (*Continued*)

Variable	Total (%)	Nongay (%)	Gay/lesbian (%)
Works well with others	21.3	23.3	14.1
Is male	.3	.4	0
Is female[a]	7.5	5.6	14.0
No response checked[b]	9.1	11.4	1.0
Did *not* vote for an assembly candidate because s/he			
Ran a dirty campaign	13.1	12.8	14.2
Is too radical	5.4	6.0	3.2
Ran single-issue campaign	15.1	16.0	12.2
Is hard to work with	1.8	1.9	1.7
Is homosexual	1.6	2.1	0
Is heterosexual[b]	1.7	.6	5.7
Is too aggressive	2.8	3.3	1.2
Is male	0	0	0
Is female	.9	1.2	0
No response checked	68.6	67.8	71.4
Contacted by which campaigns in last few days			
Deborah Glick[a]	32.1	29.4	41.9
Liz Shollenberger	25.6	24.9	28.1
Kathryn Freed	18.4	19.2	15.5
Tony Hoffmann	17.9	16.9	21.5
Robert Rygor	7.4	6.6	10.2
None	44.7	45.3	42.8
Total number of campaigns contacted by in the last few days			
None	44.7	45.3	42.8
One	27.7	29.0	23.2
Two	16.3	15.9	17.6
Three to five	11.3	9.8	16.4

SOURCE: Columbia University/Hunter College primary election study.
[a] Significance level = .05.
[b] Significance level = .01.
[c] Significance level = .001.

TABLE 5.4.
Significant differences between lesbian and gay male respondents, Democratic primary for New York State Assembly, Sixty-first District, September 1990

Item	Gay male (%)	Lesbian (%)	Significance	Nongay (%)
Age			.05	
18–29	14.6	5.7		7.2
30–49	71.4	52.9		52.9
50 and older	14.0	41.4		39.8
Sexual orientation			.05	
Bisexual	.7	16.4		2.4
Mostly homosexual	18.8	34.4		1.0
Exclusively homosexual	79.0	49.2		1.9
Tenants' rights a top issue	4.4	28.0	.01	28.2
Important that candidate				
Knows the district	28.5	55.8	.05	55.2
Works well with others	8.5	30.4	.05	23.3
Is female	3.6	44.5	.001	5.6
Used no endorsements	16.5	42.0	.05	35.3
Neared statistical significance				
Abortion a top issue	15.2	34.6	.071	27.9
Postgraduate study	53.7	76.2	.086	53.9
Religion			.081	
Jewish	19.6	50.2		49.8
Protestant	32.5	13.2		20.1
Catholic	22.2	21.5		18.3
Other religion	17.0	3.8		5.9
No religion	8.6	11.3		5.9
(N)	(55)	(19)		(265)

SOURCE: Columbia University/Hunter College primary election study.

NOTE: Significance levels are assessed between gay men and lesbians; results among nongay respondents are given for comparative purposes only and are not included in the computation of significance levels.

TABLE 5.5.
Frequency distribution of endorsements cited by respondents as having an important effect on their vote choice, and comparison between self-identified lesbians and gay men and other voters, Democratic primary for New York State Assembly, Sixty-first District, September 1990

Organization	Endorsee	Total (%)	Nongay (%)	Gay/lesbian (%)
Publications				
General circulation dailies				
New York Times	Glick	35.6	34.6	39.0
Daily News	—	2.4	2.8	.9
New York Post	Shollenberger	2.3	2.9	0
New York Newsday	Freed	4.3	4.1	4.7
General circulation weekly				
Village Voice[a]	Glick	13.4	11.3	20.9
LGB-oriented weeklies				
New York Native	—	1.3	1.5	.5
Outweek[b]	Glick	5.8	1.4	21.2
Political clubs				
General membership Democratic clubs				
Village Independent Democrats (VID)	Hoffmann	13.2	13.0	13.9
Village Reform Democratic Club (VRDC)[a]	Shollenberger	8.6	10.2	2.6
Downtown Independent Democrats (DID)	Freed	7.8	9.1	3.3
LGB-oriented Democratic clubs				
Gay/Lesbian Independent Democrats (GLID)[b]	Glick	4.6	1.3	16.1
Stonewall Democratic Club[a]	Shollenberger	4.5	3.0	9.7
Candidate's personal club				
New Frontier Democrats	Rygor	.1	0	.4
None of the above were checked[a]		32.6	35.3	23.0

SOURCE: Columbia University/Hunter College primary election study.
[a] Significance level = .05.
[b] Significance level = .001.

TABLE 5.6.

Percentages of lesbian and gay respondents voting for Deborah Glick, after demographic, attitudinal, and campaign-related variables are controlled for, Democratic primary for New York State Assembly, Sixty-first District, September 1990

(Total N = 74)

Variable	Yes (%)	No (%)	N "Yes"
Demographic variables			
Gay male (vs. lesbian)	73.9	85.5	55
In unmarried couple	75.7	77.7	31
Christian background	80.4	71.9	36
Religious attendance			
Never	80.1		42
Once or twice a year	69.9		23
Once a month or more	80.6		8
Attitudinal variables			
Among two most important issues			
AIDS	77.3	76.4	38
Gay/lesbian rights[c]	88.0	51.2	52
Important qualities in State Assembly member			
Is gay or lesbian[c]	94.4	58.0	38
Knows the district[b]	59.7	86.3	26
Is female	100.0	73.1	10
Effect of activist groups such as ACT UP on the cause of gay/lesbian rights[a]			
Have helped more	83.9		58
Have had no effect	53.7		7
Have hurt more	50.9		8
Campaign-related variables			
Contacted by Glick campaign within last few days	83.1	72.4	31
Knows Glick is lesbian	79.8	54.6	66
Voted against a candidate because s/he			
Ran single-issue campaign[c]	29.2	83.5	9
Is heterosexual	100.0	75.5	4
Endorsements influenced by			
New York Times[a]	89.5	68.8	29
Village Voice[a]	95.8	71.8	16
Outweek	94.5	72.1	16
VID[b]	39.3	82.9	10
GLID	80.9	76.1	12
Stonewall[a]	45.3	80.3	7
Past voting behavior			
Voted for Koch, 1989	53.5	80.1	11

SOURCE: Columbia University/Hunter College primary election study.

[a] Significance level = .05.
[b] Significance level = .01.
[c] Significance level = .001.

TABLE 5.7.
*Sources of endorsements important to respondents, Democratic primary for New York State
Assembly, Sixty-first District, September 1990*

Variable	Total (%)	Nongay (%)	Gay/lesbian (%)
Sources and media[a]			
Nongay publication(s) only	29.5	30.8	24.9
Gay publication(s) only	1.2	.3	4.5
1 gay, 1 nongay publication	3.4	1.1	11.6
Nongay club(s) only	17.1	19.1	9.7
Gay club(s) only	1.9	.1	8.2
1 gay, 1 nongay club	3.2	2.3	6.3
Nongay club *and* publication	7.2	8.3	3.3
Gay club *and* publication	.6	0	2.8
Nongay club, gay publication	.7	.7	.5
Gay club, nongay publication	2.6	1.9	5.2
No endorsements cited	32.6	35.3	23.0
Endorsement sources[a]			
Nongay sources only	53.8	58.2	37.9
1 gay, 1 nongay source	9.9	6.0	23.6
Gay sources only	3.7	.4	15.5
No endorsements cited	32.6	35.3	23.0
Endorsement media			
Publication(s) only	34.1	32.2	41.0
1 publication, 1 club	11.1	10.9	11.8
Club(s) only	22.1	21.6	24.1
No endorsements cited	32.6	35.3	23.0

SOURCE: Columbia University/Hunter College primary election study.
[a] Significance level = .001.

TABLE 5.8.
Logistic regression of initial model of support for Deborah Glick, Democratic primary for New York State Assembly, Sixty-first District, September 1990

Variable	Total sample (N = 339)				Gay/lesbian subsample (N = 74)			
	B	S.E.	Wald	Significance	B	S.E.	Wald	Significance
Sexual self-identification	.8316	.48612	.9270	.0871	(redundant; not included)			
New York Times endorsement	1.8766	.3177	34.8991	.0000	2.4130	1.2763	3.5746	.0587
Village Voice endorsement	.9897	.4647	4.5371	.0332	1.6402	1.6416	.9983	.3177
Want gay/lesbian legislator	2.9608	1.0340	8.1997	.0042	3.6279	1.6989	4.5600	.0327
Gay rights a top issue	1.2470	.5155	5.8518	.0156	1.4901	.9803	2.3105	.1285
Against one-issue campaign	-1.4940	.4832	9.5615	.0020	-2.5866	1.3914	3.4560	.0630
Stonewall endorsement	-2.6946	.9676	7.7551	.0054	-2.0517	1.4507	2.0003	.1573
Voted for Koch, 1989	-.6920	.3414	4.1091	.0427	-1.2439	1.2532	.9853	.3209
Contacted by Glick campaign	.1940	.3245	.3574	.5500	1.8123	1.1082	2.6746	.1020
Know Glick is lesbian	.3091	.3073	1.0115	.3146	.4657	1.0721	.1887	.6640
AIDS a top issue	.1711	.3696	.2143	.6434	.5949	1.0311	.3329	.5639
Outweek endorsement	.1175	1.0848	.0117	.9138	-1.9751	1.8962	1.0850	.2976
GLID endorsement	-.2546	.8690	.0859	.7695	-1.3119	1.3937	.8861	.3465
Constant	-6.9902	3.1899	4.8021	.0284	-6.8011	5.8003	1.3749	.2410
% correct	79.70				88.00			

SOURCE: Columbia University/Hunter College primary election study.

TABLE 5.9.
Logistic regression of refined model of support for Deborah Glick, Democratic primary for New York State Assembly, Sixty-first District, September 1990

Variable	Total sample (N = 339)				Gay/lesbian subsample (N = 74)			
	B	S.E.	Wald	Significance	B	S.E.	Wald	Significance
Sexual self-identification	.9178	.4774	3.6957	.0546	(redundant; not included)			
New York Times endorsement	1.8526	.3144	34.7211	.0000	2.2218	1.0571	4.4174	.0356
Village Voice endorsement	1.0072	.4518	4.9695	.0258	(not included)			
Want gay/lesbian legislator	2.9026	.9768	8.8311	.0030	2.4699	1.0568	5.4618	.0194
Gay rights a top issue	1.2808	.4908	6.8090	.0091	1.1724	.8265	2.0123	.1560
Against one-issue campaign	-1.4706	.4823	9.2982	.0023	-3.0779	1.3196	5.4404	.0197
Stonewall endorsement	-2.7197	.9636	7.9659	.0048	-1.7490	1.1522	2.3042	.1290
Voted for Koch, 1989	-.7232	.3374	4.5944	.0321	(not included)			
Contacted by Glick campaign	(not included)				1.2962	.8788	2.1752	.1403
Constant	-6.3064	2.3404	7.2605	.0070	-3.9897	3.7305	1.1438	.2849
% correct	79.46				90.54			

SOURCE: Columbia University/Hunter College primary election study.

 S I X

Into the Mainstream: The Lavender Vote Helps Elect a President

There is no serious question but that the 1992 presidential election was the most important up to that time for the gay, lesbian, and bisexual communities in the United States. As discussed earlier in this work, for the first time the major presidential contenders gave serious attention, positive or nega-tive, to the LGB rights movement and its political goals. As widely reported on 1992 election night and in the days thereafter, 72 percent of self-identified lesbian, bisexual, and gay voters surveyed gave their support to Bill Clinton. This figure led to the exuberant, if erroneous, claim by David Mixner and others that one Clinton voter in six was gay or lesbian, which although insupportable was taken to heart by the new president's lavender constituency and some of its right-wing detractors.

Presidential electorates and off-year electorates have been found to differ in that less motivated voters and those of lower socioeconomic status tend to go to the polls (if at all) in presidential years, but not in other elections (Wolfinger and Rosenstone 1980). One question, therefore, is whether this was true of self-identified gay, lesbian, and bisexual voters as well.

A second set of questions arises from the inclusion of bisexual self-identifiers in the sample for the first time. Because the self-identifier question condensed all three self-identification categories (gay, lesbian, and bisexual) into one, there is no way, regrettably, to tell how the views of the bisexual self-identifiers might differ from those of the gay and lesbian self-identifiers except by inference. The best we can do is see whether, with the bisexuals included, the "lavender" self-identifiers in 1992 voted pretty much the same as did the gay and lesbian self-identifiers in 1990.

175

Aside from the inclusion of bisexuals, the format of the 1992 VRS national exit poll creates some difficulty for the researcher. In 1990, we noted, there were *two* versions of the national exit poll conducted, with a small number of identical, overlapping questions. In 1992, there were *three* such variations, named Version W, Version Y, and Version P, each of which comprised mostly questions not asked in the other versions.[2]

Fortunately, the self-identifier question was included in all three versions. However, some essential questions that would make the survey useful after election night were not included. For instance, there is no way a retrospective model can be tested using the 1992 data. The usual question about approval of the president's performance in office is not included in the survey. Version Y does include a question asking the respondent to rate the president's performance in handling the economy, so it would still be possible to test something resembling a retrospective model—except that the respondent's evaluation of the condition of the nation's economy (as opposed to Bush's handling of it) is in Version W.

Another difficulty is the exclusion or revision of certain questions important in our study of 1990. No feminist self-identification item is included in the 1992 survey, which seems odd given the fact that Hillary Rodham Clinton's independent legal career, political influence, and alleged "radical feminism" became an issue in the campaign. In addition, the two religion questions have been folded into a single question on "religious affiliation," which can refer either to religious background or upbringing or to current religious practice. The very interesting transformation over time in religious beliefs and practices related to sexual identity, therefore, cannot be assessed using the 1992 data. Finally, the interesting phenomenon of third candidate voting in House races, mainly by lesbian feminists, cannot be tracked not only because of the absence of the feminist self-identification question, but also because votes for independent or third party candidates for the House were not included in the data base in 1992.

The final major problem with the 1992 data set is that in only two states, California and New York, did state-level general election exit polls include the self-identifier question, down from twenty-one in 1990. Of these two states, New York's total LGB sample size was below the thirty respondents I previously set as the minimum number of respondents from whom any meaningful analysis could be drawn. Therefore, while usable results from California are available, no state-to-state comparisons are possible, and I have chosen not to spend time on the California state-level data from 1992 for that reason. We are left only with the aggregated national data.

With these changes in mind, let us look at these national results in light of the 1990 findings reported in chapter 3.

Hypothesis 1: Rate of Identification

Lesbians and gay men will self-identify in political surveys at rates equivalent to those found in previous random-sample research, about 1.0 to 1.5 percent of the population. When bisexuals are included, the share of self-identifiers will increase by an additional 2 to 3 percent.

The overall rate of identification with bisexuals included in the self-identifier question was somewhat lower than previous surveys would have led one to estimate: 2.5 percent of all respondents self-identified, and this share fell to 2.2 percent once the weighting factors were applied. Previous random samples would have led one to expect a self-identification rate of 3 to 4 percent. Even so, the LGB sample was about as large as the Hispanic/Latino sample (2.3 percent) and twice as large as the Asian sample (1.0 percent).

Edelman (1993) believes this 2.2 percent figure is an underestimate. As he notes, between 10 and 20 percent of respondents do not answer any of the questions in the "grab bag" section. Controlling for this drop-off at the end of the survey, Edelman estimates that 3 percent of all voters were gay, lesbian, or bisexual self-identifiers. He reports independent confirmation of this finding in a *Los Angeles Times* exit poll from the same election, in which a sexual self-identifier question was included in a different format; each respondent was asked to check either a box marked "Gay or lesbian" or a box marked "Not gay or lesbian." Three percent of those responding checked the "Gay or lesbian" box in the *Times* survey (Edelman 1993).

I have chosen to take the conservative course and report the lower figure, owing to the difference in the question wording and the fact that the precise number of respondents who failed to answer the "grab bag" question because of drop-off remains uncertain. I believe it is highly likely, however, that Dr. Edelman is correct.

Hypothesis 2: Demographic Characteristics

LGBs who do self-identify will be possessed of the equivalent of "group consciousness." Therefore, the demographic correlates of group conscious-ness found among women and African Americans—youth, high educa-tion levels, and strong partisanship—should be disproportionately great among self-identified LGBs. Also, given the results of prior sex surveys, men may significantly outnumber women among self-identifiers.

The Essential Differences and Similarities

Table 6.1 shows the demographic breakdown of the 1992 sample by sexual self-identification. The most notable findings follow.

Age. Once again, self-identification was largely a function of age in 1992, although the clustering of identification rates differed somewhat from those found in 1990, as seen in table 6.2.

As expected, self-identification peaked in the twenty-five to twenty-nine age group; both those younger (eighteen to twenty-four), who presumably often are unsure of their sexual identity, and those slightly older (thirty to thirty-nine) self-identify at a somewhat lower rate. These three age groups taken together— all voters born between about 1953 and 1974—have a mean self-identification rate of 3 percent (that is, 3 percent of all respondents aged eighteen to thirty-nine identified themselves as gay, lesbian, or bisexual). In contrast, 1.7 percent of those aged forty to sixty-four (born roughly between 1928 and 1952) self-identified. Within the oldest age group, those sixty-five or older (born in 1927 or before), only 0.8 percent of 1 percent self-identified.

When a comparison is made with the 1990 figures, a pattern emerges that indicates that the inclusion of bisexuals is particularly important. In 1990 the eighteen-to-twenty-nine age group was a distinctive cluster, with 2.5 percent self-identifying as gay or lesbian, whereas only 1.4 percent of the thirtysomethings so identified themselves. The thirty-to-thirty-nine group in 1990 was part of a distinctive cluster—those aged between thirty and forty-nine—which had a total self-identification rate of 1.5 percent. With the addition of the "bisexual" element to the self-identification question, however, those in the thirty-to-thirty-nine group have a rate of identification much closer to those of the younger age groups.

The same holds true for older voters. The third distinctive cluster of self-identification rates in 1990 comprised those fifty or older: a mere 0.3 percent of these voters identified themselves as gay or lesbian. But in 1992, 1.8 percent of voters aged fifty to fifty-nine, and 1.7 percent of those aged sixty to sixty-four identified as gay, lesbian, *or bisexual,* in close accord with the self-identification rates for the two "fortysomething" age groups. Only the oldest group, those sixty-five and above, self-identified at a rate of less than 1 percent, and even here the rate was substantially higher than in 1990.

There appear, therefore, to be distinct "comfort levels" with self-identification that relate directly to age. As a general rule, the younger one is, the less one is inclined to hide one's sexual orientation. But there appear to be three distinct generational clusters of willingness to self-identify as gay or lesbian. With the addition of bisexuality as a self-identification option, the upper age range of each cluster increases.

Education. The 1990 exit polls found that self-identifiers as a group were considerably better educated than the rest of the voting population. Returning to table 6.1, the 1992 exit polls still find significant educational differences between the LGB and non-LGB samples, but these differences are greatly reduced. The number of self-identifiers with a high school education or less is far greater than the minimal figure of 1990. There still are more LGB voters who went on to college, and among those who graduate college there are a larger number of LGB voters who go on to postgraduate study (nearly one LGB voter in four), but the differences in education are far less pronounced than among the lesbian and gay self-identifiers in the 1990 off-year election.

Sex. Another notable difference between the 1990 and 1992 samples is the narrowing of the "gender gap" in self-identification. A majority of LGB identifiers were male in 1992, as in 1990, but the difference between the sexes was nine and a half points in 1992, versus about nineteen points in 1990. (Among non-LGB voters in 1992, there was a six and a half point difference, with women outnumbering men.)

Once again, self-identification tends to be concentrated in the younger age groups, although the addition of bisexual self-identification appears to have increased particularly the rate of self-identification among older age groups, and the three distinct clusters of self-identification rates have aged accordingly. The distinctively high education level expected of self-identifiers in Hypothesis 2 was found again in 1992, but the sharp distinctions of 1990 were dulled. Finally, the sharply distinct finding of 1990 that men self-identified at a higher rate than did women also was less sharp in 1992. With respect to Hypothesis 2, then, one may conclude that it was confirmed in 1992, but less conclusively than in 1990.

Other Demographic Findings

Several additional demographic findings of note deserve comment here:

Region. The 1992 LGB sample looked far more like the rest of America with respect to region of residence. Although there remained a significant preference for the West, as well as for the East (not noted in 1990), over the Midwest and the South, there was nothing remotely resembling the 1990 finding that three in seven lesbians and gays lived in the Western states. The LGB population in 1992 is found spread all over the country.

Size/type of locality. In like manner, in part because of the larger number of women, Midwesterners, and Southerners in the 1992 LGB sample, the proportion living in central cities was somewhat reduced: only about two-fifths of the LGB respondents reported living in a city of fifty thousand or more, versus more than half in 1992. However, this may partly reflect the simple fact that the sample as a whole was somewhat less urban, and more suburban and rural, than in 1990. Compared with the rest of the population, LGB voters, especially men, remained far more likely to be urban dwellers.

Income. It has been widely stated, both by LGB advocates and their opponents, that because of a hypothesized tendency among LGBs toward double-income householders in professional and managerial occupations without children to look after, LGB people have much more disposable income than do non-LGBs. The 1990 data, however, produced no evidence to support this theory: no statistical or apparent difference was found between lesbian/gay and nongay incomes. In 1992, indeed, the exact *reverse* of the anecdotal hypothesis was found: LGB self-identifiers had significantly *lower* incomes than did the rest of the voters in the sample (first reported in Edelman 1993).

Because of the disproportionate youth of the LGB sample, a control test was run by age category. Although part of the difference is attributable to the large number of young people, there is no significant difference between the incomes of "baby boomers" based on their sexual self-identification—and older LGBs have generally lower incomes than non-LGBs in the same age bracket. Also, there is no significant difference in incomes between LGB men and women that would account for these differences.

Occupation. Homemakers and retirees continued to be underrepresented among LGB voters, although not to the same extent as in 1990. Interestingly, in the 1992 sample, disproportionately large shares of LGBs are either full-time students or unemployed people seeking work, which was not the case in 1990.

A most curious statistic for which I cannot account is that, in 1992 (unlike 1990), a disproportion of the self-identifiers (22 percent) said they were schoolteachers. This group appears to account for the disproportion of LGBs among union members in 1992, which was not found in 1990. Given that there is no evidence of, and no theoretical reason to suspect, a huge influx of open lesbians, gay men, and bisexuals into the teaching profession in the last two years of the Bush administration, I treat this as an anomaly of the sample unless and until it is confirmed in later studies.[3]

Religion. Because, as noted, the "religion then" and "religion now" variables from 1990 have been folded into one, "religious affiliation," no direct replication of the 1990 results is possible. One notes with great interest, however, that twice as many LGBs as non-LGBs in 1992 identified as non-Christian, and that one-third fewer LGBs than non-LGBs identified as Protestant or "other Christian" (not Protestant or Catholic). The fact that the proportion of Catholic identifiers was virtually identical among the two groups cannot readily be explained in light of the 1990 data without further investigation, but one can speculate that, like Judaism, Catholicism is considered by many Catholics to be a quasi-ethnic element of their identity, which remains with them even if they do not practice the religion or even reject it altogether.

As with many of the demographic indicators, the trends of 1990 with regard to religious participation go in the same direction, but with less force, in 1992. Significantly fewer LGBs attended religious services regularly than did the rest of the voters in the sample, but the drop-off in attendance based on sexual self-identification is only about 19 percent in 1992 (32.4 percent for LGBs, 40.1 percent for non-LGBs), as opposed to a 43 percent drop-off in 1990 (24.4 percent for lesbians and gays, 43.4 percent for nongays). Given that the 1990 indicator read "once a month," whereas the 1992 indicator read "once a week," it appears that the 1992 sample drew in far more religiously inclined people than did the 1990 sample.

Once again, curiously, there was no difference between LGBs and the rest of the voting population in identification as a "born-again or fundamentalist Christian": about one-fifth of each group called itself born-again or fundamentalist.

Marriage and family. Here the greatest differences with 1990 were found. Three in ten LGBs in 1992 reported that they were presently legally married. It seems most likely that the inclusion of bisexuality in the self-identification question is principally responsible for this tremendous increase, a tripling of the 1990 figure, which included gay men and lesbians alone.

Further, contrary to the belief that people with same-sex orientations are largely childless, one-quarter of the LGB respondents (as against one-third of the non-LGB respondents) reported having children under eighteen *living at home.* Also, unlike in 1990, when there was a huge gender gap in childrearing between lesbians and gay men (lesbians were three times as likely as gay men to have children at home), in 1992 there was no significant difference between LGB men and women in this regard, although in raw figures lesbian and bisexual women continued to outnumber gay and bisexual men as custodial parents of minor children.

First-time voting. At the end of the demographic statistics we find a clear, significant difference between LGB and non-LGB voters that is greater than it was in 1990. In the midterm elections there was no difference between the groups in the rate of first-time voting. In 1992, however, two of every nine LGB voters reported they were casting their ballots for the very first time, as against one in ten non-LGB voters. This was not confined to the younger age groups, either: one of every six LGB voters aged thirty or more was voting for the first time—in addition to three in eight of those aged eighteen to twenty-nine! Only minimal numbers of non-LGB baby boomers and pre-boom voters had never stepped into the booth before. One initial impression, certainly, is that the salience of gay rights issues in the 1992 campaign brought voters "out of the closets and into the polls."

The self-identified lesbian, gay, and bisexual electorate in 1992 looks more like the rest of America than did the self-identified lesbians and gay men who voted in the midterm elections in 1990. The reasons for this cannot be known with certainty, but one important reason that can be hypothesized readily is the inclusion of bisexuals in the sexual self-identification question; this appears to have moderated the demographic disparities found when lesbians and gay men alone were permitted to self-identify. Such factors as the tripling in the percentage of married self-identifiers, the doubling in the percentage who have children at home, the increase in self-identification among older, less affluent, more religious people, especially in the Midwest and South, and the narrowing of the "gender gap" in self-identification all indicate the likelihood that the inclusion of "bisexual" as an option gave more "mainstream" persons with same-sex attractions sufficient comfort to identify themselves.

Be this as it may, the fact remains that LGB voters in 1992 were distinctively younger, better educated, more urban and coastal, and less religious than their non-LGB counterparts in the electorate. Although the distinctiveness is not as great as in 1990, when bisexuals were not included in the self-identification item, the direction of the distinctiveness remains consistent. The only counterintuitive finding was that LGB voters appear to have lower household incomes as a group than do non-LGBs.

The other important finding was that between a fifth and a quarter of all LGB voters in 1992 said they were voting for the first time—including one-sixth of those aged thirty and older. This, again, was more than double the proportion of the rest of the population voting for the first time; and four times as many LGBs as non-LGBs aged thirty and older said they were first-time voters. Bill Clinton's overt campaigning for LGB votes, the Republicans' numerous forays into antigay rhetoric, and the very public mixed messages of Ross Perot taken together appeared to have the predicted effect on voter turnout among LGBs.

Hypothesis 3: Political Attitudes

The general political orientation of LGB voters will be liberal or leftist and Democratic, in keeping with the pattern found among African Americans, feminists, and non-Cuban Latinos, and will be highly distinctive from that of non-LGB identifiers.

[handwritten margin note: what we expect from LGB]

Table 6.3 shows a breakdown in political attitudes of LGB and non-LGB respondents. Given the moderation in the demographic distinctiveness of LGBs found in the 1992 numbers, it may be expected that the distinctively liberal attitudes of the 1990 gay and lesbian sample may also have moderated somewhat. This was confirmed if we stress the word *somewhat*, for self-identified LGBs remain far more liberal than the rest of the electorate.

Ideology and Partisanship

The sample as a whole in 1992 is about four points less conservative than it was in 1990, with liberals and moderates benefiting evenly. The LGB sample remains far more liberal than non-LGBs, but a shade less so than in 1990; there is a seven-point increase in self-identifiers who call themselves moderates and a corresponding drop of six points in those calling themselves liberals. In both years, self-identified conservatives are in the single digits among LGBs. Nonetheless, roughly half of all LGBs in 1992 called themselves liberals, as against only one-fifth of the rest of the sample.

Interestingly, however, there were only minimal changes from the rates of partisan identification found in 1990, within the sample as a whole and within the subsamples. Indeed, there was a slight increase in the share of 1992 LGB respondents identifying as Democrats over the 1990 lesbian/gay respondents.

Issue Stands and Priorities

Approval ratings. There were no questions on overall approval of the president or of Congress in the 1992 survey. However, the one "institutional trust" question in the 1992 battery is of interest: a (small) majority of respondents, including nearly two-thirds of LGB respondents, said the country would be better off "if all new people were elected to office."

The important issues. Large pluralities of both groups checked "economy/jobs" as one of the two most important issues in determining their vote choice for the White House. Unlike the non-LGB voters, however, whose secondary issue concerns lagged rather far behind the economy, health care was nearly as important to the LGB respondents: 39 percent cited this issue, versus 19 percent of non-LGBs. Significantly lower were the federal budget deficit (Ross Perot's issue) and the GOP issues of taxes, foreign policy, and "family values." Also much lower was the environment. The reader will recall that ecological questions were rated as the top issue in 1990 by one-quarter of gay men and lesbians, and as the first-place item (with 45 percent) in the list of one or two most important issues that year. In 1992, the environment was named as one of the two top issues by only 8 percent of LGB respondents. This is a remarkable vanishing of what in 1990 was a highly distinctive issue concern of this group of voters.

Social issues. This was the area of the greatest LGB distinctiveness in 1990, and remains an area of considerable distinctiveness today. Especially noteworthy are the results with respect to government's role in encouraging, discouraging, or remaining neutral with respect to certain kinds of values.

Abortion. In the 1990 polls, in the first congressional elections after the 1989 *Webster* decision, about two American voters in five believed abortion should always be legal, and large majorities of two-thirds to three-quarters (depending on the specific question's wording) of gay men and lesbians agreed. By 1992, a large number of Americans appeared to have shifted to a position supporting limited restrictions on abortion, but keeping the procedure "mostly legal." Thus, about one-third of U.S. voters in 1992 still essentially supported abortion on demand, whereas another one-third believed abortion should be "mostly legal," and the remaining third favored either serious restrictions or a complete ban on the procedure. In apparent conformity with this trend and the apparent moderation of previous distinctiveness among LGBs, the distinctive support for the absolute pro-choice position among LGBs remained significant, but somewhat diminished, at 56 percent. An additional 30 percent of LGBs would make the procedure generally available with some restrictions. Only 14 percent sided substantially with the right-to-life movement.

Traditional values and social problems. Some of the clearest lines on issues were drawn in three questions relating to the government's role in promoting or encouraging traditional social structures and morality (sometimes iterated as "family values"). These questions, the closest of any in the survey to gauging attitudes toward the gay rights movement, produced split results among the non-LGB voters surveyed but clear results from the LGBs.

Two related questions were asked in Version P of the survey. One asked the respondent to choose, between two statements, the one closer to her own views; the choices were (1) the government should promote traditional values or (2) the government should not favor one set of values over another. The total sample split down the middle, with a small majority choosing the second option. In the other question, respondents were asked to pin the greater blame for social problems on (1) the breakdown of the traditional family or (2) government neglect of social needs. Again, the result was split, with a very small majority choosing the first option. However, in one question in Version Y the result was far more decisive. Again asked to choose between two options—(1) it is more important for the government to encourage traditional family values, or (2) it is more important for the government to encourage tolerance of nontraditional families—three-fourths of the respondents chose the first option.

Thus, among the voting population in 1992, there appeared to be three distinct views. Roughly half felt that the family was in trouble, that its break-down was chiefly responsible for our social ills, and that government should actively promote traditional values and family structures. Another quarter believed that government neglect was chiefly responsible for social decay and that government should not be in the business of favoring one set of values over another—but, if it were to do so, traditional families were to be preferred. The third group, also accounting for a quarter of the voters, appeared to believe that government actively should encourage tolerance of those whose ways of life differ, in reality or perception, from those of the majority and that government action to reduce hunger, homelessness, and hopelessness, not a new campaign for traditional values, was the solution to social decay.

In this dispute, consistent 69 to 70 percent majorities of LGB voters found themselves agreeing with the third group, the most liberal or nontraditional group.

The economy. Unlike in 1990, interestingly, in 1992 the LGB respondents held significantly more negative evaluations of the country's economic condition than did the rest of the respondents, even given that the economic evaluations of the voters were negative indeed. Whereas a plurality of all voters said their personal financial conditions were about the same as they were four years before, nearly half of the LGB respondents said they personally were worse off. In 1990 there was no significant difference in personal economic evaluations between self-identified gay men and lesbians and the rest of the population, and the raw numbers showed the self-identifiers somewhat better off than the rest of the respondents.

As for the national economy, 11 percent of LGBs, as against 19 percent of non-LGBs, thought its condition was "excellent" or "good"; the rest labeled the economy "not so good" or "poor." This differs little from the 1990 numbers, in which 14 percent of lesbians and gay men, and 20 percent of the nongay respondents held a similarly bleak assessment of the economy.

The voters' evaluation of the president's handling of the economy was sharply negative, and bad marks were even more likely to be given by "lavender" voters. Only a third of non-LGB voters and one-sixth of LGB voters approved of Bush's performance in this area. Two-thirds of LGB respondents said they "disapproved strongly."

The reasons for this increased negativism among LGB voters are not readily apparent. There is no evidence to suggest that Americans with same-sex affections were hurt more in the Bush-era recession than were heterosexuals, so one must look elsewhere for explanations. The changes in the composition of the sample certainly may be a factor, especially given that the 1992 LGB sample as a whole was somewhat poorer and less educated, and more composed of families with children, than the lesbian/gay sample of 1990. Another factor, however, may well have been spillover from the Republicans' sometimes harsh antigay rhetoric, leading many LGB voters to view the Republican administration in a negative light on noncultural issues.[4]

Trees versus jobs. One final economic variable ought to be noted. In 1990 three-quarters of the gay/lesbian self-identifiers held that preserving the environment should be given priority over economic growth when the two came into conflict. After two difficult economic years, although a majority of LGBs still supported that position, the fifty-nine to forty-one margin by which they did so in 1992 was substantially lower than the 1990 lesbian/gay figure.

Taxes and services: The role and priorities of government. The LGB and non-LGB publics seriously disagreed about the basic question of what the government ought to do in general. Whereas three-fifths of non-LGB voters said they preferred a smaller government that provided them with fewer services in return for lower taxes, a five-to-four majority of LGB voters disagreed, opting for higher taxes in exchange for more government services.

This was reflected in a second question about what the top priority for the next president should be. Among the three options of cutting taxes, cutting the federal deficit, and expanding domestic programs, 59 percent of non-LGBs opted for cutting the deficit, but a 44 percent plurality of LGBs wanted increased domestic programs first; only 36 percent of LGBs put cutting the deficit first. (Cutting taxes ran a poor third among both groups.) This emphasis carried over into specific policy questions. Large majorities of both groups said they would be willing to pay more taxes to improve health care programs, and both split down the middle on doing so for infrastructure improvements. The LGB voters, however, were significantly more inclined than non-LGB voters to support an increase in their taxes to improve job training and placement. Most notably, whereas about half of non-LGBs said they would be willing to have higher taxes go to reduce the federal deficit, only three in ten LGBs supported this position.

Therefore, whereas the priorities of the voters taken together were rather a muddle, the priorities of the lesbian, gay, and bisexual voters taken together were somewhat clearer. The largest number of people in this group, if not a majority, favored bigger government doing more about economic and social problems, and were willing to pay more in taxes to achieve these goals. (This is consistent with the finding that a huge majority of LGBs blamed government neglect rather than the breakdown of the family for social problems.) They also were much less concerned about the deficit and wanted any tax increases used to provide government services rather than reduce debt service.

Any small degree of moderation from 1990 notwithstanding, the LGB sample was again distinctively liberal in 1992, and not merely with respect to social issues; in the Clinton election, the LGB identifiers were considerably more inclined to support a big, economically active government than was the rest of the sample.

Voting Behavior

Table 6.4 displays the aggregate vote choices of the sample and the reasons given for their decisions. Most noted by the popular press was the thirty-point gap between the preferences of the "lavender vote" and the rest of the sample in the presidential contest. Equally striking, however, given the results in 1990, is the more consistent support for the Democrats across the board in contests for senators, governors,[5] and representatives;[6] in each set of contests, the aggregate non-LGB vote for Democratic nominees nationwide was between 51.5 and 53.6 percent, whereas the aggregate LGB vote was between twenty-one and twenty-five points higher for the Democrats, ranging between 74.2 and 78.3 percent.

The role of Ross Perot is worthy of note. Virtually identical shares of LGB voters (42 percent) and non-LGB voters (39 percent) indicated that during the campaign they once thought they might vote for Perot, and similar margins of each—38 percent of LGBs, 36 percent of non-LGBs—said they would have voted for Perot if he had had a chance to win, despite his very public wavering on LGB rights issues (and so much else) during the campaign. The vote totals, therefore, are not uniformly good news for the Democrats, given that most of this underlying Perot support would have been at the expense of Bill Clinton. Even if Perot had not been in the race, only about a third of the LGBs who actually did give him their votes would have gone to Clinton; nearly all the rest would either have voted for a third party candidate or, more commonly, would not have voted at all.

Nonetheless, the rejection of George Bush even by his former LGB supporters is manifest. Only half of LGB Republicans voted for their party's president; of those who split away, roughly half went to Clinton, half to Perot. Even more notable, nearly two-thirds of those LGBs who reported voting for Bush in 1988 split from him in 1992; a plurality of 1988 Bush voters supported Clinton. Indeed, seven in ten LGBs who reported having voted for Ronald Reagan in 1984 rejected Bush in 1992; a majority voted for Clinton. Only two-thirds of LGBs who voted for GOP House candidates voted for Bush; of LGBs who chose Democrats in the House races, 90 percent voted for Clinton. Bush lost among LGB conservatives, right-to-lifers, and "born-again" or fundamentalist Christians as well.

It is not surprising that LGB voters differed from non-LGB voters in virtually every category on the question of the most important candidate qualities; those Clinton stressed were more frequently cited and those his opponents used to attack him were less frequently cited. Of greater interest were two other sets of questions about factors important in each respondent's vote choice. Close to half of the LGB respondents cited Supreme Court appointments as an important factor, and twice as many LGBs as non-LGBs cited the candidates' wives and the party conventions as important factors. Significantly fewer LGBs than non-LGBs cited a pair of issues related to the Democratic nominee's past: the candidates' marital fidelity, and the draft status and Vietnam protests of Clinton personally.

Interestingly, there was no significant difference between the LGB and non-LGB respondents about when they made their respective final decisions on how they would vote. Although only half as many LGBs as non-LGBs were undecided going into the final week of the campaign (13 versus 25 percent), more than a third of LGB voters did not make up their minds until after the presidential debates in October. A large number of these apparently were prospective Perot voters who, while having no intention of voting for Bush, were not yet comfortable with Bill Clinton.

Hypothesis 4 (Part): Gender

Lesbians and bisexual women, whether feminists or not, will be more opposed to the use of force in politics, and therefore will be more likely to vote for Democrats than are gay and bisexual men. (The portion of the hypothesis relating to feminism cannot be tested here.)

Interestingly, unlike in 1990, no especial pattern of differences based on sex was discernible in 1992. Although LGB women and men did show statistically significant differences on a number of items, we learn very little from them. There was no difference in vote choice at any level between the sexes. Nor were there any differences on any indicator related to foreign policy, nor on the preeminent controversial "women's issue," abortion.

As in 1990, women took a somewhat more pessimistic view of the national economy (45 percent rated its condition "poor," versus 31 percent of men). Women also were more inclined than men to favor increased domestic spending as the top priority for the new president; self-identified gay and bisexual men, like the non-LGB majority, held cutting the deficit to be most important (43 percent, as against 32 percent for increasing domestic spending and 26 percent seeking lower taxes), whereas two-thirds of self-identified lesbians and bisexual women wanted domestic programs beefed up and only one in six said cutting the deficit was more important. However, the men were significantly more likely (55 to 37 percent) to rate "economy/jobs" as one of the two most important issues in the campaign—and to view Clinton as most likely to raise their taxes. Thus, one cannot clearly interpret any economic effect on the LGB vote based on sex.

Any analysis of gender effects in 1992 is seriously hindered by the absence of any direct indicator of feminism. As reported earlier, the "feminism gap" appears to be much more significant than any "gender gap" among the LGB population, especially given the extraordinary rate of identification with feminism among self-identified lesbians. Taking differences in sex in and of themselves, the 1992 data give us no basis on which to reconfirm Hypothesis 4.

Hypothesis 5: Voting Blocs within the Community

Given the divergent concepts of group identity among LGBs, and their differing notions of what the goals of the LGB movement should be and the best means for achieving them, LGB voters will not be monolithic; although the large majority will vote for Democrats, significant minorities will support Republicans or leftist third candidates.

Table 6.5 displays the statistically significant differences within the LGB sample as broken down by party affiliation. As discussed above, the most notable difference is the near-unanimous support for Bill Clinton among LGB Democrats, whereas only half of the rather small band of LGB Republicans voted for George Bush.[7] Although the GOP figure shows a remarkably high degree of intrapartisan desertion, it fits into the previously noted tendency of LGB Republicans to splinter their tickets, which carried over into other contests: two in five "lavender" GOP identifiers voted for Democrats for the U.S. Senate and one-quarter did the same in House races. In contrast, the LGB Democrats in all contests held together remarkably well, with at least 91 percent voting for their copartisans.

Also of interest is the more consistent support for Democratic nominees among LGB independents. In the three-way presidential contest, Clinton won the votes of five in eight LGB independent and third party identifiers; Ross Perot pulled one-fourth, and George Bush about one in nine for a poor third place. In the congressional contests, fully three-quarters of this group voted for Democratic nominees,[8] and in the small number of gubernatorial contests, seven in ten voted Democratic. Although they behaved like true independents in most cases, splitting their tickets, the LGB independent vote was more strongly tilted in favor of the Democrats in 1992 than it had been in 1990.

A few of the demographic differences reported here might be expected: Republicans are wealthier, more rural, more white, and more Christian than are Democrats and independents. The contrast in religious affiliation by party affiliation, however, is rather stark. Only 10 percent of LGB Republicans identified themselves as non-Christians, compared with 35 percent of LGB Democrats and 45 percent of LGB independents. Three LGB Republicans in eight identify as "born again," as against one in five Democrats and one in nine independents.

Also of interest are the LGB employment statistics. The Democrats include disproportions of students and retirees, the Republicans a disproportion of homemakers, and independents disproportions of part-time workers and the unemployed. Oddly, the disproportion of schoolteachers in the LGB sample noted previously appears to be heavily concentrated among self-identified Democrats.

Finally, Republicans with same-sex attractions were half again as likely to have been legally married at some point in their lives, and more than half again as likely to be married presently, as were LGB independents and Democrats. There was no significant difference, however, among the partisan categories in having children living at home.

The 1992 figures on political attitudes by party are most notable for their confirmation of the 1990 finding that, unlike most of their non-LGB copartisans, LGB Republicans were decided moderates; only one in seven called herself a conservative, not many more than the single-digit totals found among the Democrats and independents. GOP issue concerns and attitudes, as may be expected, were significantly more conservative than those of other LGBs, especially with respect to taxes and the economy. Yet there was no mistaking them for the "average" non-LGB Republican.

As for independents, they were significantly more likely to view abortion as an important issue, and to support the absolute pro-choice position, than were the major party identifiers, and along with the Republicans they were much more likely to view the federal deficit as an important problem than were the Democrats. (Not surprisingly, LGB independents who cited the deficit constituted the subgroup most likely to vote for Ross Perot.) As may be expected, independents were also three times as likely as major party supporters to say that divided government—having a president and congressional majorities of different parties—was better than single-party government, Perot's complaints about partisan "gridlock" notwithstanding.

One question, therefore, remains to be answered. After a campaign in which Republicans overtly opposed LGB rights and spoke disparagingly of LGB people, why did roughly three hundred thousand self-identified lesbian, gay, and bisexual Americans vote for George Bush in 1992? The pro-Bush group was demographically and ideologically very much like the Republicans who voted against Bush: it did not comprise right-wing extremists, and it contained a share of ticket-splitters as well as straight-ticket Republicans.

Only four major characteristics set this group apart. First, nearly half of LGB Bush voters were small-town or rural residents, and fewer than a quarter lived in central cities; this is directly contrary to the general trend. Second, half of the Bush voters said the national economy was doing well, and a large majority approved of Bush's handling of the economy; they thus gave a retrospective reward to the president, just as the models say they should have.

Third, they were uniformly negative about Bill Clinton personally, all saying they would be either "concerned" or "scared" if Clinton were elected. Fourth, about half of Bush's voters said, as did three in seven Perot voters, that they were voting more *against* their candidate's opponents than *for* their candidate. In contrast, a three-to-one majority of Clinton's supporters said they were voting for Clinton, not against his opponents.

The essential findings of 1990 with respect to Hypothesis 5 were confirmed. As a rule, most LGB Democrats were strongly liberal on all issues, not just social issues, and partisan in their voting behavior. LGB Republicans, on the other hand, were centrists whose attitudes and voting behavior were more like those of conservative-leaning moderate independents than like the main branch of their own party. The mean LGB independent, meanwhile, was a shade less liberal than her LGB Democratic neighbors and far more inclined to split her ticket, but even when the ticket was split most of her votes went to the Democrats.

In addition, I replicated the age cohort analysis of 1990, seeking to find whether the differences in attitudes and voting behavior based on generational lines in that year would be found again in the Clinton election. These are not the "coming out" cohorts spoken of at the beginning of the chapter; they are instead the more clearly drawn generational lines discussed widely in the social science literature and the popular press among "baby boomers" (those aged roughly thirty to forty-four at the time of this study), the "post-boom" or "baby bust" generation (those under thirty), and the "pre-boomers," those born during or before World War II (those roughly forty-five and older).

Table 6.6 shows the results. Unlike the 1990 results, there are few interesting attitudinal or behavioral differences this time around. However, some demographic divergences are worth discussing.

Almost two in five LGBs aged forty-five and up in 1992 had not had more than a high school education—but of those who did go on to college, nearly half had done some postgraduate work. In contrast, only a handful of LGBs of the baby boom generation reported having had no college classes at all. Two-thirds of LGBs aged eighteen to twenty-nine had some college, but a third did not.

Fully a third of LGBs forty-five and older were retired, not far off the rest of the sample. An additional one in eight in that age group were homemakers. Among those seeking work, unemployment was low. This last was not the case in the under-forty-five category, in which one in eight baby boomers, and one in six baby busters, were unemployed and seeking work. In addition, 10 percent of "boomers" and 14 percent of "busters" were employed only part-time. Given that full-time students fell into a separate category (nearly a quarter of the eighteen to twenty-nine group were students), this is a significant degree of unemployment and underemployment in the younger age brackets.

As age decreases among LGBs, so does Christianity, religiosity, and the inclination for whatever reason to marry a person of the opposite sex. An absolute majority (52 percent) of the under-thirty LGBs were non-Christians; 22 percent held no religious affiliation at all. This is a steep drop from the 79 percent of LGBs forty-five and older and the 70 percent of LGB baby boomers who give a Christian affiliation. Interestingly, it is Protestant affiliation that suffers most dramatically, falling from 45 percent among the oldest cohort to 14 percent among the youngest; in contrast, Catholic self-identification remains even across the age groups. As may be expected given these numbers, weekly attendance at religious services drops off precipitously as well, from 47 percent among the oldest cohort to 28 percent among the boomers and 21 percent among the busters.

As for marriage, three in seven self-identified LGBs aged forty-five and older were in a legal heterosexual marriage in November 1992, along with 30 percent of baby boomers and 18 percent of the youngest cohort. Nearly two-thirds of the older self-identifiers had been married at some point in their lives, as had three in seven baby boomers but less than a quarter of the baby busters (mostly those presently married). It is not known, of course, how many spouses in such relationships knew that their partners were gay, lesbian, or bisexual.

One last demographic item of interest is that 27 percent of LGBs aged forty-five and up say they do not have a friend or relative who is gay, lesbian, or bisexual, as against minuscule shares of the other two age groups that report the same.

The one observed pattern of difference in responses to the attitudinal questions related to the Vietnam War and to Bill Clinton's draft evasion and protests against the war as a young man. Whereas seven-eighths of the oldest age group and seven-tenths of the boomers opposed the war, less than half of the busters (some of whom had not been born when the war ended) opposed it, and it was among the youngest cohort that significantly more concern was raised about Clinton's activities: nearly a quarter of those eighteen to twenty-nine named it as very important in their vote choice, as opposed to single-digit shares of the two older groups. However, seven-tenths of the busters thought Clinton had told the truth about his Vietnam-related activities, as did five-sixths of the oldest group. (Interestingly, only half of the LGBs from the "Vietnam generation" believed Clinton had been entirely forthcoming about this, although it did not affect his level of support among this group.) In a related demographic difference, 27 percent of the oldest cohort said they were military veterans, versus 12 percent of boomers and 16 percent of the youngest cohort.

One additional finding related to voting behavior. Although virtually identical shares of all three age groups voted for Clinton, Bush, and Perot, half of those LGBs eighteen to twenty-nine said they once thought they might vote for Perot, and would have done so if he had had a chance to win.

Hypothesis 6: The "Sexuality Gap"

> LGB voting will be sufficiently distinctive as to have an independent effect on vote choice after controlling for attitudes, partisanship, incumbency, and demographic factors significantly correlated with LGB self-identification. Thus, there will be an authentic "sexuality gap," meaning that self-identified LGBs will be more liberal and Democratic in their voting than will their liberal, Democratic cohorts who do not identify as lesbian, bisexual, or gay.

The results presented in table 6.7 should not at this point surprise the reader. After controlling for the variety of differences in demographics, party affiliation, and ideology found between the self-identified lesbians, gay men, and bisexuals and the rest of the sample, we see that sexual self-identification standing alone helped explain and predict how Americans would vote in the 1992 presidential election.

Two findings warrant additional comment in this context. One is the relative strength of this one factor after all the control variables have been added to the mix of explanations. Although it is possible that the addition of a feminism indicator (which was missing in the 1992 questionnaire) would have reduced the strength of the sexual self-identification factor, it does not appear likely from the data reported here that feminism could "wipe out" the independent effect of LGB identification. The other finding of note is the extent to which even Ross Perot's independent candidacy was hindered by his public waffling specifically on issues of concern to LGB voters.

One question, regrettably, cannot be answered. As reported in the 1990 state-level studies, retrospective evaluations did not appear to negate the independent effect of lesbian/gay identification in state gubernatorial contests. Retrospective modeling was designed, however, specifically to explain and predict voting in presidential elections. But the data base in 1992 again hinders us, in that there is no direct measure of presidential approval. Further, the economic evaluation questions are found in one version of the survey, but the question on approval of President Bush's economic performance is in a different version. No retrospective voting analysis is possible, therefore, using the 1992 exit polls, and we can neither confirm nor deny that sexual self-identification would have an independent effect in determining the two-party vote for president after controlling for the factors in a retrospective evaluation model. Such a determination will have to wait until at least 1996.

The Lavender Vote in the Election of Bill Clinton

This litany of numbers, boiled down to essentials, confirms much of what we learned in earlier chapters. There is a distinctive voting bloc comprising self-identified lesbians, gay men, and bisexuals in the United States, who together cast roughly two and one-quarter million votes in the 1992 presidential election. Of these, a bit more than 1.6 million were cast for Bill Clinton, as opposed to roughly 300,000 each for George Bush and Ross Perot. Similarly three-to-one shares of this vote were cast for Democratic candidates for Congress and for a dozen state governorships.

This group of voters is distinctively young, well educated, urban, secular, liberal, and Democratic. But above and beyond that, their self-identification as gay, lesbian, or bisexual has an independent effect on how they will vote. In the 1990 election it was demonstrated that a pro-LGB Republican could win the overwhelming support of self-identified lesbian and gay voters over a Democrat perceived to be hostile to the LGB community. In the 1992 election, however, the Republican side was decidedly (and, perhaps, with deliberate calculation) negative on LGB rights, and insulting and provocative toward LGB people; Governor Weld was a minority voice within his party. At the same time, Bill Clinton appealed directly and openly to lesbian, gay, and bisexual voters as had no major party presidential nominee before him. Thus, in 1992, the direction of the "lavender vote" was thoroughly predictable and logical.

Perhaps more interesting, then, is the fact that even with the inclusion of bisexuals in the self-identifier item and an influx of LGB first-time voters of all ages—which factors together muted many of the demographic differences between gay and nongay found in 1990—the distinctive ideological tilt, issue positions, and partisanship of LGB voters were not much affected. This less wealthy, less educated, less urban, less politically interested, less male, and more family-oriented set of LGB voters, who by self-identification were some-what less liberal as well, still were substantially more liberal in actual attitudes than their non-LGB counterparts.

In 1990 we saw that urban lesbians and gay men voted rather like their liberal urban nongay neighbors, whereas suburban and rural gays and lesbians were nearly as distinctively liberal as their urban counterparts and, therefore, much more liberal than their nongay neighbors. A similar lesson can be learned from the 1992 data. Sexual self-identification appears to be an extremely important factor in the formation of political attitudes that can override our expectations based on a voter's demographic profile. Further, even self-identification as a bisexual can help make a voter almost as distinctively liberal as one who identifies as a lesbian or a gay man.

Even absent the GOP's antigay rhetoric, it is likely that this group would have given many more of its votes to the Democrats than to the Republicans. The GOP's rhetoric and the Democrats' overtures, however, apparently did three things. First, they are by far the most logical explanation for the vastly greater turnout of first-time voters among LGBs. Second, they shattered the Republican Party's support among LGB Republicans and independents: nearly two hundred thousand of the four hundred thousand self-identified LGB Republicans casting ballots in the election, for the clearest example, voted against their president. Third, the election may have had an important effect in sealing an alliance between the Democratic Party and the "lavender vote"; as discussed in the next chapter, we shall have to await the results of the 1996 election to see whether this is so.

This concludes the discussion of the exit polling data from 1990 and 1992. I now try to pull all this information together and, in the last chapter, say what it all means and why it matters.

TABLE 6.1.
Demographic comparison of gay, lesbian, and bisexual voters with other voters, 1992 U.S. general election

Data base(s)	Variable	Non-LGB (%)	LGB (%)	Data base(s)	Variable	Non-LGB (%)	LGB (%)
All	Age[c]			All	Household income[c]		
	18–24	10.5	14.4		Less than $15,000	14.3	23.9
	25–29	9.9	15.6		$15,000–29,999	24.1	27.0
	30–39	23.8	31.4		$30,000–49,999	29.6	29.2
	40–44	12.2	8.5		$50,000–74,999	19.7	12.8
	45–49	10.4	9.5		$75,000 or more	12.3	7.1
	50–59	12.3	9.9				
	60–64	7.1	5.5	W	Employment status[c]		
	65 or older	13.8	5.2		Unemployed,		
					seeking work	5.4	11.1
W	Education[a]				Employed		
	Not high school				full-time	55.5	55.2
	graduate	6.7	6.4		Employed		
	High school				part-time	9.8	8.4
	graduate	27.8	20.1		Full-time student	4.4	9.8
	Some college	27.7	30.7		Homemaker	8.2	4.4
	College graduate	22.5	19.2		Retired	16.8	11.0
	Postgraduate work	15.3	23.6				
				W	Labor union member		
All	Sex[b] (% male)	46.8	54.7		in household[a]	18.2	25.1
All	Race			W	Religious affiliation[c]		
	White	87.5	84.6		Protestant	41.8	28.6
	Black	8.1	10.1		Catholic	27.0	27.9
	Hispanic/Latino	2.3	3.5		Other Christian	14.4	9.7
	Asian	1.0	.7		Jewish	3.9	4.2
	Other	1.1	1.1		Other religion	6.4	13.9
					No religion	6.6	15.7
All	Region[b]						
	East	23.2	29.5				
	Midwest	27.4	21.0	W	Attend religious services at least		
	South	29.4	25.5		once a week	40.1	32.4
	West	20.1	24.0	W	Born-again or fundamentalist		
					Christian	19.3	20.9
All	Size/type of locality[c]						
	500,000 or more	9.1	17.9	W	Married[c]	67.3	30.3
	250,000–499,000	3.2	6.7		Have children under		
	50,000–249,000	12.4	15.1	W	18[b]	34.5	24.9
	Suburbs	40.2	39.8				
	10,000–49,000	10.7	4.2	W	First-time voter[c]	10.2	22.4
	Rural area	24.5	16.4	W, Y	Military veteran	17.3	17.9

NOTE: Data are presented as weighted percentages. "All" indicates combined responses to identical questions from the W, Y, and P versions of the poll.
[a] Significance level = .05.
[b] Significance level = .01.
[c] Significance level = .001.

TABLE 6.2.

Differences in age clusters between gay or lesbian self-identifiers, 1990, and gay, lesbian, and bisexual self-identifiers, 1992

	% of total sample	
Age group	1990	1992
18–29	2.6	3.2[a]
30–39	1.4	2.9
40–44	1.6	1.5
45–49	1.5	2.1
50–59	0.3	1.8
60 and older	0.3	1.1[b]

NOTE: Data represent the weighted percentages of all respondents to the 1990 and 1992 national general election exit polls in each age cluster who self-identified as gay or lesbian (1990) or as gay, lesbian, or bisexual (1992). The 1990 exit polls had only six age categories; the 1992 exit polls had eight, which are compressed above into the six 1990 categories. The 1992 data are further broken out below.

[a] 1992 figures: 18–24, 3.0 percent; 25–29, 3.5 percent.

[b] 1992 figures: 60–64, 1.7 percent; 65 and older, 0.8 percent.

TABLE 6.3.

Political attitudes of gay, lesbian, and bisexual voters compared with other voters, 1992 U.S. general election

Data base(s)	Variable	Non-LGB (%)	LGB (%)	Data base(s)	Variable	Non-LGB (%)	LGB (%)
All	Party affiliation[c]				About same as life		
	Democratic	37.7	50.4		today	32.7	18.4
	Republican	34.9	17.7		Worse than life today	36.6	48.1
	Independent	23.6	22.4	P	More important to		
	Other	3.8	9.4		Preserve environment	49.3	59.3
W	Ideology[c]				Preserve economic		
	Liberal	20.7	49.3		growth	50.7	40.7
	Moderate	48.8	42.3		*Taxes and services*		
	Conservative	30.5	8.4	Y	Would rather have[b]		
					More services,		
W	One of two most important issues				higher taxes	39.4	55.3
	Health care[c]	19.1	39.0		Fewer services,		
	Federal budget				Lower taxes	60.6	44.7
	deficit[a]	21.4	14.7	P	Highest priority for next president should be:[b]		
	Abortion	12.0	11.8				
	Education	12.7	16.3		Cut taxes	16.4	20.6
	Economy/jobs	42.1	46.2		Cut federal deficit	58.7	35.8
	Environment	5.6	8.4		Expand domestic		
	Taxes[c]	14.4	6.0		programs	24.9	43.6
	Foreign policy[a]	7.8	3.1				
	Family values[b]	15.1	8.0	P	I would pay more taxes to		
					Reduce federal		
Economy					deficit[b]	49.8	29.1
W	Evaluation of national economy[c]				Improve health care		
	Excellent	.9	3.0		programs	69.1	80.1
	Good	18.4	7.7		Improve		
	Not so good	47.9	51.6		infrastructure	49.6	55.8
	Poor	33.1	37.8		Improve job training/		
					placement[a]	59.1	75.3
W	Compared to four years ago am financially[b]			*Social issues*			
	Better off	24.8	20.0	W	Abortion should be[c]		
	About the same	41.3	34.0		Always legal	34.6	56.0
	Worse off	33.9	46.0		Mostly legal	31.2	29.5
					Mostly illegal	25.0	8.6
Y	Bush's handling of economy[c]				Always illegal	9.2	5.8
	Approve strongly	9.0	3.4				
	Approve somewhat	26.2	14.2	Y	Government should[c]		
	Disapprove somewhat	24.2	16.9		Encourage		
	Disapprove strongly	40.5	65.5		traditional values	74.2	30.0
					Encourage tolerance		
P	Life for next generation will be				of other values	25.8	70.0
	Better than life today	30.7	33.5				

TABLE 6.3. *(Continued)*

Data base(s)	Variable	Non-LGB (%)	LGB (%)	Data base(s)	Variable	Non-LGB (%)	LGB (%)
P	Government should[c]				*Miscellaneous*		
	Promote			Y	Opposed Vietnam War[c]	31.1	67.5
	traditional values	47.9	30.3				
	Not favor one set of			W	Clinton has told whole truth about what		
	values over another	52.1	69.7		he did in Vietnam		
					era[c]	43.5	65.2
P	Main reason for our social problems[b]						
	Breakdown of the			W	Bush has told whole truth about his		
	family	51.4	30.8		role in Iran-Contra[a]	27.6	16.8
	Government neglect	48.6	69.2				

Institutional trust

Y	Would be better off if all new people were elected to office[b]	51.1	65.6

NOTE: Data are presented as weighted percentages. "All" indicates combined responses to identical questions from the W, Y, and P versions of the poll.

[a] Significance level = .05.

[b] Significance level = .01.

[c] Significance level = .001.

TABLE 6.4.

Voting behavior and rationales of gay, lesbian, and bisexual voters compared with other voters, 1992 U.S. general election

Data base(s)	Variable	Non-LGB (%)	LGB (%)	Data base(s)	Variable	Non-LGB (%)	LGB (%)
All	Vote for president[c]			W	One or two most important qualities in presidential candidate		
	Bill Clinton (D)	42.9	72.2				
	George Bush (R)	37.9	14.2		Has the right experience[c]	19.1	7.4
	Ross Perot (I)	19.2	13.6				
	Other candidates	<.1	0		Will bring needed change[c]	35.6	53.2
All	Vote for governor				Is my party's candidate	4.8	6.0
	Democratic	53.5	74.2				
	Republican	43.6	22.7		Cares about people like me[c]	13.1	25.9
	Other	1.0	0				
					Is honest and trustworthy[c]	14.4	5.4
All	Vote for U.S. Senate[c]						
	Democratic	51.5	75.7		Has best plan for country	24.4	29.0
	Republican	43.1	17.8				
	Other	2.8	3.1		Would have good judgment in a crisis[c]	16.6	6.9
All	Vote for U.S. House[c]				Choice of vice president[c]	8.1	15.3
	Democratic	53.6	78.3				
	Republican	46.4	21.7		Has strong convictions[a]	14.1	9.0
	(No data on vote for third candidates)						
All	Self-reported 1988 presidential vote[c]			Y	Factors very important in vote choice for president		
	George Bush (R)	55.4	27.8				
	Michael Dukakis (D)	27.0	45.0		Supreme Court appointees[b]	30.1	45.1
	Other	2.5	3.6		Gulf War	23.3	19.7
	Did not vote in 1988	5.1	23.6		Age of candidates	8.9	11.9
W	Reported voting for Ronald Reagan in 1984[c]	42.8	26.9		Vice presidential candidate	24.9	32.0
W	Once thought I might vote for Perot	39.3	42.2		Candidate's marital fidelity[a]	11.7	4.6
					Debates	35.1	26.5
W	If Perot had not been on ballot, would have voted for[c]				Bush breaking tax pledge	21.3	26.2
	Bill Clinton (D)	49.3	77.0		Clinton's draft status and Vietnam protests[a]	19.1	11.4
	George Bush (R)	44.6	15.0				
	Someone else	2.2	3.0				
	Would not have voted	3.9	4.9	P	Factors that helped me decide in presidential election		
Y	Would have voted for Perot if he had a chance to win	35.5	38.2		Candidates' wives[b]	16.3	32.5
					Campaign ads	24.6	28.7

Data base(s)	Variable	Non-LGB (%)	LGB (%)	Data base(s)	Variable	Non-LGB (%)	LGB (%)
	Candidates on TV talk shows	46.0	52.7	Y	If Clinton is elected I will feel[c]		
	Preelection polls	6.6	8.9		Excited	14.9	35.8
	Party conventions[b]	23.1	39.8		Optimistic	26.1	29.9
	Debates	62.8	75.4		Concerned	28.6	19.3
					Scared	30.4	15.0
Y	Vote was more						
	For my candidate	71.7	72.7				
	Against his opponents	28.3	27.3				

NOTE: Data are presented as weighted percentages. "All" indicates combined responses to identical questions from the W, Y, and P versions of the poll.
[a] Significance level = .05.
[b] Significance level = .01.
[c] Significance level = .001.

TABLE 6.5.
Differences among self-identified gay, lesbian, and bisexual respondents based on party identification

Data base	Item	Dem (%)	Rep (%)	Ind/O (%)
Demographics				
All	Race (% white)[b]	78.7	93.4	89.3
All	Size/type of locality[a]			
	(compressed from 6 categories)			
	Central city (50,000 or more)	45.8	30.7	33.4
	Suburbs	40.0	37.5	41.7
	Small town or rural	14.2	31.8	24.8
All	Income[d] (compressed from 5 categories)			
	Under $30,000	54.0	36.8	53.0
	$30,000–49,999	30.4	33.1	25.4
	$50,000 or more	15.6	30.1	21.7
All	Employment status[a]			
	Unemployed, seeking work	7.5	9.7	17.4
	Employed full-time	52.8	62.8	54.3
	Employed part-time	5.6	5.1	14.6
	Full-time student	14.7	4.4	5.6
	Homemaker	3.4	9.0	3.4
	Retired	16.0	9.0	4.7
Y, P	Schoolteacher[b]	33.6	15.1	7.4
Y, P	Religion[c]			
	Protestant	30.2	54.6	11.6
	Catholic	22.4	20.6	40.2
	Other Christian	11.9	14.6	3.6
	Jewish	4.6	2.7	4.5
	Other religion	13.7	4.2	19.8
	No religion	17.3	3.4	20.3
Y, P	Born-again/fundamentalist[b]	21.2	37.8	10.7
Y, P	Marital status[a]			
	Presently married	25.1	45.3	29.4
	Ever married	42.0	59.7	39.1
Voting behavior				
All	Presidential vote[c]			
	Clinton (D)	95.9	23.2	62.2
	Bush (R)	1.7	53.7	10.7
	Perot (I)	2.4	23.1	27.1

TABLE 6.5. (*Continued*)

Data base	Item	Dem (%)	Rep (%)	Ind/O (%)
Y	Would have voted for Perot if he had a chance to win[a]	26.8	56.9	54.6
All	Voted for Democrat			
	In Senate race[c]	91.2	40.5	75.4
	In House race[c]	99.0	26.3	74.9
	In gubernatorial race[c]	100.0	12.8	70.3
W	One or two top candidate qualities			
	Has right experience[c]	1.7	25.5	5.5
	Has best plan for U.S.[a]	28.1	14.7	38.4
	Would have good judgment in a crisis[b]	2.8	19.9	5.6
Y	Very important in vote choice			
	Supreme Court appointments[d]	54.7	50.9	25.6
	Vice presidential candidates[a]	44.3	20.0	16.5
	Clinton's Vietnam-era activities[c]	1.5	36.1	18.7
	Bush's role in Iran-Contra[b]	56.9	6.6	35.9
Y	My vote was more for my candidate than against opponents[a]	82.5	47.0	68.9
P	TV ads helped me decide[d]	20.7	10.5	47.7
P	Talk shows helped decide[a]	54.4	12.8	70.7
Y	Bush ran more unfair ads[a]	62.8	21.6	40.2
Y	Wore a campaign button[a]	58.9	48.4	16.7
Y	Contacted this year by a presidential campaign[a]	50.8	2.9	30.1
Y	Have participated in antiwar protests[b]	44.6	28.9	16.3
Political attitudes				
W	One of two most important issues			
	Federal budget deficit[d]	8.8	23.2	18.7
	Abortion	8.9	4.1	20.5
	Taxes[c]	4.3	19.3	1.1
	Foreign policy[a]	.9	9.3	2.8
	Family values[c]	6.6	24.4	.8
W	Abortion (% "always legal")[b]	54.1	43.6	65.6

Data base	Item	Dem (%)	Rep (%)	Ind/O (%)
W	Ideology[b]			
	Liberal	60.0	20.0	50.6
	Moderate	31.1	66.4	44.7
	Conservative	8.9	13.6	4.6
W	National economy excellent/good[c]	5.3	30.9	7.1
W	Personal economic condition better[c]	14.0	41.7	16.6
W	Foreign trade loses jobs[a]	25.0	31.9	70.0
W	Prefer more taxes, services over lower services, taxes[b]	74.6	6.6	47.8
P	Government should do more to solve our economic problems[c]	80.6	20.2	65.3
P	Would pay more taxes to improve job training/placement[d]	89.1	47.2	70.4
P	Economy is in long-term decline, not just normal downturn[d]	68.5	29.1	72.7
Y	Approve Bush's economic performance[c]	4.8	50.6	22.2
Y	Government should encourage tolerance of nontraditional families[b]	86.0	54.4	47.5
P	Government should not favor one set of values over another[a]	54.3	57.4	91.6
W	Clinton has told truth about his Vietnam-era activities[b]	77.6	26.9	66.3
W	Bush has told truth about his role in Iran-Contra[c]	5.7	48.2	13.6
Y	Better to have president, Congress of different parties[b]	24.9	21.1	63.0
Y	Feelings if Clinton elected (% positive)[c]	93.0	13.8	41.1
Y	Clinton more likely to raise my taxes[b]	23.4	77.3	26.9

NOTE: Data are presented as weighted percentages. "All" indicates combined responses to identical questions from the W, Y, and P versions of the poll.
 [a] Significance level = .05.
 [b] Significance level = .01.
 [c] Significance level = .001.
 [d] Relationships significant at .051 to .099 (approaching statistical significance).

TABLE 6.6.
Differences among self-identified lesbian, gay, and bisexual respondents based on age cohort, 1992

Data base	Item	18–29 (%)	30–44 (%)	45 + (%)
Demographics				
W	Education[c]			
	Not high school graduate	5.4	.9	12.9
	High school graduate	29.7	7.5	26.4
	Some college	35.5	37.2	19.4
	College graduate	14.9	25.5	15.8
	Postgraduate study	14.5	28.9	25.6
All	Household income[b]			
	Less than $15,000	33.4	16.8	24.3
	$15,000–29,999	34.7	24.9	21.3
	$30,000–49,999	21.3	31.9	34.0
	$50,000–74,999	6.4	18.4	11.9
	$75,000 or more	4.2	8.0	8.5
W	Employment status[c]			
	Unemployed/seeking work	16.5	12.9	3.4
	Employed full-time	44.6	72.4	44.7
	Employed part-time	14.1	9.3	2.1
	Full-time student	23.6	5.0	3.0
	Homemaker	1.3	.3	12.3
	Retired	0	0	34.5
W, Y	Military veteran[a]	16.1	12.2	27.1
W	Religious affiliation[a]			
	Protestant	13.5	27.0	44.8
	Catholic	28.8	29.5	25.3
	Other Christian	5.3	13.2	9.1
	Jewish	6.3	3.3	3.3
	Other religion	23.7	12.4	6.7
	No religion	22.4	14.7	10.8
W	Attend religious services at least once a week[b]	20.9	28.0	47.4
W	Marital status[c]			
W	Presently married	18.2	29.5	42.1
W	Ever married	23.5	43.1	64.1
Y	Have an LGB friend or relative	95.6	98.7	73.0
Political attitudes				
Y	Opposed Vietnam War[a]	47.9	69.7	87.5

Data base	Item	18–29 (%)	30–44 (%)	45+ (%)
Y	Factors very important in vote choice			
	Bush breaks tax pledge[d]	26.2	17.6	42.5
	Clinton's draft status			
	and Vietnam protests[a]	23.9	6.9	4.7
W	Clinton has told whole truth about what			
	he did in Vietnam era[d]	69.5	53.8	84.4
P	I would pay more taxes to			
	reduce federal deficit[d]	13.4	47.3	20.8
Voting behavior				
W	Once thought I might			
	vote for Perot[a]	56.7	37.5	35.1
Y	Would have voted for Perot is			
	he had a chance to win[d]	47.8	25.2	49.8

NOTE: Data are presented as weighted percentages. "All" indicates combined responses to identical questions from the W, Y, and P versions of the poll.

[a] Significance level = .05.
[b] Significance level = .01.
[c] Significance level = .001.
[d] Relationships significant at .051 to .099 (approaching statistical significance).

TABLE 6.7.

Logistic regression analysis of effect of gay, lesbian, and bisexual self-identification on voting behavior when controlled, in succession, for demographic variables, party affiliation, and ideology, 1992 general election

	Explanatory measures				Predictive measures	
	B	S.E.	Wald	Significance	Mean	% Correct
Presidential context (N = 6,729)						
Voted for Bill Clinton (Democrat)					42.09	
Self-identification alone	1.4496	.1809	64.2117	.0000		57.91
Add demographics	1.4024	.1898	54.6181	.0000		67.23
Add party identification	1.4425	.2202	42.9191	.0000		78.75
Add ideology	1.2320	.2178	32.0058	.0000		79.13
Voted for George Bush (Republican)					37.22	
Self-identification alone	−1.3625	.2256	36.4688	.0000		62.78
Add demographics	−1.2354	.2335	28.0032	.0000		67.25
Add party identification	−1.0871	.2590	17.6185	.0000		79.01
Add ideology	−.8055	.2585	9.7070	.0018		80.09
Voted for Ross Perot (Independent)					19.34	
Self-identification alone	−.7247	.2512	8.3234	.0039		80.66
Add demographics	−.7686	.2559	9.0224	.0027		80.66
Add party identification	−.7941	.2591	9.3925	.0022		80.82
Add ideology	−.7952	.2598	9.3666	.0022		80.87

SOURCE: VRS W data base.

SEVEN

What It All Means and Why It Matters

This study was undertaken to find out whether we have overlooked a significant factor in determining whether, and how, Americans cast their votes: the factor of sexual identity. It has long been speculated that a "lavender vote" exists that leans strongly toward liberal and Democratic Party candidates. My aim was to see how many voters would identify themselves as lesbian, gay, or bisexual; whether and to what extent they differed in their demographics, attitudes, and voting behavior from the rest of the American electorate; whether in fact they voted as a cohesive bloc; and what the underlying reasons were for any distinctive voting.

In answering these questions, I return to the nine hypotheses laid out at the end of chapter 2. I first present again each of these hypotheses, state whether the hypothesis was confirmed or not (or confirmed only to a limited extent), and discuss what we have learned. After this, I devote a few pages to findings of interest beyond those bearing on these hypotheses. At the end I attempt to answer the question, "So what does this mean and why does it matter?"

Hypothesis 1: Rate of Identification

Lesbians and gay men will self-identify in political surveys at rates equivalent to those found in previous random-sample research, about 1.0 to 1.5 percent of the population. When bisexuals are included, the share of self-identifiers will increase by an additional 2 to 3 percent. *Confirmed in part.*

The discussion that follows must be tempered by the simple fact that the share of the total electorate we are discussing is small. The national data bases and the pooled twenty-one-state data confirm that, in 1990, only one American voter in ninety identified her- or himself as gay or lesbian, and when we add in bisexuals, this confirmable share increases to about two voters in ninety.

These numbers confirm the initial hypothesis that, because of the severe legal and social penalties for self-identification, the number of those willing to call themselves gay or lesbian would be comparatively small. As noted above, the number of gay and lesbian self-identifiers, at 1.1 percent, is in the expected range (1.0–1.5 percent). Although there were variations based on region and size or type of locality, in no state did the total reach even 3 percent, and in the areas with the largest share of such voters, the urban centers of the West, the total self-identified lesbian and gay electorate remained in the single digits as a percentage of the whole.[1]

When bisexuals are added as part of the self-identification category, one finds that their share is indeed smaller than predicted based on prior random-sample research: self-identified gay men, lesbians, and bisexuals added together accounted for just 2.2 percent of the 1992 electorate, well below the hypothesized figure between 3.0 and 4.5 percent. (We should make note again, however, of Edelman's estimation [1993] that the figure would reach 3 percent if we account for those respondents who "dropped off" the survey before answering the "grab bag" questions in which the LGB self-identifier was found.)

That said, the portion of the LGB population willing to identify as such is growing significantly. The single factor that correlated consistently with self-identification across all the surveys examined in this study was age. The very youngest voters did not self-identify at a much greater rate than that of the rest of the population; but people in their mid- to late twenties were more than four times as likely to identify themselves as LGB, and nearly ten times as likely to call themselves gay or lesbian as were those in the oldest age category. Indeed, they were two-thirds more likely to call themselves lesbian or gay, and twice as likely to call themselves LGB than were the fortysomething members of the "baby boom" generation immediately preceding them.

The few studies on homosexuality and bisexuality available do not indicate that the rate of homosexuality or bisexuality is growing. They show, rather, that the rate of homosexual behavior is constant among age groups and races, and that among men the rate of admission to homosexual experimentation increased only among the well-educated (Fay et al. 1989). Although much more work needs to be done in this area, it appears from the evidence at hand that the increase in self-identification results from an increase in comfort with

LGB self-identification among the young, which appears to have resulted from the activity of the LGB movement, particularly in the past quarter century. More simply put, more young people "come out" not because there is any more homosexuality among the young, but because it is somewhat safer these days to be honest about it.

A corollary factor is the addition of bisexuality to the self-identification category. Not only did this double the overall number of self-identifiers, it also led to disproportionately large increases in the rate of self-identification among older respondents. I noted that there appear to be three distinct, age-determined "comfort levels" with self-identification. When "gay or lesbian" was the wording of the question in 1990, these "comfort levels" consisted of those aged eighteen to twenty-nine (2.5 percent self-identified), those thirty to forty-nine (1.5 percent self-identified), and those fifty and older (0.3 percent self-identified). With the addition of bisexuals in 1992, self-identification rates increased rather dramatically among thirtysomethings and among those aged fifty to sixty-four. The three "comfort levels," therefore, aged as well: eighteen to thirty-nine (3.0 percent), forty to sixty-four (1.7 percent), and sixty-five and older (0.8 percent).

Already the LGB vote is as large as the Latino vote and twice the size of the Asian vote. If the progress of the LGB movement continues, we can expect that the combined "lavender vote" will reach 4 to 5 percent of the total voting population within the next twenty years. At such a level, self-identified LGB voters will constitute a potential bloc of votes surpassing Jews (currently about 3.5 percent of the voters) and every racial minority other than African Americans.

Hypothesis 2: Demographic Characteristics

LGBs who do self-identify will be possessed of the equivalent of "group consciousness." Therefore, the demographic correlates of group consciousness found among women and African Americans—youth, high education levels, and strong partisanship—should be disproportionately great among self-identified LGBs. Also, given the results of prior sex surveys, men may significantly outnumber women among self-identifiers. *Confirmed as to age and education. Mixed results as to sex. Not confirmed as to partisanship.*

Our ability to examine the hypothesis that LGB self-identification was a valid substitute indicator for levels of group consciousness—that the fact of self-identifying demonstrated that one was possessed of "gay consciousness"—was considerably limited. The sole indicators at hand are simply correlates with group consciousness, not direct measures of such concepts as perceptions of "polar power" or "internal political efficacy." The correlate variables available were age, education level, and partisanship. (An augmented level of political interest was assumed in 1990 from the mere fact of voting in an off-year congressional and/or gubernatorial election.) An attempt to make an initial assessment of the truth or falsity of the hypothesis, nonetheless, was undertaken.

As expected in the hypothesis, the LGB samples, as noted above, were skewed heavily toward the younger end of the age scale. An additional factor was the exceedingly high education level of the gay/lesbian respondents in the 1990 national data base: an absolute majority were college graduates and a very large share had some postgraduate education. Although these extreme levels were not replicated in 1992, the LGB sample remained significantly better educated than the non-LGB sample. Again, these data appeared to support the hypothesis. Partisanship was more questionable; although the national data showed a partisan tilt toward the Democrats and away from the Republicans, the degree of partisanship per se was no greater, and the rate of independent self-identification no smaller, among the LGB voters than among the rest.

The 1990 state and local-level data, however, seem to shred the hypothesis of uniformly high education levels among the self-identifiers. In Texas, where the legal and social climate for gay men and lesbians is considerably harsher by objective measures than in California and Massachusetts, education levels did not differ significantly between the gay and nongay groups. Further, in two of the three state-level polls examined in depth, there were no significant differences between the gay and nongay groups either in degree of partisanship or even in party affiliation. (In the Glick poll, of course, all respondents were registered Democrats voting in their party's primary.)

Finally, there is the first-time voting factor. In 1990 there was no significant difference in the rate of first-time voting between the gay and nongay samples. In 1992, however, LGB self-identifiers were more than twice as likely as non-LGBs to be voting for the first time, and this trend was found in all age groups, from the youngest to the oldest. This indicates that the level of political interest among the LGBs in 1992 was relatively *low* and that their participation had been triggered by the high salience of LGB issues during the presidential campaign.

Therefore, there is no uniform confirmation that the demographic correlates of group consciousness can be found among LGB self-identifiers. Additional work on this line of research, employing indicators of actual elements of group consciousness on presumptive self-identifiers, is being undertaken by the present author.

The data do show that gay men consistently make up a disproportionate share of lesbian and gay self-identifiers, nationally and in all regions, and that this disproportion, in which men make up three-fifths to two-thirds of the gay and lesbian samples, is consistent with the findings of sex research with regard to both sexual self-identification and continuing or frequent homosexual activity. However, in the 1992 data, there is no discernible "gender gap" in LGB self-identification rates. Men still outnumber women slightly, but the difference is small and not statistically significant. A clue to the possible reason for this disparity, "lesbian bisexuality," was found in the Glick poll and will be discussed later in this chapter.

Hypothesis 3: Political Attitudes

> The general political orientation of LGB voters will be liberal or leftist and Democratic, in keeping with the pattern found among African Americans, feminists, and non-Cuban Latinos, and will be highly distinctive from that of non-LGB identifiers. *Confirmed, with qualifications.*

The issue attitudes of most LGB self-identifiers were distinctively liberal; a majority of self-identifiers both called themselves liberal and held liberal attitudes on specific issues. In addition, an absolute majority of lesbians in 1990 called themselves strong feminists. Logistic regression analysis showed that, indeed, when the factors of liberalism and feminism were controlled for, there was no independent effect of self-identification as gay or lesbian on attitudes toward economic or defense/foreign policy issues.

However, on domestic social issues, the self-identified LGBs were significantly more liberal or libertarian than were liberal and feminist heterosexuals. Indeed, otherwise conservative and Republican LGBs tended to take liberal stands on domestic social issues other than the death penalty, and to call themselves moderates rather than conservatives. There is, therefore, a "sexuality gap" on these issues that cannot be accounted for otherwise.

Partisan affiliation, as noted above, was not nearly as distinctive as this augmented liberalism and feminism would predict. Neither, in 1990, was voting behavior in the aggregated results on the national level. Although a disproportion of lesbian and gay straight-ticket voters supported the Democrats, versus a near-even split among nongay identifiers in this category, two-thirds of voters, straight and gay alike, split their tickets in states with simultaneous contests for the Senate, the House, and the governor's mansion. In the House races, indeed, one self-identifier in six voted for a third candidate. Although these voters were profoundly liberal, they were not apparently voting against Democratic incumbents any more often than Republican incumbents, nor were they motivated by any particular issue concern.

This changed dramatically in 1992. Whereas independents and Republican LGBs still split their tickets as frequently as did the rest of the population, the one-half of LGBs who identified as Democrats were in the main straight-ticket voters, and a large disproportion of the LGB independents who did vote a straight ticket went with the Democrats. This cohesion among LGB Democrats was as great as that among black Democrats. It remains to be seen whether this is a one-time phenomenon or the start of a long-term trend.

Hypothesis 4: Gender and Feminism

> Lesbians and bisexual women, whether feminists or not, will be more opposed to the use of force in politics, and therefore will be more likely to vote for Democrats than are gay and bisexual men. In addition, lesbian feminists will hold different issue priorities from LGB men and women who do not identify with feminism, and thus are far more likely to hold liberal positions on abortion and other feminist issues; they will be more inclined to vote for Democrats than will other women. *Confirmed as to the "feminism gap." Limited confirmation as to the "gender gap."*

Because of the absence of feminism and use-of-force indicators in the 1992 data base, this discussion is confined to the data from 1990.

I proposed that actual differences in candidate selection and issue stands between lesbians and gay men would be minimal, other than in the area of defense and foreign policy, but that issue emphasis would differ. With respect to the national sample, this hypothesis was confirmed in large part, although the variations from the predicted pattern should be noted. As predicted, the greatest differences were found in the two questions relating to the Persian Gulf deployment, which strong majorities of men supported and equally strong majorities of women opposed. Again, as predicted, women were three times as likely as men in the VRS data to name abortion as one top issue; men were more likely to name the environment and the deficit. Interestingly, however, the lesbians were significantly more skeptical about the economy and the overall direction of the country, and were far less inclined to approve of the deficit compromise than were the gay men. This was not predicted based on the Gilens (1988) gender gap model.

Many more significant differences in attitudes and voting behavior, however, were found based on identification as a strong feminist, a categorization that included five of every eight lesbians in the national sample. Approval of George Bush was in the single digits among this group, and five of six said they probably would vote for the Democrat in 1992, as against 41 percent of the nonfeminists. 78.5 percent voted for the Democrat for the Senate in 1990, versus just over half of the nonfeminist gay folk, and three-quarters of feminists (as against just under half of nonfeminists) called themselves liberals. Even personal economic evaluations were far worse among the feminist identifiers than among the nonfeminists. Nearly all lesbian feminists supported abortion on demand, and fully half named it as one of the top two issues in the congressional race.

As noted in the chapter on the national polls, feminism was one of three indicators that appear to explain most of the differences in issue attitudes between LGB and non-LGB samples. This is a testament in hard numbers to the continuing vitality of lesbian feminism as a movement within the broader feminist and LGB communities.

Hypothesis 5: Voting Blocs within the Community

> Given the divergent concepts of group identity among LGBs, and their differing notions of what the goals of the LGB movement should be and the best means for achieving them, LGB voters will not be monolithic; although the large majority will vote for Democrats, significant minorities will support Republicans or leftist third candidates. *Confirmed.*

A small but significant minority of the self-identified LGB respondents voted Republican. Half of the LGB Republicans even voted for George Bush after the antigay GOP campaign of 1992. Although sharing the cultural liberalism of the Democrats and independents on abortion, drugs, and the environment, they were considerably more conservative on economic issues, the death penalty, and defense and foreign policy, and strongly supported President Reagan in 1984 and President Bush in 1988, before the Republican "family values" campaign of 1992 drove them into exile. In 1990 they tended to stick with their party in the congressional contests, but about half split away in gubernatorial contests. In 1992, about two in five split from their Senate candidates, although a large majority stuck with GOP nominees for the House. (Too few LGB Republicans voted in the small number of 1992 governor's races to draw any conclusions.)

Independent self-identifiers were only marginally less liberal in philosophy and issue positions than were self-identified Democrats. They were, nonetheless, authentic ticket-splitters relative to their Democratic counterparts, strongly supporting Democrats for state governors in 1990 but in many cases looking to other candidates for Congress. (We should at this point distinguish voters who identified with neither major party from those referred to above who sided with third candidates in the contests for the House of Representatives. As many Democrats as independents [and a few Republicans!] were found among the latter group.) In the Clinton-Bush-Perot contest, however, pro-Democratic sentiment was much stronger: five in eight LGB independents voted for Clinton, and between 70 and 75 percent of them voted for Democrats for statehouses and for both houses of Congress.

Hypothesis 6: The "Sexuality Gap"

LGB voting will be sufficiently distinctive to have an independent effect on vote choice after controlling for attitudes, partisanship, incumbency, and demographic factors significantly correlated with LGB self-identification. Thus, there will be an authentic "sexuality gap," meaning that self-identified LGBs will be more liberal and Democratic in voting than will their liberal, Democratic cohorts who do not identify as lesbian, bisexual, or gay. *Confirmed with respect to high-salience elections.*

Hypothesis 7: Results in Specific Contests

LGB voting will remain highly distinctive in particular individual contests, not merely in aggregated national partisan results for governorships and seats in Congress, and will be particularly distinctive in high-salience contests. *Confirmed with respect to high-salience elections.*

The simple crosstabular results make clear that self-identified LGBs think and vote differently from the rest of the population. What was in question, however, was the extent to which sexual self-identification had an independent effect on political attitudes and voting behavior. The 1990 gay and lesbian sample was more liberal and more feminist than was the rest of the sample in 1990. It therefore could be postulated that those lesbians and gay men who were "out of the closet" were those who started off with less conventional opinions and practices, and that when compared to heterosexuals of the same description, the differences would disappear. This seemed to be borne out by the aggregated national results in chapter 3.

But the state-level results reported in chapter 4 put the lie to this. Sexual self-identification had an independent effect on vote choice in the five specific high-salience gubernatorial and Senate contests we examined, even after we had controlled for demographics, party affiliation, ideology, and feminism. The perceived closeness of each contest did not appear to affect these findings: Ben Parmer clearly was believed to have no chance against Senator Phil Gramm in Texas, but a "sexuality gap" was found just as strongly in that high-visibility contest as in the three hotly contested governor's races examined here. Indeed, in a retrospective voting model, self-identification had an independent effect on vote choice for governors and senators in all five of these contests, above and beyond its influence on the retrospective indicators.

There is no need to repeat oneself too much concerning the Clinton election of 1992. In this most salient election for LGB people, the effect of sexual self-identification not only remained significant, but strongly so, after controlling for the demographic, partisan, and attitudinal variables.

It must be noted that, in lower-salience elections in 1990, the solidity of the gay and lesbian vote dissipated. Although the trend in favor of Democratic nominees held up, considerable splitting of votes to Republicans and, in the case of the House races, to third candidates appeared. Indeed, in one of the two lower-salience Texas contests, even sexual self-identification standing alone had no significant effect on vote choice. In this respect, the gay and lesbian vote was not nearly as cohesive as, say, the African American vote; the same flexibility that allowed gay/lesbian voters to switch parties *en masse* in a high-salience election also inhibited party loyalty in lower-salience contests.

This was not true in 1992. As noted earlier, LGB Democrats were nearly monolithic in their support for their party's ticket across the board, and LGB independents were considerably more likely to vote a straight Democratic ticket than they were in 1990. Because individual-level results were not available in state-level contests, one cannot draw any conclusions from the 1992 numbers with respect to Hypothesis 7, but certainly if anything these numbers give a firmer confirmation to Hypothesis 6 than do those from 1990.

Interestingly, in the Glick contest, the independent effect of sexual self-identification was supplanted by the effect of the desire for a gay or lesbian representative.

The central question for practical politicians is whether there is a "lavender vote" that can be mobilized in favor of candidates supportive of LGB issues, or in opposition to candidates who take antigay positions. The answer clearly is yes. In the 1990 governor's races in California, Massachusetts, and Texas and the Glick primary race in New York City, the candidate in a high-salience contest who was perceived to be the most progay took a remarkably similar 77 to 78 percent of the votes of the lesbian and gay communities. In the three-way presidential contest of 1992, when bisexuals were added to the exit polls' self-identification item, Bill Clinton won 72 percent of the homosexual and bisexual self-identifiers (George Bush and Ross Perot won 14 percent apiece), as against a split of 43, 38, and 19 percent for Clinton, Bush, and Perot, respectively, in the rest of the sample.

The most remarkable fact, perhaps, about this LGB vote is that it can be mobilized against a Democratic nominee, as seen in the case of John Silber's ill-fated gubernatorial campaign in Massachusetts—at least provided that the Republican nominee makes the sort of strong and direct appeal to the LGB community that William Weld did. The LGB vote, although inclined toward the Democrats, was by no means uniformly Democratic or guaranteed to the Democratic nominee in the same way as were the votes of most African Americans. Despite the strong Democratic tide in voting behavior in 1992, the presidential contest did nothing to alter the basic partisan alignment and issue attitudes of LGB voters compared with those in 1990. Those Republicans who write off the LGB vote as hopelessly lost, therefore, appear to be making a serious strategic mistake in close contests.

Hypothesis 8: Symbolic versus Substantive Voting

> LGB voters will seek both substantive and symbolic gains. Therefore, in a high-salience contest between a "progay" and an "antigay" candidate, they will vote for the "progay" candidate; and in a contest in which there is little difference between the candidates on LGB issues, substantive issue differences will be of greater concern. *Confirmed, except that in the instance of an LGB candidate, the desire for a seat at the table tends to outweigh substantive issue concerns.*

There is no question from the results that, in contests between a "progay" and an "antigay" candidate, regardless of party or political philosophy, the voters will unite around the "progay" candidate.[2] The question before us is how self-identified LGBs will vote in an election in which there is no such clear bifurcation.

There is only one individual contest we could examine in which the public attitudes of both major candidates were positive toward their gay and lesbian constituents, the race for governor of California. In that contest, partisan cohesion was at its highest: a huge majority of lesbian and gay Republicans supported their party's nominee, as did a huge majority of lesbian and gay Democrats. It was the numerical superiority of the Democrats, combined with the liberal issue stands of California lesbian and gay independents, that led to the large majority for Dianne Feinstein among self-identifiers.

I note as well that the self-reporting of presidential voting in 1988, in which neither major candidate took antigay stands, found a third of lesbian and gay self-identifiers, and a plurality of those in Texas, reporting they voted for George Bush. In the event that a relatively "progay" Republican, or at least one with neutral feelings on LGB issues, were nominated for high office in Texas, with its large number of conservative and Republican lesbian and gay self-identifiers, it is possible that a real cleavage would occur within the community in that state.

These indicate that in contests in which there is no visible cleavage among candidates on LGB issues, substantive issue concerns and party loyalties will be the basis of voting decisions, rather than membership in the LGB community. This is not, however, to discount the independent effect of LGB self-identification on liberalism and (among women) feminism, which in turn directly affect issue stands and party affiliation.

The one exception to this rule appears to be the instance in which an open LGB is seeking election; in that case, the "symbolic" desire for a seat at the table of power and the respect it brings with it appears to override issue concerns. All candidates in the New York primary contest we examined supported lesbian and gay rights, were pro-choice on abortion, and wanted the state to do more about AIDS. However, given a viable lesbian candidate, the logistic regression showed that these substantive concerns were overridden utterly by a desire for a lesbian or gay elected representative in Albany.

Hypothesis 9: Role of Political Leadership

The extent of LGB voting cohesion in any given contest will depend on the unity of LGB political leaders, who, if united, should be able to mobilize LGB voters independently of any outside political force. *Not confirmed.*

Because of the presumption that group identification among LGBs would correlate strongly with group consciousness, I opined that the LGB vote would be mobilized by LGB political actors, without reference to the endorsements (or lack thereof) of heterosexuals. If the Glick poll can be generalized, in no respect was I more wrong. Certainly in the case of a district with a very large open lesbian and gay population, encompassing the neighborhood that is the LGB "Mecca" of eastern North America, with an extremely well educated, well-off population and some of the longest, most well established LGB-oriented publications and political organizations in the world, it is surprising indeed to see the extent to which the endorsement of the *New York Times* was deemed essential to the voting decisions of lesbian and gay voters. The *Times* served as a badge of "legitimacy," legitimacy in this case being defined as sufficient support from a major heterosexual-oriented source either to make Glick a serious contender or to affirm a previously uncertain predilection to vote for her.

At the same time, the failure of an LGB-oriented club (albeit one formed largely out of personal opposition to Glick and her friends) to endorse "the gay candidate" and the perception that she was a "one-issue" candidate took support away from her in her own lesbian and gay community. The former indicates that there is some importance, even within the core community, to unanimity; the near unanimity of the LGB endorsers was not enough for a small number of respondents. The latter indicates, again, the extent to which legitimacy in the eyes of the heterosexual majority is viewed as important within the homo-sexual and bisexual community. As noted in the Glick chapter, of the gay and lesbian respondents who indicated that at least one endorsement was important, just one in five cited only LGB-oriented political clubs or publications; and a majority cited *only* predominately heterosexual clubs or publications.

In each of the governor's races we have examined, as well as in the Glick primary, there was considerable doubt as to who the winner would be, and a perception that the pro-LGB candidate could win—bestowed in the latter case by non-LGB endorsements.

This raises an interesting question. Earlier we saw that a considerable share of the LGB voters appeared to be acting for reasons more symbolic than substantive, some supporting Glick in her high-salience contest in order to get the seat at the table, others supporting third candidates with no hope of winning in lower-salience congressional races. Yet in the Glick race we also see the vital importance of outside legitimation. Was it the outside endorsements, particularly by the *Times,* that in fact made the Glick race a high-salience election in the LGB community, bringing out voters who otherwise might not have voted? We cannot know at present, but this may be an explanation for the anomaly.

Additional Findings

Beyond the specific hypotheses, three unexpected findings are of interest and should be pursued in greater depth by political science, sociology, and psychology.

The Role of Religion

The relative secularism of the LGB self-identifiers is apparent throughout, and given the negative attitude of the Western religions toward homosexuality, this is hardly surprising. What is notable, and cause for study, is that there was in 1990 a significantly lower rate of lesbian and gay self-identification among those raised in the predominant religious tradition in a particular community — Protestantism in California and Texas, Catholicism in Massachusetts.

A similar finding with respect to Judaism in the Glick contest was ruled out, as lesbians, who tended to be long-term residents of the district, were just as Jewish as their nongay neighbors; it was gay male immigrants who were responsible for the disproportionately small Jewish share of the LGB sample. It is possible, therefore, that in the cases we have examined, especially those of California and Massachusetts, a considerable share of the religious disparity is attributable to interstate migration.

However, this cannot explain the finding on the national level; there is certainly no evidence that LGBs raised in the Protestant faiths are emigrating from the United States, and no reason to believe that they refrain from voting more than do self-identifiers of other backgrounds. The reasons a significantly smaller share of Protestants self-identify as LGB are deserving, therefore, of greater study.

Coalition Formation and Political Culture

Elazar's theory (1965) of "political culture" differences among the states, as discussed in chapter 5, appeared to be validated with respect to gay and lesbian voting behavior in California and Massachusetts, but not in Texas. In California, with its structural factors and political mores that encourage statewide coalition politics, white and nonfeminist lesbians and gays voted very much like nongay blacks, Latinos, and feminists. In Massachusetts, however, with a relatively permeable political structure and mores supporting group competition, there was a significant split even between gay and nongay feminists in the governor's race. (Only one gay respondent was not of European descent.) In Texas, however, where the political climate for coalition building and even internal cohesion among lesbians and gay men would seem to be the worst, "Anglo" and nonfeminist self-identifiers voted Democratic in the high-salience contests at rates equivalent to those of nongay Latinos and feminists.

Adam (1987) enunciated the theory that LGBs make up an essential part of the leftist coalition of "new social movements," in which are included feminists, "New Left" intellectuals, and group-conscious members of the labor movement and of previously disinherited racial and ethnic minorities. This postulated coalition crosses boundaries of race and class and has its theoretical basis in neo-Marxian notions of resistance to a dominant coalition comprising (1) capitalists seeking to maintain economic dominance through exploitation, and (2) traditionalist forces, particularly white Christian ultraconservatives, which seek to maintain the existing social order (see Adam 1987; Young 1990). That most feminists, union members, African Americans, and non-Cuban Latinos voted in most cases for the Democrats in 1990, as did most self-identified lesbians and gay men, is not surprising. This, however, tests the theory only in the most superficial way.

First, merely voting alike is not equivalent to belonging to a coalition. The existence of a coalition can be tested by the extent to which the members of each group in the purported coalition support the general aims and goals of the other groups. In this case, if a coalition exists, we would expect that heterosexual union members, feminists, and people of color would give some significant degree of support to LGB issues and candidates, and that LGB voters would likewise give support to campaigns for labor, racial justice, and women's rights. Based on the evidence at hand, we cannot be certain such a coalition exists.

We see that LGB voters are strongly pro-choice and that a huge share of lesbians are feminists, but we have no indicators with regard to race-related issues, and on labor issues we find mixed results: a somewhat larger share of lesbian and gay voters believed unemployment was the most significant economic problem in 1990, but by a tremendous margin they also said preserving the environment was much more important than preserving jobs; even after two years of economic stagnation, a three-to-two majority agreed with the latter proposition. Then we find in the Glick poll no stronger support for the winning candidate among union members, blacks, or Hispanics than among white, nonunion heterosexuals, and utterly minimal citation of LGB rights as an important issue by nongay members of these groups (data not shown). No indicator of feminism was available in the Glick poll.

Second, even if a coalition did exist, can we tell whether it was a liberal, integrationist coalition or a leftist, cultural-pluralist coalition as Adam postulates? One indicator is the degree of support given by voters with liberal or leftist views to third candidates as opposed to "mainstream" major party nominees. As previously noted, one lesbian or gay voter in six supported a non-major party candidate in the 1990 House elections, and this group was very liberal and almost unanimous in its support of Democratic nominees for governors. Yet we do not find such divergences among the other postulated coalition partners (data not shown). Further, perhaps more to the point, five gay/lesbian voters in six voted for the "mainstream" candidates. We further have seen the extent to which LGB voters, even in Deborah Glick's district, looked for validation of their LGB candidate by the "straight" media. This evidence is too scanty to reach any firm conclusions, but it indicates the likelihood that, whatever may be said by intellectuals and theorists, the large majority of LGB voters—and the other postulated coalition members—are pragmatic liberals rather than neoleftists.

Lesbian Bisexuality and the Gay Male Disproportion

Finally, the nineteen lesbian respondents to the Glick poll give us an interesting question to ponder with respect to the reasons for the relatively small number of lesbians compared to gay men, both in these political surveys and in sex research. Half of the lesbian self-identifiers, as against 20 percent of the self-identified gay men, reported in the second self-identification question that they were *not* exclusively homosexual. This interesting point is reinforced in the 1992 national data, in which the male-female gap in sexual self-identification was largely eliminated and—at the least coincidentally—bisexuals were included in the self-identification item.

The factors I cited earlier as possible reasons for the relative absence of lesbian respondents were (1) actual physiological differences that result in fewer women than men having same-sex attractions, (2) different social rules regarding acceptable same-gender intimacy between women and men, which make men more likely to recognize their desire for closeness to other men as sexual in nature, and (3) the fact that in the 1990 polls a disproportion of self-identified lesbians reported having children at home, which if generally true might inhibit lesbians disproportionately from reporting their sexual orientation on surveys completed anonymously but not in absolute privacy. What this "lesbian bisexuality" gives us is a fourth possible explanation that requires research: women with same-sex attractions may be more inclined to bisexuality, for reasons either physiological or sociological (or both), whereas men with same-sex attractions may be more inclined to exclusive homosexuality.

In conclusion, then, here is what practical politicians and the media who cover them ought to know:

There is a "lavender vote" in America, as opposed merely to gay, lesbian, and bisexual voters. It is characterized mainly by strong liberalism on domestic social issues among those who openly identify themselves as bisexual, lesbian, or gay. Although most self-identified LGBs are generally far more liberal and (among women) feminist than the rest of the population, some of their greater liberalism on social issues can be attributed solely to sexual identity. That is, regardless of their stands on other issues, LGB-identified people are more liberal than the rest of the population on cultural issues—including abortion rights, the environment, and drug policy—because of the experience of being lesbian, bisexual, or gay and facing the hostility of cultural conservatives.

The LGB vote is remarkable for its partisan fluidity. Although, all other things being equal, they tend to vote for Democrats in high-salience elections in which one candidate is clearly more "progay" than the other, LGB voters can be counted on to support the progay candidate, *regardless of party,* by margins of about three to one. Absent a high-salience contest, the vote splinters: two-thirds of self-identified LGBs split their tickets in 1990, exactly the same proportion as the rest of the population. About one in six LGB voters in lower-salience contests may support liberal or leftist independents as opposed to Democratic nominees. About one in four LGB voters appear to support Republicans, at least in contests in which the economy or foreign policy issues are paramount as opposed to social issues, and in a traditionalistic Southern state such as Texas many more LGBs may vote Republican.

Therefore, the lavender vote is up for grabs. Its social liberalism does not equate with voting for the Democrats. Democrats who take LGB voters for granted and Republicans who write off or deliberately alienate them both are making a serious mistake.

When we consider voters who *identify themselves* as gay or lesbian, the proportion of the gay and lesbian vote is small, just over 1 percent of the national voting population in 1990. When self-identified bisexuals are included this figure doubles, and equals the share of Latino voters in the United States. The rate of identification by age group tells us that its size may grow to about 4 or 5 percent of the total in the next twenty years.

Although LGB-oriented political activists do appear to have some effect in drawing attention to certain important contests, in a race in which an openly LGB candidate is seeking election, a majority of LGB voters appear to require the validation of that person's candidacy by non-LGB-oriented media and/or organizations in order to consider the candidate "serious."

What We Do Not Know

The most essential question left in the air is precisely how many homosexual and bisexual voters there actually are in the United States, and whether those who do not self-identify on the survey forms in fact vote the same as, or differently from, the self-identifiers. Therefore, there is no factual basis for claims such as the one bandied about after the 1992 election that one in six Clinton supporters were gay or lesbian and that this group was responsible for Clinton's election.

We can ascertain differences between objective membership in the working class and working-class/middle-class self-identification because survey respondents willingly tell us their incomes and job status. It is exceedingly unlikely that a survey on political attitudes and voting behavior will include questions about the respondents' hidden sexual attractions or behavior; or that, in the unlikely event such questions were asked, they would be answered. Our dilemma therefore appears likely to remain fixed. Existing sex research, indeed, has failed to probe this fundamental question sufficiently to draw any firm conclusions, although the Chicago study (Laumann et al. 1994) has made a welcome start. We are left to look only at the self-identifiers.

A second, related question is the extent to which those who do self-identify are possessed of the psychological mobilizing force called group consciousness. One correlate variable (high political interest) was assumed from the fact of voting in 1990, but the reverse appeared to be found in 1992 from the extremely large share of LGB first-time voters that year. A second correlate, relative youth, was consistently found in the data. A third correlate variable, education, was found in the national data, but found only inconsistently at the state level. The fourth, an augmented level of partisanship, was not found, even though the partisan tilt of the LGB voters was distinctive. Although these spotty effects may have resulted principally from small sample sizes, we cannot be certain. With no direct elements other than group identification available in the data sets examined, further exposition must await studies that specifically probe group consciousness among LGB self-identifiers.

We can make no certain claims, either, regarding the share of the LGB vote represented by the various theoretical strains we have discussed; nor can we say whether, and to what extent, a true electoral coalition has been established between LGB voters and other groups in the population. These too must be left to future research.

Prospects for 1996

At this writing no data were yet available from the 1994 general election exit polls, so we cannot say whether the trends found in 1990 and 1992 held up in the recent Republican sweep. However, it is possible to reach some conclusions about the lavender vote and for whom it is likely to go in 1996.

The Clinton Record on LGB Issues

Bill Clinton's strong appeals to LGB voters in the 1992 election were rewarded with strong support. In his first six months in office, however, he squandered much of the goodwill of the LGB community by vacillating on his pledge to lift the military ban and finally retreating into the "don't ask, don't tell" compromise, which, by the president's own account, may have left no one happy on any side of the issue.

The military issue was emblematic of Clinton's mixed record. He did appoint more open lesbians and gay men to influential posts than all previous presidents combined, including the first out-of-the-closet federal judge and the first two assistant cabinet secretaries. Yet after the midterm elections he withdrew or canceled the appointments of a gay man to an ambassadorship and of a progay heterosexual man as an assistant attorney general, and when he deemed an openly gay White House staffer too outspoken, the aide was sent into exile in a midlevel post in the Interior Department.

He did achieve substantial increases in AIDS research spending. He also appointed a national AIDS policy coordinator; but the post was ill-defined, access to the president was limited, and the initial coordinator's statements on safe sex were toned down after political pressure from her superiors. It was not the "AIDS czar" Clinton had promised. He also fired his outspoken surgeon general, Dr. Joycelyn Elders, who had encouraged frank discussion of sexuality and advocated condom distribution in high schools.

He did meet with national LGB leaders and, after intervening with the National Park Service to allow the demonstrators to use the Mall, sent a welcoming message to the April 1993 LGB march on Washington—the first president ever to embrace the gay rights cause even in part—although he hastily arranged an out-of-town speaking engagement for the Sunday on which the march took place.

He did publicly condemn the antigay ballot initiative efforts that proliferated in 1994, and Attorney General Janet Reno sent federal mediators to Ovett, Mississippi, to try to stop the violent harassment of a lesbian couple who had opened a women's retreat center there. Yet Reno's Justice Department continued its vigorous appeals of federal trial court decisions holding the military ban unconstitutional and failed to file a supporting brief when the Amendment 2 case went to the U.S. Supreme Court.

Taken together, the president's reputation as a "waffler," which appeared to play a significant part in the Democrats' midterm disaster, was manifested in his ambivalent support for the LGB cause. Early in the administration, ACT UP founder Larry Kramer bluntly asked the crowd at the march on Washington, "Why are we kissing this president's ass? He may be *saying* all the right things, but he isn't *doing* anything!" Yet many LGBs who were disappointed and angry about the policy defeats still appreciated the fact that Clinton's words and some of his deeds came down on their side; few doubted he was personally progay. One comic reportedly commented thus on Clinton after the gays-in-the-military defeat, "For the first time we got kissed before we got f—ed."

Alternatives to Clinton

LGB voters who are turned off by Clinton's substantive record have relatively few alternatives. The president's only somewhat serious challenger in his own party, who withdrew early on, was former Pennsylvania Governor Robert Casey, a devout Roman Catholic and social conservative best known for his unyielding opposition to abortion. Given the apparent conservative ascendancy in the country and the perception of Clinton among many voters as a "big-government liberal"—which also contributed to the Republican sweep—no serious candidate has emerged to challenge Clinton from the left; nor, if one should emerge, is that candidate likely to harm in the general election.

Among the likely Republican challengers, most were unsympathetic, if not downright homophobic. Columnist Pat Buchanan, for instance, has asserted that a "visceral recoil from homosexuality is the sign of a healthy society trying to preserve itself." The most moderate Republican on LGB issues, California Governor Pete Wilson, withdrew from the contest in late 1995. Wilson had signed a bill banning employment discrimination, but only after vetoing a more comprehensive nondiscrimination measure; he later vetoed a state domestic partnership bill. Another potential moderate on LGB issues, Pennsylvania Senator Arlen Specter, campaigned openly against "the intolerant right" as a pro-choice, libertarian conservative, although he is anathema to many women's rights supporters after his aggressive grilling of Anita Hill during the Clarence Thomas hearings, Specter too withdrew early.

Many LGB Republicans could comfortably have supported Specter in the primaries. But he was never likely to win the party's presidential nomination, given the preponderance of Religious Right activists and other cultural conservatives in the GOP nominating process. (Wilson was widely thought in 1995 to be a plausible nominee for vice president; Specter was not.) The prospective nominee, Senate Majority Leader Robert Dole of Kansas, is a social conservative with a record generally opposing LGB rights, despite waffling over acceptance of a campaign contribution from LGB republicans; he is not identified personally with the Religious Right but who has its confidence and support.[3]

The alternatives for the socially liberal majority of LGB self-identifiers in the fall of 1996, therefore, seem to be confined to (1) voting to reelect Clinton, (2) casting protest votes for leftist third party candidates who have no chance of winning, (3) staying home on election day, or (4) voting for a centrist independent with a chance of winning, à la Ross Perot, provided it is one who tends to support LGB civil rights. There is no indication at this point that the fourth option will emerge—but then, through the early part of the 1992 election cycle, Perot was not even thought of as a contender. (If Perot himself should run again, LGB Republicans may take refuge under his wing if they cannot countenance either Clinton or their own party's choice.)

The Democrats: How Far Can We Go?

Among the socially liberal activists who predominate in the Democrats' nominating process, the debate is less about what public policy toward LGB people ought to be—they are agreed on the need for and desirability of basic antidiscrimination laws, an end to the military ban, and some protection or benefits for same-sex couples—than about how far they can go in enacting these policies without alienating their more socially conservative copartisans and the moderate independents they need to win elections. After the gays-in-the-military flap of 1993 and the results of the 1994 elections, LGB rights supporters expect no legislative progress at the federal level until at least after the next elections, and the president certainly will propose no new LGB rights initiatives. The question for the Clinton campaign in 1996 is whether it should again make a strong appeal for LGB support, as one way of energizing the Democrats' base of progressive activists, or whether in appealing to the center Clinton should backtrack from his previous stands.

There is danger in both strategies, and not just as they apply to LGB voters. As noted previously, Clinton's main problem with the American public is the perception that he is a big-government, socially permissive liberal at heart (a "counterculture McGovernick," in House Speaker Newt Gingrich's colorful phrase), who nonetheless has a weak personal character, lacking the courage of his convictions and retreating at the first sign of opposition. If he reaches out to his LGB constituency and other social progressives as he did in 1992, albeit then as a "new Democrat," he will reinforce the perception that he is a permissive liberal. If he backs away from them, he will reinforce the perception that he is spineless. The record of his administration on LGB issues indicates that Clinton is trying to split the difference in order to help hold a dissatisfied left flank and a dissatisfied center together behind him.

The Republicans: Divided over LGB Issues

An interesting battle over homosexuality and gay rights has emerged within the GOP among three distinct groups of Republicans, somewhat reflective of the battle over cultural issues taking place in American society as a whole. Which group gets the upper hand in this intraparty battle probably will determine the extent to which the movement of more conservative and moderate LGBs to the Democrats in 1992 was a onetime phenomenon or the first manifestation of a long-term trend.

At one end of the scale, the Religious Right and its allies characterize homosexuality as an "abomination" and a threat to society, and advocate strong governmental action to clamp down on open homosexuals. This includes retaining or reinstituting criminal sodomy laws, repealing all gay rights and domestic partnership legislation, expelling all LGBs (open or closeted) from the military, denying permits for LGB-oriented restaurants, bookstores, and bars, banning public display of "homoerotic" art and defunding artists who create it, removing books and periodicals with positive or neutral depictions of homosexuality from libraries, denying LGB groups access to meeting space in public buildings and permits for parades and marches, banning or defunding LGB college and youth support groups and programs, forbidding discussion of homosexuality or "safer sex" in public school curricula, firing LGB teachers, and banning open LGBs from either conceiving or keeping custody of children— including their own.

At the other end of the scale, libertarian Republicans, mostly moderates and liberals from the Northeast but including "Mr. Conservative" Barry Goldwater of Arizona (who has an openly gay grandson), support gay rights legislation to varying degrees. Republican governors Wilson, Weld, Arne Carlson of Minnesota, and Lincoln Almond of Rhode Island all have signed statewide gay rights laws, and they and Christine Whitman of New Jersey have appointed open lesbians and gay men to significant positions in state government and in their campaigns, as have New York Mayor Rudolph Giuliani and Los Angeles Mayor Richard Riordan.

Midway between the two stand the "tolerant" (but not accepting) conservatives. This preponderant stream in the GOP appears to include both old-style "Main Street" Republicans such as Dole and Bush, and those "New Right" conservatives who emphasize economic opportunity, such as Quayle and Gingrich (the latter has an openly lesbian sister). In Gingrich's words, "Our position should be toleration; it shouldn't be condemnation and it shouldn't be promotion." Toleration as this group defines it does not include antidiscrimination laws, open LGBs in the military, or government funding for LGB artists; these are viewed as government action that "promotes" homosexuality or its acceptance.

The mainstream of Republican thought holds that heterosexuality is the natural and moral norm; that the causes of sexual orientation are unclear; and that society and government therefore should seek to push those who may be on the fence toward heterosexuality and "normal" marriage and family life. It also holds, however, that people who do become lesbian, gay, or bisexual should not be persecuted or cast out, rather allowed to live their lives, albeit with limitations. For example, "tolerant" social conservatives would not allow same-sex marriage or domestic partnership, and would not permit open LGBs to adopt or provide foster care for children, or to conceive them through artificial insemination or surrogacy. Yet they would not take LGB parents' own children away from them, and they appear to hold to a "don't ask, don't tell" policy with regard to schoolteachers and others who work closely with children.

The Lavender Vote in '96: Where Will It Go?

Perhaps the most important finding of this study for the average reader is that a significant share of the LGB vote is up for grabs between the two major parties. That this was true in 1990 is clear; it was less clear in 1992. What about after 1996, when LGB rights will likely be a major issue dwarfing 1992 and with the Religious Right holding a dominant position in the Republican nominating process?

The Republicans can maintain their substantial foothold of LGB support only if they do not cater to the demands of the Religious Right for the public condemnation of homosexuals. Postconvention and postelection surveys indicated that the 1992 Bush-Quayle campaign was tarnished, even among middle-of-the-road heterosexuals, by the perception of intolerance and narrow-mindedness as a result of the hard-right tone of that year's Republican convention. In this context, the ability of more gay-sympathetic congressional Republicans to keep conservative and moderate LGB voters in their electoral coalitions will depend largely on two factors: the extent to which the 1996 congressional elections become national rather than local in nature, and the extent to which the GOP national ticket plays up or plays down LGB and other "family values" issues.

In all likelihood, the 1996 congressional election will be nationalized. It will offer not merely a referendum on the president's performance, which usually does not significantly affect local congressional contests, but a direct choice between Bill Clinton's record and that of the Republican Congress, which codified its promises in unprecedented detail in its 1994 "Contract with America."

The remaining question, then, is whether the Republican nominee—unlikely in the extreme to embrace the libertarian position of public acceptance and civil rights advocated by Barry Goldwater and William Weld—will seek to energize his Religious Right supporters with antigay rhetoric, follow the path of "tolerance" most appealing to mainstream conservatives, or attempt, as Bush and Quayle did with questionable success, to split the difference. The GOP nominee will have far more flexibility in this regard than does the Democratic president, owing to the strong desire among Republicans to consolidate their newfound dominance of Congress and regain the White House to top off their success.

Therefore, whether Republicans maintain a significant share of the lavender vote will depend greatly on the personal feelings, expressions, and actions of one individual in one time frame: the 1996 presidential nominee. Given the likelihood of an uncommonly nationalized election, a GOP nominee who goes too far in alienating moderate and conservative LGBs may drive these voters permanently into the arms of the Democrats, just as (ironically) Barry Goldwater's opposition to federal civil rights laws in 1964 drove all but a smidgen of the remaining black Republicans into the Democratic Party. In like manner, a Republican nominee who shows personal respect for LGB voters and speaks against intolerance, even if he also praises "family values" and sees no need for federal nondiscrimination laws, probably will regain the LGB voters George Bush won in 1988 and lost in 1992, and regain them not just for the national nominees but for gay-sympathetic Republicans further down the ticket.

This study could not have been done a mere half-dozen years ago. We had no usable data on LGB voters, because no one would ask the essential self-identification question. Even today, standard national political surveys, and even the National Election Studies, do not include a self-identifier question. There was until the last few years a practical reason for this, other than mere concern about respondent objections: it was not certain that enough respondents would indicate a homosexual or bisexual identity to make the question worth asking. It is likely that some pollster reticence will continue until, within the next five to ten years, it becomes clear that roughly as many American voters will identify as gay, lesbian, or bisexual as will identify as Latino or Jewish.

Political surveys with samples of 1,000 or more—certainly those with samples of 1,500 or more—should include a self-identifier question, for this study has shown us beyond doubt that we have found a relatively small but potentially important force in American electoral politics. The addition of sexual identity to the repertory of standard demographic variables in political polls will give everyone interested in U.S. politics a greater ability to explain American elections, especially the voters' stands on important domestic social issues, and to predict who will vote for whom and why.

This study presents not "the truth" about the lavender vote, but a first draft of a few truths. Study in this field must continue, and each new random-sample survey will tell us more. I commend this topic strongly to all whose interest lies in general voting behavior and in the study of minority politics.

Even more, I commend the study of this topic to all who wish to advance this country's understanding of its gay, lesbian, and bisexual citizens. The same ancient prejudices, the same preference not to think about this group, and the same fears of being tainted by association with gay people that exist in the larger society, manifested in both law and custom, have worked their way hard into the breast of American political science. Such fear, if we allow it to rule us, will condemn us to being second-rate scholars and citizens. In spelling out the philosophy of the university he founded, Jefferson proclaimed what we should honor and live by as the scholar's credo: "Here we are not afraid to follow truth wherever it may lead, nor to tolerate any error so long as reason is left free to combat it."

Appendix: Methods

Because this study is the first of its kind on this group of voters, the source material comprises polling data from 1990 and 1992, the first years for which comparable polls are available. As noted previously, the number of probability-sample data bases available to researchers and usable for this study is extremely small, and I have employed most of them here.

The 1990 national data bases serve as the basis of my initial analysis, found in chapter 3, and a similar analysis of the 1992 data is reported in chapter 6.[1] I also look at five additional data sets. Of the state-level exit polls from 1990, three are from states in which the number of self-identified lesbian and gay respondents exceeded thirty; these are California, Texas, and Massachusetts. (Because only one state met this criterion in 1992—the LGB self-identifier item was included that year in only two state-level polls—no comparative analysis is possible, and I leave it aside.) In chapter 4 I examine these three state polls in detail, and also look briefly for comparative purposes at the pooled results from all twenty-one state exit polls from 1990 in which the gay/lesbian self-identifier question was asked, to determine whether they tend to reflect the national poll results. Finally, to examine the effects of various organizational influences on gay voting, I look in chapter 5 at what I have called the "Glick poll," an exit poll taken in a New York State Assembly primary in a lower Manhattan district in September 1990.

All the data bases examined here employed the same essential methodology. Within each sampling frame (be it nation, state, or assembly district), precincts were selected at random. Every Nth voter leaving the polling place at the selected precinct was handed a form by an employee or volunteer for the polling organization; the voter was asked to complete the form at an adjoining table, then to fold the completed form and place it in a designated box. Respondents were instructed both orally and in writing not to put their names or other identifying information on the forms.

Each form consisted of a single letter-size sheet of paper printed on two sides, in two columns on each side. Answers to questions were indicated by checking a box beneath each question. No open-ended answers were sought, and volunteered answers falling outside the categories in the check-off boxes were not tabulated.

In each instance the gay/lesbian or LGB self-identifier question was asked in a so-called grab bag section in the second column on the back page of the survey. In all the VRS polls, this was the last batch of questions asked. The "grab bag" section opened with the words "Which Of The Following Describe You? (Check All That Apply)." Beneath this heading appeared several demographic or attitudinal self-categorizations not asked about in other parts of the survey; examples include "First-time voter," "Strong feminist," "Married," "Live in rent-controlled/rent-subsidized housing," "Veteran," and "Fundamentalist or evangelical Christian." The actual items in the "grab bag" varied from survey to survey.

In the 1990 VRS surveys the last such item listed (and therefore the last item on the form) read "Gay or lesbian." In 1992 the self-identifier read "Gay, lesbian or bisexual." The Glick poll included the "Gay or lesbian" item toward the middle of its grab bag.

In addition, the Glick poll alone asked a second, separate question at the end of the form: "Which of the following best describes your sexual orientation?" Responses permitted were, in order, "Exclusively heterosexual," "Mostly heterosexual," "Bisexual," "Mostly homosexual," and "Exclusively homosexual."

The Data Sets

With the exception of the Glick poll, all data were collected, tabulated, and analyzed initially by Voter Research and Surveys, Inc. (VRS) of New York City, a polling consortium of the four major broadcast news organizations in the United States (ABC, CBS, CNN, and NBC). (VRS merged in 1993 into the new Voter News Service.) The 1990 VRS data bases were obtained from the Roper Center (Storrs, Connecticut), and the 1992 data bases from the Inter-University Consortium for Political and Social Research (Ann Arbor, Michigan). In addition to the usual demographic weighting, all VRS-connected data sets at the state level were weighted to reflect the actual official outcome of the elections for governor and U.S. senator in each state; no such weighting based on election returns was done to the national surveys.

The Glick poll was provided to me in July 1992 by the joint courtesy of its principal creators: Dr. Robert W. Bailey, then of Columbia University (now with Rutgers University, Camden Campus); Dr. Kenneth S. Sherrill of Hunter College, City University of New York; and Dr. Murray S. Edelman, then director of surveys for VRS (now editorial director of Voter News Service).

The 1990 national exit polls. Two versions of a national exit survey were conducted on the date of the general election, 2 November 1990. The four networks belonging to VRS originally formulated a single set of national and state-level surveys. CBS chose in addition to formulate its own national questionnaire, which included far fewer demographic variables than did the joint four-network (ABC-CBS-CNN-NBC) poll but a far larger number of questions about the voters' attitudes on issues. The gay/lesbian self-identifier question, fortunately, was included in both versions.

As discussed in chapter 3, the four-network national survey in 1990 has been referred to as the VRS form, and the additional CBS national questionnaire as the CBS form. A number of questions, however, were identical, both in wording and in placement, on the VRS and CBS forms. The pooled responses to such questions have been referred to as the U.S.A. data. The number of respondents (N) to the VRS form was 10,565; to the CBS form, 9,323; and to the combined U.S.A. questions, 19,888.

The CBS and VRS versions of the poll were administered to different voters in the same sample precincts. There were not, therefore, two separate samples drawn; this is simply two different versions of the same poll, not two separate, simultaneous polls.

Every respondent to the national surveys was asked how she or he voted in the election for the House of Representatives in her or his congressional district; rather than listing the specific candidates, the voter simply was asked whether she had voted for the Democrat, the Republican, someone else, or whether she had not voted in the House race. Using the same format, the voter was asked about her vote in the contest for U.S. senator and/or governor in the states in which such contests were being held. Common demographic questions asked in both forms included race, gender, party affiliation, and a few of the grab bag questions, including the gay/lesbian self-identifier. Additional questions, broken out by the specific survey in which they were asked, will be set forth later in this appendix.

The 1990 state exit polls. The four networks also agreed on a format for the exit polls taken on specific contests in each of the forty-two states in which a governor or U.S. senator, or both, was being elected;[2] the questions largely resembled the national VRS (four-network) form. VRS used a "short form" of a single page in half of these states, which did not include the "grab bag" and, therefore, excluded the gay/lesbian self-identifier.

Initially I examined the surveys from all twenty-one states in which the gay/lesbian self-identifier was asked. In many of these states, the small numbers of respondents made the data useless.[3] In the manner of Edelman (1991), I then pooled the responses; these are reported in tables 4.1 and 4.2 in chapter 4 for descriptive purposes only.

As noted above, California (eighty-six gay/lesbian respondents), Texas (fifty respondents), and Massachusetts (thirty-three respondents) had a sufficient number of gay/lesbian self-identifiers to make rudimentary comparative analysis possible. As it happens, these three states also hosted close gubernatorial contests in which issues of concern to lesbians and gay men were on the candidates' agendas, as discussed in chapter 4.

The state-level polls did not ask respondents about their votes for the House of Representatives, in that none of the networks thought it useful to survey the number of respondents necessary to attempt to call individual House contests with exit poll results.

Additional specific questions asked on each state's poll are addressed in chapter 4.

The 1992 national data sets. The 1992 presidential exit polls were conducted jointly for the four participating networks by VRS. However, in order to ask a larger number of questions without making the poll form overly lengthy, VRS developed three different versions of the poll, labeled Version W, Version Y, and Version P, which were administered to different respondents at the same sample precincts. The dependent variables, party affiliation, and a few essential demographic variables were included in all versions; other dependent and attitudinal variables were found in one or (sometimes) two versions. The sample sizes for each version, interestingly, were very different. The total sample N for all three versions was 15,300. But Version W included more than half the respondents, 8,277; Version Y had an N of 4,089; and Version P had an N of 2,934.

The Glick poll. The Glick poll is discussed in detail in chapter 5. Total sample N was 516, of whom 339 voted in the contest studied.

Data Analysis

All data analyses were carried out using SPSS-X (for the national and state-level exit polls) or SPSS-PC (for the Glick poll). Both crosstabulations and logistic regressions were employed. All figures reported (with two exceptions) employ weighted data, and in all instances statistical significance was measured using weighted data. Significance was established at the level of .05 using two-tailed tests. Because of the small gay/lesbian sample sizes in some cases, I also report some relationships significant at the level of less than .10, which approach but do not reach statistical significance according to the .05 standard above.

In the case of the crosstabulations, Pearson's chi-square was used to measure significance.

In the case of the logistic regressions, I report the B (odds ratio) statistic, standard error (SE), and the Wald statistic, which equals $(B - SE)^2$ and which measures the relative strength of relationship among each of the independent variables on the dependent—that is, the higher the Wald, the stronger the variable is in the mix. Statistical significance was determined using a two-tailed Student's t-test of the Wald statistic. When models were respecified, total percentage improvement in predictive power was used to assess the corrections to each model.

The Empirical Tests

The next pages discuss the measures employed to test each of the nine hypotheses set out at the end of chapter 2. Following the description of the testing procedure is a section setting out and discussing each of the indicators employed.

Hypothesis 1: Rate of identification. An initial frequency distribution was run of each data set to determine the number of gay/lesbian or LGB self-identifiers and their proportion of the total sample. In each case a breakdown by sex was done as well. In the case of the 1990 national surveys, the VRS and CBS data sets were compared to determine consistency of results. The results from the twenty-one state-level data sets from 1990 were added together, with breakdown by sex and by region of the country.

Hypotheses 2 and 3: Comparisons with non-LGB voters. A crosstabulation by sexual self-identification of all demographic, attitudinal, and voting behavior variables employed in the surveys then was undertaken, and most of these results are reported, along with statistically significant results at the levels of .05, .01, and .001. These specific variables are set forth and discussed in the "Indicators" section later in this appendix.

Hypotheses 4 and 5: Intragroup divisions. Next, the same method was used to crosstabulate gay and lesbian or LGB self-identifiers alone by sex, party affiliation, and, in 1990, identification as a "strong feminist." In addition, because of unexpected differences found based on age categories when the data were examined, I created three age cohorts and tested these for significant differences as well; this is explained further in chapter 3. Only significant and near-significant (less than .10) differences based on sex, age, party, and feminism are reported.

Independents and the small number of third party identifiers were grouped together for analysis. Also, as discussed in chapter 3, because of the unusually large share of the lesbian and gay subsample that voted for third candidates for the House of Representatives in 1990, these voters were tested as well for their demographics, attitudes, and voting behavior in the Senate and governor's races.

In the case of feminism, which was measured only in the 1990 battery of polls, because of the minimal number of gay men who identified themselves as strong feminists ($N = 6$), the independent variable was coded into three responses: gay men, nonfeminist lesbians, and feminist lesbians. At the national level, only respondents to the VRS form could be included in the feminism tests, because the "strong feminist" indicator was not included in the CBS form; at the state level, all respondents were included.

In the three state-level polls, an additional set of crosstabulations of the entire polling sample was run, showing any differences in voting behavior in individual contests between the gay and nongay populations broken down by race and by feminist identification, in order to test whether vote choice among self-identified lesbians and gay men was consistent with that of nongay feminists, Latinos, and African Americans. This was done to assess the Adam (1987) hypothesis that lesbians and gay men form part of a neoleftist coalition with feminists and members of racial minorities, noted in chapters 1 and 2, and additionally as a means of assessing the effect of state "political culture" in Elazar's reckoning (1965) on self-identified lesbians and gay men in each state (see chapter 4).

In the case of the Glick poll, all respondents were registered Democrats, almost all gay and lesbian respondents were white, and no feminism indicator was included; therefore, the only intrasample breakdown of this kind was done by sex.

Hypothesis 6: The "sexuality gap." The next tests employed logistic regression analysis of all respondents. The first logit test sought to determine the demographic indicators that correlated with sexual self-identification and the extent to which they had any power to predict whether a respondent would self-identify as gay or lesbian (1990) or as gay, lesbian, or bisexual (1992). I included in this analysis any demographic indicators that were found to be statistically significant in the crosstabular analysis and that had any sound theoretical basis for inclusion. Indicators with nominal values were recoded into bivariate "dummies."[4]

Once the demographic correlates were determined, I sought to create a model incorporating theoretically sound demographic and political orientation variables that would wipe out any independent effect of sexual self-identification on issue stands and vote choice. In other words, I sought to determine whether, once one had controlled for the right factors, self-identifications as gay men, bisexuals, and lesbians still had an independent effect on American elections.

A four-step test of the effect of gay/lesbian or LGB self-identification on vote choice was undertaken. First, the independent effect of gay/lesbian or LGB self-identification, without more, on vote choice was assessed. The demographic correlates were added to determine whether the independent effect of sexual self-identification remained significant. Because party identification (Campbell et al. 1960) and incumbency (Jacobson 1983) are considered the most important factors in determining the vote for Congress, I then in like manner added these variables to the model. Finally, because of the augmented levels of liberalism and feminism found in the gay and lesbian sample (chapter 3), these two additional variables were included in the 1990 analyses as well. No feminism indicator was included in the 1992 data, so only ideology was controlled for in this last step in the 1992 contests.

The final set of tests of the 1990 data examined the independent effect, if any, of sexual self-identification on congressional or gubernatorial voting when a standard retrospective voting model, originally applied to presidential elections (Campbell et al. 1960; Fiorina 1981), is employed; this model is discussed in chapter 3. As discussed in chapter 6, owing to a lack of valid indicators, no retrospective analysis of the 1992 presidential election could be performed.

Hypotheses 7, 8, and 9: Voting in individual contests and the role of leaders. The same logistic regression tests were performed on seven individual contests included in the three state-level exit polls from 1990 that were examined. These were designed specifically to confirm or refute the results found in the aggregated national polls on individual contests. The state results were compared with each other to determine consistency with the national result, and to attempt to explain any state-by-state variations.

The Glick poll also assisted in evaluating Hypothesis 8, on the weight of symbolic versus substantive factors in the way lesbians and gays cast their votes. Initial crosstabulations determined the share of voters who cited gay/lesbian rights, AIDS, and abortion as top substantive issue concerns, and asked respondents about the ("symbolic") importance of having a gay/lesbian representative. These factors were included in the logistic regression analysis discussed next.

The only direct test of Hypothesis 9, on the role of LGB political leaders, could be made using the data in the Glick poll; respondents were asked whether each campaign had contacted them within the "past few days," and which of thirteen local periodical and political club endorsements, if any, had been important in their voting decision. The latter list included clubs and publications with both "gay" and "mainstream" orientations. An initial crosstabulation determined significant differences between the gay and non-gay samples and, as discussed above, within the sample between the gay men and the lesbians. Another crosstabulation determined significant differences, among the sample as a whole and among the gay/lesbian subsample, using a vote for or against Deborah Glick as the dependent variable.

Then, incorporating the indicators upon which significant differences were found, an initial model to explain voting for Glick was created. This model was tested first using the entire sample of voters, then tested again using the gay/lesbian self-identifiers only. A revised model, excluding indicators that were clearly insignificant, then was run, again first with the entire sample, then with the gay/lesbian subsample only; thus the different effects of group leadership and symbolic and substantive factors on the gay/lesbian subsample could be assessed.

Indicators

The unique indicators in the Glick poll are detailed in chapter 5. This section discusses the indicators in the national and state-level exit polls reported in chapters 3, 4, and 6.

Demographics. All national and state exit polls asked respondents about each of the following demographic factors: age,[5] sex, race, sexual self-identification, frequency of religious attendance (phrased "Attend religious services at least once a month"), and whether the respondent was a first-time voter. The state exit polls and the 1990 VRS national poll form additionally asked about the respondent's education and household income levels,[6] in which religion she was *raised,* and whether she was married, belonged to a labor union, or had a family member in the armed forces or reserves.[7] The CBS form asked the respondent's type of employment and whether she was a government employee, her religious affilia- tion *today,* whether she was a "fundamentalist or evangelical Christian," had children under age eighteen, was a military veteran, a gun owner, or the victim of a crime within the last year. In addition, based on the location of the sample precinct, each case was coded for region of residence (East, Midwest, South, or West) and the size of the locality.[8] The 1992 national survey versions contained an identical question asking one's "religious affiliation" which folded together the two questions from 1990.

Once demographic relationships were established, those found in the cross- tabulation to have a significant relationship (at .05) with sexual self-identification were placed in a logistic regression model with sexual self-identification as the dependent variable to determine whether, and to what extent, they had the power to predict gay/lesbian self-identification. (In the case of the 1990 national data, three such equations were run, using the VRS, CBS, and U.S.A. indicators, respectively.)

Attitudes. The 1990 VRS form and state polls asked two questions important for our purposes that were not included in the 1990 CBS form: the respondent's self-stated ideology on a three-point scale (liberal, moderate, or conservative), and whether the respondent was a strong feminist. The ideology scale was carried over into the 1992 Version W; no feminism question was asked in any form of the 1992 poll. The VRS national demographic indicators were used to construct logistic regression models that attempted to determine likelihood to identify as a liberal and as a strong feminist; sexual self-identification first was tested alone, then with the other hypothesized indicators.

Two attitudinal questions were asked of all 1990 respondents to both of the national polls and all state exit polls studied: their party affiliation and whether they approved of President Bush's performance in office.

Another set of questions may be classed as "the same thing asked in different ways." In 1990, the CBS form asked respondents to name the single most important issue in their vote for Congress, whereas the VRS form asked them to name up to two. The four-network form asked whether abortion should be legal always, sometimes, or never; the CBS form broke the middle category into two: "in most cases" and "in cases of rape, incest, or to save the life of the mother." VRS asked whether the country was "right" to be in the Persian Gulf at present, whereas CBS asked whether we should stay there even at the risk of U.S. lives. CBS asked whether "most" members of Congress deserve reelection; VRS asked voters, in separate questions, whether they approved of Congress's performance and whether they supported congressional term limits.

The 1992 poll asked three not-quite-identical questions regarding the role of family and traditional values and how the neglect of these might relate to the country's social problems.

The questions in the 1990 VRS form were better suited to testing retrospective models of voting behavior (Fiorina 1981). The respondents were asked to assess the current condition of the national economy, predict its condition next year, and give a personal retrospective assessment of whether they were better off, worse off, or "about the same" as they were two years before; they also were asked whether they thought the country was seriously off track.

The CBS questions, in contrast, sought more to tie vote choice to issue attitudes. In addition to the issue questions noted above, CBS asked its respondents their attitudes on the death penalty, defense spending, and the relative merit of law enforcement as against education and treatment in controlling drug abuse. Its economic-related questions asked whether unemployment or inflation was more in need of control, whether the president or Congress was better able to handle the deficit, and whether saving the environment was more important than saving jobs. CBS also did ask a general institutional trust question regarding the federal government.

As noted previously, the 1992 battery included no question on general presidential performance, which precluded any retrospective analysis.

The state-level attitudinal questions were tailored to the circumstances of each state and are discussed individually in chapter 4. However, the VRS questions on ideology, feminism, abortion attitude, and whether the country was seriously off track were carried over into each state survey. (No CBS-specific questions appear in any of the state polls.) As in the VRS national form, each state survey contained a list of seven to nine issues, from which the respondent could choose up to two that were the most important in her vote *for governor,* as opposed to her vote for Congress as in the national polls. An additional list of seven to nine questions was asked in each state relating to personal impressions or qualities of the candidates or campaign factors such as televised debates, from which the respondent could choose, again, up to two that had an important effect on her vote choice for governor.

Voting behavior. The 1990 and 1992 national forms asked respondents their vote choice, by party (not by name), for U.S. representative and, in the appropriate states, for U.S. senator and/or state governor. The 1992 vote choice for president was asked by name of candidate and party. The state polls asked the vote choice, by name and party, for Senate and governor, but *not* for the House (because VRS was not attempting to call individual House races on election night on the basis of exit polls). In most state polls in which statehouses were contested, respondents were asked when they had made up their minds in the gubernatorial contest: within the past three days, the past week, the past month, or before then.

In addition, the state polls, the 1990 VRS national form, and all three 1992 national forms asked respondents to report their vote (if any) in the 1988 presidential election. In all cases this resulted in an apparent overreporting of support for George Bush. The VRS national form asked voters to look ahead to 1992 and indicate their likely presidential vote choice (Bush, "the Democrat," or "not sure"), and their preference among seven listed candidates for the Democratic nomination.[9] The 1992 version asked whether each respondent had voted for Ronald Reagan in 1984.

CBS asked respondents to its 1990 national form three specific questions about their congressional vote choice: whether their vote was pro- or anti-Bush (or whether Bush was not a factor in their decision), whether effectiveness, stand on issues, or party affiliation was most important in the vote choice, and whether campaigns "this year" (1990) were more positive, more negative, or about the same as campaigns in the past.

For purposes of testing predictive models using logistic regressions, several multivariate indicators were broken out into a number of bivariate "dummies," most significantly vote choice in each contest (dependent variable) and party affiliation (both dependent and independent). Several independent nominal variables also were broken into "dummies," including region, size of locality, the religion variables, and partisan incumbency—whether a Democratic incumbent, a Republican incumbent, or no incumbent was seeking reelection to the office in question.

NOTES

Notes to Chapter One

1. This dubious number had its basis in the 1992 VRS national exit poll, discussed at length in chapter 6, which showed that 72 percent of self-identified lesbians, gay men, and bisexuals (the bisexual category was added that year) voted for Clinton. It also showed that 2.2 percent of the weighted sample (2.5 percent of the raw sample) self-identified as gay, lesbian or bisexual. Mixner and other gay leaders, however, employed the Kinsey-based, often abused 10 percent estimate and claimed that gay people who had voted for Clinton accounted for 7.2 percent of all American voters—roughly one-sixth of the 43 percent of the national popular vote that Clinton received.

2. The observant reader will note that "gay" sometimes is used in its generic sense as a nickname for all persons with romantic attractions to members of their own sex, and sometimes is used solely to delineate homosexual men, as opposed to homosexual women, who in the main prefer to be called lesbians. For the sake of simplicity and clarity I often will refer to the "gay rights" movement, because this is what it is called in the press and how it is referred to in general conversation.

3. The exact percentage of Americans who are homosexual or bisexual is uncertain, but it is possible to state a range. Kinsey's nonrandom-sample studies in the 1940s (Kinsey et al. 1948; Institute for Sex Research 1953) estimated that 14 percent of American men and 6 percent of women were exclusively homosexual *in behavior* for at least three years of their lives. From this was derived the much-used estimate that homosexuals make up 10 percent of the population. Fay et al. (1989), using 1970 random-sample data, estimated that 6 percent of U.S. men were exclusively or predominately homosexual; women were not studied.

Janus and Janus's quota sample (1993) found that 9 percent of U.S. men and 5 percent of women reported either ongoing or "frequent" homosexual activity. In a separate question, again 9 percent of the men and 5 percent of the women self-identified as either homosexual or bisexual. (Four percent of men and 2 percent of women called themselves homosexual; 5 percent of men and 3 percent of women called themselves bisexual.) The self-identifiers and the actors did not precisely overlap; Janus and Janus state (but do not present data) that many persons who reported frequent or ongoing gay experiences still identified as "heterosexual." (Twenty-two percent of men and 17 percent of women reported having had at least one homosexual experience.)

Most reliably and recently, the random-sample, nationwide "Chicago sex survey" (Laumann et al. 1994) found that 10.1 percent of men and 8.7 percent of women exhibited either same-sex desire, same-sex sexual behavior, or homosexual or bisexual self-identification, or some combination of the three. Interestingly, only 2.6 percent of the men and 1.3 percent of the women self-identified as gay, lesbian, or bisexual in this in-person survey—less than half of all those of each sex who reported having engaged in same-sex behavior. This question will be discussed in greater depth in chapter 2.

4. The only voting behavior data collected on self-identified bisexuals are the "Glick poll" discussed in chapter 5 and the 1992 battery of primary and general election exit polls. The bisexuals are grouped together with lesbians and gay men in a single self-identification item in the latter poll, leaving no way to distinguish among them.

5. This usage may irritate some readers, so let me explain my conscious decision to employ it. Endless repetition of the term "lesbians, gay men, and bisexuals" would be cluttersome. "Gay" or "homosexual" is not an option: it is inaccurate to call bisexuals "gay" or "homosexual," and some lesbians are offended by being called "gay" rather than "lesbian" (interestingly, to a much lesser extent, the reverse is true as well). Some of the all-inclusive terms that members of the movement have adopted, however, such as "lambda," "rainbow," "lesbigay," "queer," or even "lavender," used in the title, are sufficiently obscure, slangy, or full of other meanings that to use them here would likely lead to the study being dismissed as frivolous. "LGB" was the happiest medium I could find.

In like manner, because the non-self-identifiers presumably include homosexuals and bisexuals who do not choose to self-identify for the reasons discussed later, it would be inaccurate to call them "straight" or "heterosexual" voters. In most instances, therefore, I call them "non-LGBs" when comparing them to lesbians, gay men, *and* bisexuals, and "nongay" for simplicity's sake when comparing them to lesbians and gay men in the 1990 data sets, which do not allow for bisexual self-identification.

6. Particularly good summaries are found in Schmalz 1992a and Turque et al. 1992.

7. The number of marchers is in dispute. The District of Columbia government estimated that 1.1 million persons took part in the 25 April march. The National Park Service, however, estimated three hundred thousand. March organizers claimed that the latter figure resulted from political pettiness by former Bush administration employees still in charge of the Park Service, who had planned to reseed the Mall that weekend and allowed the marchers to use it only after the intervention of the Clinton White House and Interior Secretary Bruce Babbitt. The National Gay and Lesbian Task Force, the country's second largest gay rights organization, later settled on a split-the-difference figure of seven hundred thousand.

8. As an example of some newspapers' sensitivity: in March and April 1993, Lynn Johnston's comic strip about a Canadian family, "For Better or for Worse," featured a five-week story line about a seventeen-year-old boy who "came out" as gay to friends and parents. As a result, nineteen newspapers in the United States canceled their subscriptions to the strip permanently, and another fifty refused to run the gay story line (Kramer 1993).

9. Given that this is so, and given the complete absence of published work on LGB people as voters, it is quite possible that the former is responsible in large part for the latter—in other words, it may be that fear by researchers of being associated with a study

of homosexuals is the reason for the absence of any such study up to now. I hope that, the ground now having been broken, fruitful future research on this important topic may take place with less hesitation.

10. It is notable as well that the union movement in the United States increasingly is dominated by white-collar professionals, particularly teachers and other government employees, whereas blue-collar unionism has declined dramatically in the past forty years.

11. The question was first used on an experimental basis in the New York Democratic presidential primary. Four percent of New York primary voters identified themselves as gay or lesbian, and of this predominantly white group, 57 percent cast their ballots for Jesse Jackson, who had made strong appeals for gay and lesbian support. The question was asked thereafter in all ten Democratic presidential primaries remaining that year, including those in Pennsylvania, Ohio, California, and New Jersey.

12. Robert W. Bailey, interview, 28–29 July 1992.

13. The U.S. Census found about 145,000 U.S. households in 1990 constituting same-sex "unmarried couples" (DiLallo and Krumholtz 1994).

14. The question appeared on the second page of the two-page form, in a "grab bag" of demographic and attitudinal descriptions headed, "Which of the following describes you? (Check all that apply)"; the answer item, appearing at the bottom of the list of eight to ten items (depending on the state) such as "union member" and "first-time voter," read "gay or lesbian."

15. VRS merged in 1993 with the News Election Service, which reports actual returns on election nights, to form Voter News Service (VNS).

16. This data set, regrettably, was not publicly available at the time of this study, and has not been examined here.

Notes to Chapter Two

1. This last alternately is expressed in voluntary "working-class" self-identification and/or in membership, not always voluntary, in a labor union.

2. There is not universal agreement on this. Young (1990), synthesizing New Left thinking on the subject, wholly redefines "oppression" as systemic and essentially organic, requiring no oppressing group or ideology and no conscious intent to oppress. For her, oppression is the result of unquestioned adherence to "norms, habits, and symbols" that diminish certain human beings because of their membership in groups, which membership is an integral and inseparable part of what they are. Further, like a virus, oppressive assumptions infect and are reproduced in nearly all economic, social, and political institutions and, therefore, oppression cannot be done away with by changing laws or even systems of government.

3. Interestingly to the non-Marxist, a (fairly simplistic) Times Mirror cluster analysis of a survey of roughly fifty-seven thousand American voters in 1987 found that, of their eleven clusters, the two that formed the support base of the Republican Party were "enterprisers," voters most concerned with maintaining free enterprise and limiting

government intervention in the economy, and "moralists," those most concerned with using government to reinforce traditional Christian moral teachings and to fight what they consider to be moral degeneration (Ornstein et al. 1988).

4. All members of the Mattachine Society initially were men. The Daughters of Bilitis, founded in 1955, was the first lesbian organization in America (Martin and Lyon 1972).

5. Illinois became the first state to remove its consensual "sodomy" law from the books in 1961. To date, twenty-eight states (most recently, at this writing, Nevada) and the District of Columbia either have repealed their laws through the legislative process or had them struck down by state supreme courts as unconstitutional. The U.S. Supreme Court, in *Bowers v. Hardwick* (1986), ruled five to four that homosexual acts between consenting adults in private are not protected by the federal Constitution's right to privacy enunciated in previous rulings on contraception and abortion, and therefore twenty-two states retain laws criminalizing such behavior (Murdoch 1993).

6. The use of this term sticks in the craw of every LGB organization and every serious researcher on the subject of homosexuality and bisexuality. Sexual attraction, or even sexual behavior, manifestly is not a "lifestyle" in any meaningful sense of the term; the use of the term "lifestyle" appears to be a matter of initial carelessness compounded by sloth. Any readers who plan survey research in this area are warned hereby to employ accurate terminology in order to achieve valid results.

7. So named for the National Opinion Research Center (NORC), headquartered at the University of Chicago, which conducted the survey over seven months in 1993.

8. It is curious that no objections are raised to detailed public education about narcotics on the ground that such will promote drug abuse. Sherrill (1991) points out a similar lack of congressional concern with AIDS education aimed at intravenous drug users compared to such concern with respect to "safer sex" education for homosexual adults.

9. Writing for the majority, Justice Byron White (who dissented in both *Griswold* and *Roe*) framed the issue around the conduct in question rather than on the constitutional right to privacy issue, stating, "there is [no] constitutional right to commit homosexual sodomy." Chief Justice Warren Burger concurred, and quoted the opinion of the eighteenth-century English legal commentator Sir William Blackstone that sodomy was "abominable and unspeakable" and a crime "worse than rape."

The *Bowers* decision is discussed further by Goldstein (1988) and Vieira (1988).

10. These three countries still draw a distinction between same-sex and opposite-sex marriages; same-sex couples may not be married in the state church, nor may they adopt children. The Netherlands also has national legislation recognizing same-sex "domestic partnerships" for certain purposes, but does not give them the status of legal marriages.

11. Missouri and, until 1995, Virginia, alone among the states, held the legal position that living in a homosexual relationship per se was unrebuttable proof of unfitness and, therefore, sufficient grounds to deprive a natural parent of custody. This rule was applied in 1993 in Henrico County, Virginia (suburban Richmond), in the well-known case of

Sharon Bottoms, a divorced woman living with her female lover. Custody of her two-year-old son was taken from her and given to Bottoms's mother by a trial judge, solely on the grounds of her live-in lesbian relationship. There was no allegation of abuse or neglect, and the child's father, Bottoms's ex-husband, supported Bottoms in the custody fight; but Virginia retains its felony sodomy law on the books. The Virginia Supreme Court, in a four to three decision on 21 April 1995, abandoned the rule of unfitness per se it laid down in *Roe v. Roe* (1985) but upheld the trial court, on grounds of other alleged (though unproven) deficiencies in Bottoms's character and of the possible stigma and "social ostracism" that might attach to her child as a result of the mother's living arrangement.

12. A trial court in Denver in December 1993 ruled that Amendment 2, as the measure is known, violated the U.S. Constitution and was therefore void; this ruling was affirmed by a six to one majority of the Colorado Supreme Court. The case at this writing is on appeal to the U.S. Supreme Court.

13. For the sake of clarity, I am referring here to the child's becoming aware of the fact that differences in skin color or genitals are important to the people in her life, *not* to the political form of "group consciousness" discussed in this chapter.

14. I do not enter into the debate about what "causes" sexual attraction to one or another sex, or to both; the evidence is inconclusive, although Tripp (1975) and most subsequent researchers believe that the direction of one's sexual attraction is set in early childhood (if not before birth, by physiology), and is largely or entirely beyond the conscious control of parents. Most of the considerable share (43 percent) of the population who believe that homosexuality is "a choice" (Schmalz 1993) likely would concede that some preexisting internal inclination exists to act on homosexual attraction or "temptation," be it derived from nature, nurture, or Satan, and that the principal aim of the laws and practices we have discussed is strongly to discourage youth and adults alike from acting on this attraction.

15. The theoretical concept of "group consciousness" defined as such probably goes back to Engels's introduction to *The Communist Manifesto*.

16. Because of fears that group members could be arrested simply for discussing homosexuality, the Mattachine at first was organized into mutually anonymous cells organized from the top down, along the lines of the Communist Party. By 1953, however, partly because of concern over the rumored Communist ties of some of the leaders, partly because of a growing confidence that their activities could be pursued more publicly, the society became an open, membership-run organization. Although the organization effectively died out on the West Coast and in New York after the Stonewall riots, the Washington, D.C., branch, founded by longtime activist Dr. Frank Kameny, survived into the 1980s.

17. The American Psychiatric Association's governing board removed homosexuality from its list of mental and emotional disorders in 1972. Sharp protest in the ranks led to an unprecedented membership referendum on the issue in 1973, wherein the members voted by a margin of three to two to uphold the board. The American Psychological Association followed suit in 1975, and the World Health Organization did so in 1990.

It is well to note that Kameny was a particularly militant "homophile," organizing the first gay pickets of the White House, the State Department, and other government facilities and lobbying for an end to the Civil Service's exclusion of homosexuals from government employment. Following Stonewall, Kameny was the principal founder of the liberationist Gay Activists Alliance in Washington, and ran in the first election in the District of Columbia for a nonvoting delegate to the U.S. House of Representatives in 1971, the first openly gay candidate for Congress in the country.

18. Friedan later repented—mostly—of her remarks and joined NOW leaders in 1973 who officially proclaimed lesbian rights an essential part of the women's rights agenda. By late 1991, NOW had elected a national president, Patricia Ireland, who made headlines when she acknowledged having simultaneously a husband in Miami and a female lover in Washington, saying that she valued both relationships, that all three parties were happy with the arrangement, and that she was going to keep both partners. At this writing Ireland remains president of NOW, although numerous commentators in the popular press used her as Exhibit A in their case that NOW had become an extreme, avant-garde organization that had completely lost touch with the aspirations of the average American woman.

19. The most notorious incident involving members of ACT UP was a 1989 demonstration inside St. Patrick's Cathedral in New York during a mass said by John Cardinal O'Connor, a vociferous conservative who had led efforts to quash safer-sex education and condom distribution in city schools on the grounds that these would promote fornication, homosexuality, and condom usage, all of which the Roman Catholic Church deems sinful. A half-dozen demonstrators repeatedly disrupted the cardinal's sermon, then chained themselves to pews or lay across the main aisle while congregants were attempting to receive Communion. One person took a Communion wafer (which devout Catholics believe contains the actual body of Christ), dropped it on the floor in front of the cardinal, and crushed it under foot. The St. Patrick's incident was cheered by some people furious at conservative religious leaders whose sexual mores seemed to them more important than saving people's lives, while it appalled or enraged most everyone else.

ACT UP in New York eventually splintered in a conflict over the role of its Treatment and Data Committee, which more militant members thought was getting too powerful within the organization and too close to the government agencies and drug companies it was supposed to be confronting. Meanwhile, the ACT UP chapter in San Francisco split in two in late 1990 over differences between members who wanted to concentrate solely on AIDS issues and other members who wanted ACT UP to get involved in other causes, including opposition to the Persian Gulf War.

Notes to Chapter Three

1. There are two separate self-identification questions in the "Glick poll" discussed in chapter 5, one of which includes "bisexual" as a category. However, that question differed distinctively from the self-identification format in the other polls, and, in addition, only

fourteen persons self-identified as bisexual, three of whom also called themselves "gay or lesbian" in the other self-identification item. For these reasons I chose to use the self-identification question that more closely resembled that used in the national and state exit polls as my indicator.

2. Regrettably, no such study has appeared in the literature concerning women.

3. The percentages by age group were as follows: eighteen to twenty-nine, 2.6; thirty to thirty-nine, 1.4; forty to forty-four, 1.6; forty-five to forty-nine, 1.5; fifty to fifty-nine, 0.3; sixty and older, 0.3.

4. The term "heterosexual" or "straight" must be used with some caution, in that the "heterosexual" respondents include the probable majority of homosexual or bisexual voters who would not declare themselves. I have avoided its usage here.

5. As noted earlier in this study, about 9 percent of men and 5 percent of women in the Janus-Janus study (1993) indicated they were exclusively or predominately homosexual in behavior; 4 percent of men and 2 percent of women identified themselves as homosexual; and 5 percent of men and 3 percent of women identified themselves as bisexual.

6. Eighteen percent of self-identified lesbians reported having children under the age of eighteen in the CBS poll, as opposed to 6 percent of the gay men.

7. At the time of the survey, only the District of Columbia and three states — Wisconsin, Massachusetts, and Hawaii — had statewide laws on the books banning discrimination of various kinds based on sexual orientation. In several other states, governors had issued executive orders barring antigay discrimination in state employment and/or contracting practices. Since the 1990 survey, California, Connecticut, Minnesota, New Jersey, Vermont, and Rhode Island have added sexual orientation as a protected category in certain of their state civil rights laws.

8. The term "other Christian" is an extremely broad brush. Clearly it includes the Eastern Orthodox churches; Latter-day Saints would consider it to include them as well. However, those raised in some conservative sects of Protestant origin also may identify as "other Christian," as may some Anglicans, Christian Scientists, and Unitarians, for example.

9. The link between Christianity and certain conservative positions, however, is less easy to grasp. Although it is clear from previous studies, as well as from the present data, that some positive correlation exists between Christian identification and ideological conservatism, why Christians should be more inclined to favor the death penalty, oppose cutting defense spending, or emphasize law enforcement over drug education and treatment than are non-Christians is simply curious.

10. This being the case, the finding that nearly identical shares of the gay and nongay samples call themselves "fundamentalist or evangelical Christians" is curious indeed; one would expect that those who identify with "mainline" Protestant churches would be far more forthcoming. I can offer no explanation for this finding at present.

11. Responses rated "liberal" were those supporting decreased defense spending, opposing restrictions on legal abortion, favoring education and treatment over law en-

forcement in dealing with the drug problem, supporting protection of the environment over preserving jobs when the two conflicted, opposing the death penalty, and opposing continued deployment in the Persian Gulf. Responses rated "conservative" were the converse, including support for any restrictions on abortion and for either increasing defense spending or maintaining it at current levels.

12. Most of the lesbian/gay Republican voters, we may note, were George Bush supporters in 1988, and tended to approve of Bush's conduct in office—but two-thirds were undecided as to whether they would vote for him again, and one in six said they would vote for the Democrat.

13. The actual 1988 electorate gave approximately 53 percent of its votes to Bush, 46 percent to Dukakis.

14. The other listed candidates were conservative Georgia Senator Sam Nunn and Virginia's Douglas Wilder, the nation's first elected black governor and a fiscal conservative.

15. The only demographic differences of any note were the propensity of a larger share of gay men to reside in central cities, while a plurality of lesbians in the sample resided in the suburbs; a small "gender gap" in household income between gay men and lesbians, which may be attributable to living arrangements such as suburban residence in that there was no significant difference in occupational status; and the fact that three times as many lesbians as gay men had children living at home.

16. Gay men were not broken out by feminism because of the small number of gay men who called themselves strong feminists ($N = 6$).

17. Because the question on children living at home was in the CBS data base, it is impossible to determine whether there is a relationship among actual child care responsibilities, attitudes on education, and feminism among lesbians.

18. In addition, only one "strong feminist" identified as a Republican.

19. These paragraphs discuss self-identified independents and third party identifiers together. The hypothesized "green" vote for the House of Representatives is discussed separately after this.

20. Only eight respondents were in states with Senate elections, and their votes were scattered among the parties.

21. See the discussion of the William Weld-John Silber gubernatorial race in Massachusetts in chapter 4 for an illustration.

22. As noted in the table, this also gave rise to the peculiar, although highly insignificant, effect of causing the direction of the relationship to be reversed. That is, after all the control variables were added in, self-identification as gay or lesbian purportedly made one *less* likely to vote for a Democrat for the House. This appears to be a direct result of liberal (especially lesbian feminist) desertions of the Democrats for third candidates, as discussed above.

23. Named for the University of Michigan, where the four coauthors of *The American Voter* taught and did their research.

24. Race sometimes is included as a fourth independent variable in retrospective models.

25. In the three-way 1992 presidential election, Dr. Steven E. Finkel (unpublished data), using a preelection survey of Charlottesville, Virginia, area voters, found that when Ross Perot supporters were excluded from the analysis, the retrospective model was 95 percent accurate in predicting who would support Bill Clinton or George Bush.

26. The wording varies slightly in the two data sets. The VRS form asked respondents whether they approved or disapproved of the job Congress was doing; the CBS form asked whether they believed most members of Congress were deserving of reelection.

27. These VRS findings were substantially confirmed in the CBS data base, which included no question on retrospective economic evaluations and must therefore be deemed incomplete in that respect. However, in neither test run with the CBS data was the evaluation of Congress as a whole significant. Also, curiously, there *was* a statistically significant independent effect of self-identification on voting for a Democrat, *but not* on voting for a Republican (data not shown). Why this last should be so is exceedingly curious. One possible explanation, confirmed in the data, is the fact that religion was a statistically significant factor in voting for the Republicans, but was not for the Democrats.

Notes to Chapter Four

1. I employ this typology with caution. This scheme may be unsatisfactory to those seeking a strong empirical basis for Elazar's normative classifications (the present data bases certainly provide us with none), and the classifications themselves are thirty years old. I have taken into account population migrations among the states, and the veritable revolution in voting rights and representation law that have taken place in the interim.

2. It is very important that the reader not confuse "moralistic," as Elazar uses it, with the "moralistic" politics of the Religious Right. A number of the states with "moralistic" political cultures are those least inclined to be influenced by religious conservatives. A better term for this classification of political culture probably would have been "communitarian," although when Elazar wrote his book he or his editors may have thought the word too easy to confuse with, say, "communistic."

3. A few examples: The forty state senators each represent districts of about 750,000 inhabitants apiece, larger than the fifty-two U.S. House districts, and the eighty state assembly members have districts of about 375,000 persons each. Each of the five members of the Los Angeles County Board of Supervisors is elected from a separate district of 1.8 million people apiece. (Thirty percent of Californians live in Los Angeles County.) San Franciscans elect their eleven-member Board of Supervisors at large, and the fifteen Los Angeles City Council districts each comprise more than 200,000 people.

4. Shilts (1982) noted that Feinstein's warm relations with individual gay and lesbian people go back many years. In 1975, only a few weeks before facing voters citywide in

her bid for reelection to the Board of Supervisors, Feinstein, at her own insistence, hosted a lesbian wedding in her backyard; she wanted to be present for the "holy union" ceremony for two lesbian friends, but could not leave her dying first husband at home. Epstein (1986), however, took note of Feinstein's strong ties to downtown business interests in San Francisco and her leadership on the board of the six to five majority opposing the liberal, "neighborhood"-oriented forces of Mayor Moscone and Harvey Milk.

5. These included former governors John Volpe and Francis Sargent, former U.S. Senator Edward Brooke, and the late Representative Silvio Conte.

6. A third principal candidate in the primary, Lieutenant Governor Evelyn Murphy, is of interest to our discussion. Murphy dropped out of the race eight days before the primary; the most liberal candidate in the race, she was harmed by being tied to Dukakis, even though she once staged a brief (and technically constitutional) takeover of state government while Dukakis was out of state. In June 1990, a Boston gay activist accused her on live television of being a closeted lesbian, a charge on which she declined comment and for which the activist later apologized (Bull 1990). The "outing" incident was not widely publicized and apparently was not a factor in Murphy's poor showing in the polls, which led to her withdrawal.

7. Among other comments, Silber suggested that old people, once having reached a certain level of inability, should die in order to save society trouble; he also said Massachusetts had become a "welfare magnet" for those he euphemistically said were more used to "warmer climes."

8. Even the state's lieutenant governor occupies an independent power center; elected separately from the governor, he (there have been no women in the job) is the leader *de facto* and *de jure* of the state senate.

9. She was *not* the first woman governor of Texas; that distinction belongs to Miriam "Ma" Ferguson, who was elected to succeed her incarcerated husband in 1924.

10. "Big Green" may be presented as an inherent case of what Elazar might describe as Californian conflict between its desire for a more pristine "commonwealth" and its desire to let people alone. It can be argued that—the strongly individualistic tendencies of self-identified lesbians and gay men seen in chapter 3 notwithstanding—when it came to the environment the "moralistic" or communitarian tendency won out with California gay and lesbian voters.

11. The sample appears extreme in other respects as well, even among the gay and lesbian voters examined so far. Three of five claim some postgraduate education, three of seven are "strong feminists," and nearly one in four were raised in the Jewish faith. These results may reflect the fact that a large disproportion of the sample precincts were in the city of Boston; one-third of all respondents, and an absolute majority of gay and lesbian self-identifiers, are found within the city limits of Boston. It is true, additionally, that the tiny sample makes inferences to the whole self-identified gay and lesbian population of the state considerably more hazardous. Be this as it may, statistically significant differences remain even with this sample size.

12. Massachusetts has a "semi-closed" primary system; registered independents may

vote in the primary of either party, but registered Democrats or Republicans may not cross over. Among voters as a whole there is significant overreporting of voting in this particular Republican primary.

13. In the sample, of the seven gay men who evidently voted against Richards because of her sex, four were self-described moderate Democrats and three self-described liberal independents. All voted for Ben Parmer, the unsuccessful (and somewhat unknown) Democratic nominee facing Senator Phil Gramm. The only thing they appeared to have in common was an uncommonly strong opposition to abortion; all said it should never be legal. However, none rated abortion as a strong factor in their voting decision.

14. Unlike in the national data examined in the last chapter, incumbency cannot be entered as a factor in an individual contest. As it happens, only in the Massachusetts and Texas U.S. Senate races were incumbents seeking reelection; all other contests were "open seat" races.

15. It is odd that the addition of party affiliation, in the case of Massachusetts, slightly *increases* the explanatory power of sexual self-identification after demographic correlates have been controlled for.

16. Whether it does so in the governor's race depends on whether one uses a vote for Ann Richards (significant) or for Clayton Williams (not significant) as the dependent variable. I include it in the "significant" category because identifying as gay or lesbian *was* significant in determining whether or not to vote for Ann Richards.

Notes to Chapter Five

1. On 27 June 1969, police raided the Stonewall Inn, a bar frequented by younger gay men and some transvestites, on the grounds that the bar had violated its liquor license. However, numerous patrons were herded into police wagons and some were roughed up. Other patrons and onlookers who had left the bar attacked the police, first verbally, then with rocks and bottles, forcing the police to call for reinforcements. Evening skirmishes between police and gay people continued for three successive nights. "Stonewall" is widely regarded as the Lexington and Concord of the gay rights movement, the first time that homosexuals stood up to and fought back against police repression (Duberman 1993).

2. Source: personal interviews and communications with Robert W. Bailey and Kenneth S. Sherrill, July 1992 to July 1993; Philip Ryan and Laura Morrison, July 1992.

3. Owles ran in 1973 against City Councillor Carol Greitzer, a lower Manhattan Democrat who had offended the gay and lesbian community by declining to meet with community leaders, saying she "couldn't be bothered." (Revson 1978; Kenneth S. Sherrill, personal communication.)

4. Source: Philip Ryan and Laura Morrison, interview with the author, 31 July 1992. Morrison was president of GLID at the time of our conversation, and Ryan had been involved with the organization for many years.

5. Ryan and Morrison, ibid.

6. To "out" people is to disclose their homosexuality or bisexuality without their permission, particularly in a public forum. Initially its chief practitioner and advocate was *Outweek's* columnist Michelangelo Signorile, although by this writing the practice has been adopted among some in the mainstream press when deemed "newsworthy." "Outing" has remained a source of extreme controversy in the LGB community. Some argue it is justified only when a public figure uses his or her influence actively to oppose lesbian and gay civil rights; others say it is never justifiable at all. (See Mohr 1992; Signorile 1993; Gross 1993.)

7. New York has a "challenge" primary law for statewide elections. A state convention chooses the party's nominee, unless more than one candidate can succeed in winning the votes of 25 percent of the state convention delegates. The only candidate facing a primary challenge was Carol Bellamy, a former New York City Council president seeking the nomination for state controller, a post then held by a Republican; all other statewide elected offices, except for one U.S. Senate seat, were held by the Democrats. Bellamy, as expected, easily won her primary.

8. The assembly district is the principal unit of party organization in New York City; each is composed of numerous "election districts" or precincts. Assembly district leaders make up the general governing bodies of each of the four county party organizations (Staten Island excepted), which in turn constitute the citywide organizations. In the Manhattan Democratic organization, each assembly district is divided for ease of management into two, three, or four "executive parts," each of which has two coleaders, one male and one female, who are elected in the party's primary. Shollenberger was the female leader, and Hoffmann the male leader, in the northern "executive part" of the Sixty-first, and Freed the female leader of the southern part.

9. Source: Robert W. Bailey and Kenneth S. Sherrill, personal communications.

10. Source: Robert W. Bailey, Kenneth S. Sherrill, Philip Ryan, and Laura Morrison, interviews and personal communications.

11. It should be noted that Glick, although the first elected *legislator,* would not be the first openly gay or lesbian elected official in New York City. In 1989, a gay man and a lesbian both were elected to Manhattan judgeships, becoming the first "out-of-the-closet" elected public officials in the city. Tim Mains, elected to the Rochester City Council in 1985, was the first openly gay elected public official in New York state. Because New York City's Democratic and Republican district leaders are elected in party primaries, Kenneth S. Sherrill (one of the three principal cocreators of the Glick poll), who was elected a Democratic leader of an assembly district on the Upper West Side of Manhattan in 1977, holds the distinction of being the first openly gay elected official in New York.

12. Rygor, left without any significant endorsements, created a "New Frontier Democratic Club," comprising himself and a few supporters. The club promptly gave him their "endorsement," which then appeared on his campaign literature.

13. "For Assembly: Manhattan, Bronx," *New York Times,* 6 September 1990, A26.

14. The *Times* gave its blessing in 1989 to Tom Duane, the openly gay opponent of

downtown Manhattan council member Carol Greitzer, who as previously noted had offended the LGB community in the early 1970s and was never forgiven. Greitzer's council district at the time overlapped the Sixty-first Assembly District to some extent. In a court-ordered special election in 1991, in which the size of the council was expanded from thirty-five to fifty-one members, Duane was elected in an open-seat district—largely overlapping Deborah Glick's assembly district—which was drawn in order to maximize LGB influence. Greitzer was defeated for reelection in a neighboring district.

15. Glick won the November general election with more than four-fifths of the vote against token Republican and minor party opposition.

16. It is interesting to note that half of the nongay identifiers nonetheless agreed that "activist groups such as ACT-UP" had helped the cause of gay rights. Given its particularly confrontational tactics in New York, including the disruption of a 1989 service at St. Patrick's Cathedral led by John Cardinal O'Connor (chapter 2, n. 19), this is a verdict not likely to be rendered by heterosexuals in the rest of the country, nor even in much of the city.

17. I am struck by the constant recurrence of the figure 77 percent. The reader will recall that the "progay" gubernatorial candidates in California, Massachusetts, and Texas won 77, 77, and 78 percent of the gay and lesbian self-identifiers, respectively, in their general elections. The fact that Deborah Glick won 77 percent of these voters in her primary, and David Dinkins won 77 percent of these voters in this district in *his* primary, is a terribly amusing coincidence.

18. It is notable in this context that Rygor, the other openly gay candidate, was not picked by *any* of the lesbian and gay respondents.

19. One gender-based issue difference came to the fore: lesbians were as likely as nonlesbian women, and more than twice as likely as gay or nongay men, to name abortion as one of the top two issues in the election.

20. Rygor's *faux* club, the "New Frontier Democrats," was included to see if it made any impact at all. One gay respondent (who was heavily downweighted) did cite New Frontier—and that person voted for someone other than Rygor.

21. The "New Frontier Democrats" were excluded from the analysis.

22. This is not to say, however, that the GLID endorsement was unimportant. The initial base of volunteers Glick needed to contact her supporters in the lesbian and gay community came from her home club, GLID; and the voter contact apparently had some of the desired mobilizing effect.

23. Kenneth S. Sherrill (various personal communications) argues strongly that the *Times* endorsement did not necessarily persuade uncertain lesbian and gay voters, but instead "validated" their predisposition to vote for Glick and gave them ammunition to use with undecided heterosexual friends and neighbors. That this is possible I concede, and Dr. Sherrill is, saying the least, far better schooled and experienced in New York's Democratic politics and LGB politics than am I. Yet the wording of the endorsement question on the exit poll was such that the stronger inference, I believe, is that these voters may not have turned out, or may have voted for a different candidate, absent the

good word from the *Times*. The one way to test these differing interpretations would have been to ask the voters when they made up their minds, a question frequently asked in exit polls and postelection surveys. Sadly, no such question was included in the Glick poll, so the debate remains unresolved.

Notes to Chapter Six

1. Edelman (1993) reports figures differing slightly from mine. Employing a larger, combined database which incorporates both the national survey responses and the California and New York state-level respondents (weighted down to their share of the national electorate), he reports, among other findings, that 70 percent of self-identifiers voted for Clinton. The national data set made available to academic researchers by ICPSR appears to be the one used on election night, incorporating only the respondents to the three versions of the national survey.

2. Oddly, one question was included in Versions W and Y, but not in Version P, whereas three additional questions were include in Y and P, but not W.

3. I found no support, incidentally, for the notion that the proportion of LGB schoolteachers is significantly higher in states with gay rights laws preventing those teachers from being dismissed because of their sexual orientation.

4. That one's party identification has a direct effect on evaluations of presidential performance, and on "objective" national economic evaluations, is not in dispute.

5. Only thirteen states, most of minimal size, held gubernatorial elections in 1992; thirty-five held such elections in 1990. The total LGB sample from states electing governors, therefore, was minimal as well ($N = 40$), and the difference between the LGB and non-LGB groups only approached statistical significance (at .099). Little further analysis of the gubernatorial results has been undertaken.

6. As noted at the beginning of the chapter, the vote for third candidates for the House of Representatives was omitted from the 1992 data set. Given the high percentage of votes for third candidates for the House among lesbians and gay men in 1990, one cannot conclude that the two-party results presented and analyzed here are definitive.

7. Less encouraging for Clinton, however, is the finding that one-quarter of the LGB Democrats would have voted instead for Ross Perot if he had had a chance to win the election. The same was true of equal proportions of LGB Republicans and independents who did not vote for Perot.

8. Again, it is important to state that this analysis excludes any votes cast for third party and independent candidates in House races, because these votes were not coded into the data set.

Notes to Chapter Seven

1. In cities with populations of 250,000 to 499,000 in the West, self-identified gay men and lesbians accounted for 6.1 percent of the voting population in November 1990.

This was the highest figure for any region or size/type of locality. (Source: Combined 1990 national data bases [U.S.A. data.])

2. The most extreme example comes from a contest I did not examine in detail, the 1990 North Carolina Senate race between ultraconservative Senator Jesse Helms, regarded by LGB groups as the most antigay member of the Senate, and Harvey Gantt, the African American former mayor of Charlotte who quietly courted LGB support. The twenty-two gay and lesbian self-identifiers in the Helms-Gantt exit poll, nearly half of whom said they had voted for George Bush in 1988, voted unanimously for Gantt.

3. Dole—who has twice signed a Human Rights Campaign pledge that he does not discriminate against LGBs in hiring his Senate staffers—got into hot water in the summer of 1995 when his campaign returned a thousand-dollar contribution from the Log Cabin Federation, the national LGB Republican organization. A letter to Log Cabin from Dole's campaign said the group's agenda was "completely opposed" to the senator's own. (Log Cabin had also sent thousand-dollar donations to Wilson and Specter's campaigns, which had been quietly accepted.) After being criticized in the media for appearing intolerant, Dole publicly disavowed the return of the contribution and blamed it on his staff. This led to more criticism, from religious conservatives and from commentators who accused Dole of behaving like the allegedly flip-flopping president he was trying to unseat.

Notes to Appendix

1. I have chosen not to analyze the polls on the 1988 and 1992 Democratic presidential primaries, in that primary electorates do not reflect the populations of the states in which they are held—and the 1988 races have already been looked at (Bailey 1989). The Glick poll in chapter 5 is analyzed principally because of its unique independent variable indicators, and additionally because it is the only contest on which polling data were available to me that included an openly gay or lesbian candidate.

As this work goes to press, analyses of the LGB vote in the New York and Los Angeles mayoral races of 1993 are forthcoming from Dr. Robert W. Bailey of Rutgers-Camden, who performed the analysis of the 1988 Democratic primary races.

2. The sole exception was Virginia, in which Republican Senator John Warner faced opposition to his reelection only from an independent candidate allied with Lyndon LaRouche.

3. In Kentucky, to take the most extreme example, all of four respondents checked the self-identifier box. In several other states, the number of respondents was in the single digits or low teens (see table 4.1).

4. For example, region was recoded into "East" or "non-East," "South" or "non-South," "Midwest" or "non-Midwest," and "West" or "non-West." One such dummy variable was chosen as the "baseline" against which the others were measured. "Midwest" was chosen as the baseline for region, "Protestant" for religious background and religion

today, and "rural" for size of locality in the national data sets; in the three state data sets there were no "rural" cases, so "10,000–49,999" population was used as the baseline.

In later analyses, party affiliation and party of the incumbent officeholder seeking re-election also were coded into "dummies." "Independent" was the baseline for party, and "open seat" for incumbency.

5. Age groups in 1990 were clustered as follows: 18–29, 30–39, 40–44, 45–49, 50–59, and 60 or above. Translated, these produce categories of people born, respectively, in 1961 or after; 1951–60; 1946–50 (the immediate postwar period that began the baby boom); 1941–45 (the World War II years); 1931–40; and 1930 or before.

In 1992 the age groups were clustered as follows: 18–24, 25–29, 30–39, 40–44, 45–49, 50–59, 60–64, and 65 or above. This translates into groups of those born, respectively, in 1968 or after; 1963–67; 1953–62; 1948–52; 1943–47; 1933–42; 1928–32; and 1927 or before.

6. Education clusters were as follows: did not graduate high school, high school graduate, some college, college graduate, and postgraduate study. Household income clusters in 1990 were the following: less than $15,000, $15,000–$29,999, $30,000–$49,999, $50,000–$99,999, and $100,000 or more. In 1992 the last two income categories were revised to $50,000–$74,999, and $75,000 or more.

7. This last was deemed important because of the large infusion of American troops into the Persian Gulf and the possibility of war in that region at the time of the 1990 general election.

8. Size of locality clusters: city of 500,000 or more, city of 250,000–499,999, city of 50,000–249,999, suburbs, city/town of 10,000–49,999, or rural area (including nonsuburban towns of 10,000 or fewer residents).

9. In calculating and reporting these last results, I excluded Republican identifiers. The candidates listed, in order, were Texas Senator Lloyd Bentsen, New Jersey Senator Bill Bradley, Arkansas Governor Bill Clinton, New York Governor Mario Cuomo, the Reverend Jesse Jackson, Georgia Senator Sam Nunn, and Virginia Governor Douglas Wilder; an additional box allowed the respondent to indicate "someone else."

REFERENCES

Works Cited

Adam, Barry D. 1987. *The Rise of a Gay and Lesbian Movement.* Social Movements, Past and Present (series). Boston: Twayne Publishers.

Allen, Laura S., and Roger A. Gorski. 1992. "Sexual orientation and the size of the anterior commissure in the human brain." *Proceedings of the National Academy of Sciences of the U.S.A.* 89:7199–202.

Almond, Gabriel A., and Sidney Verba. 1963. *The Civic Culture: Political Attitudes and Democracy in Five Nations.* Princeton: Princeton University Press.

———, eds. 1980. *The Civic Culture Revisited.* Boston: Little, Brown.

The Alyson Almanac: A Treasury of Information for the Gay and Lesbian Community. 1990. Boston: Alyson Publications.

Alyson, Sasha. 1991. *Young, Gay and Proud.* Boston: Alyson Publications.

Arriola, Elvia Rosales. 1988. "Sexual identity and the Constitution: Homosexual persons as a discrete and insular minority." *Women's Rights Law Reporter* 10:143–76.

Bagnall, Robert G., et al. 1984. "Burdens on gay litigants and bias in the court system: Homosexual panic, child custody, and anonymous parties." *Harvard Civil Rights-Civil Liberties Law Review* 19:497–559.

Bailey, J. Michael, and Richard C. Pillard. 1991. "A genetic study of male sexual orientation." *Archives of General Psychiatry* 48:1089–96.

Bailey, J. Michael, Richard C. Pillard, Michael C. Neale, and Yvonne Agyei. 1993. "Heritable factors influence sexual orientation in women." *Archives of General Psychiatry* 50:217–23.

Bailey, Martha. 1992. "Working class identification and political attitudes, 1964–86." Paper presented at the annual meeting of the American Political Science Association, Chicago.

Bailey, Robert W. 1989. "Gay and lesbian voting behavior in the 1988 Democratic presidential primaries: Issues of method and identity." Paper presented at the annual meeting of the American Political Science Association, Washington, D.C.

Barinaga, Marcia. 1991. "Is homosexuality biological?" *Science,* n.s., 253:956–57.

Barone, Michael, and Grant Ujifusa. 1991. *The Almanac of American Politics 1992.* Washington, D.C.: National Journal.

Bauman, Robert. 1986. *The Gentleman from Maryland: The Conscience of a Gay Conservative.* New York: Arbor House.

Bawer, Bruce. 1993. *A Place at the Table: The Gay Individual in American Society.* New York: Poseidon Press.

Bell, Alan P., and Martin S. Weinberg. 1978. *Homosexualities: A Study of Diversity among Men and Women.* New York: Simon and Schuster.

Black, Earl, and Merle Black. 1987. *Politics and Society in the South.* Cambridge: Harvard University Press.

Blumenfeld, Warren. 1992. *Homophobia: How We All Pay the Price.* Boston: Beacon Press.

Bowman, Karyln, and Everett Carll Ladd, eds. 1993. "Views about homosexuality." In "The American Enterprise public opinion and demographic report." *Public Perspective* 4 (3): (insert) 82–83.

Brecher, Charles, and Raymond D. Horton, with Robert A. Cropf and Dean Michael Mead. 1993. *Power Failure: New York City Politics and Policy Since 1960.* New York: Oxford University Press.

Brown, Bruce D. 1992. "Gay staffer takes on the GOP." *Washington Post,* 24 July, D1.

Browning, Frank. 1993. *The Culture of Desire: Paradox and Perversity in Gay Lives Today.* New York: Crown Publishers.

Browning, Rufus P., Dale Rogers Marshall, and David H. Tabb, eds. 1990. *Racial Politics in American Cities.* New York: Longman.

Bull, Chris. 1990. "Boston activist 'outs' a politician but ends up doubting himself." *Advocate,* no. 555 (17 July): 12–13.

————. 1992. "Gays and lesbians fare well at Democratic convention, but will Clinton regret it?" *Advocate,* no. 610 (25 August): 18–19.

Byne, William, and Bruce Parsons. 1993. "Human sexual orientation: The biological theories reappraised." *Archives of General Psychiatry* 50:228–39.

Campbell, Angus, Philip E. Converse, Warren E. Miller, and Donald E. Stokes. 1960. *The American Voter.* New York: Wiley.

Cass, Vivienne C. 1984. "Homosexual identity formation: Testing a theoretical model." *Journal of Sex Research* 20:143–67.

Challandes, Elliot. 1992. "Theory of empowerment: A lesbian and gay perspective." Paper presented at the annual meeting of the American Political Science Association, Chicago.

Clark, Kenneth B., and Mamie P. Clark. 1947. "Racial identification and preference in Negro children." In *Readings in Social Psychology,* ed. T. M. Newcomb and E. L. Hartley. New York: Henry Holt.

Clines, Francis X. 1992. "For gay G.O.P. members, a 2d closet." *New York Times,* 4 September, A12.

Clinton, Bill, and Albert Gore. 1992. *Putting People First: How We Can All Change America.* New York: Times Books.

Comstock, Gary David. 1991. *Violence against Lesbians and Gay Men.* New York: Columbia University Press.

Cross, William E. 1971. "Negro-to-Black conversion experience: toward a psychology of Black liberation." *Black World* 20 (9): 13–27.

Crossen, Cynthia. 1989. "Shock troops: AIDS activist group harasses and provokes to make its point; 'ACT-UP,' gay and yuppie, uses raids, phone 'zaps' to spotlight health crisis." *Wall Street Journal,* 7 December, 1.

Dejowski, Edmund F. 1989. "Federal restrictions on AIDS prevention efforts for gay men." *St. Louis University Public Law Review* 8:275–98.

D'Emilio, John. 1983. *Sexual Politics, Sexual Communities: The Making of a Homosexual Minority in the United States, 1940–1970.* Chicago: University of Chicago Press.

De Witt, Karen. 1992. "Quayle contends homosexuality is a matter of choice, not biology." *New York Times,* 14 September, A17.

DiLallo, Kevin, and Jack Krumholtz. 1994. *The Unofficial Gay Manual: Living the Lifestyle, or at Least Appearing To.* New York: Main Street Books.

Downing, Nancy E., and Kristin L. Roush. 1985. "From passive acceptance to active commitment: A model of feminist identity development for women." *Counseling Psychologist* 13:695–709.

Duberman, Martin B. 1993. *Stonewall.* New York: Dutton.

Easton, David. 1965. *A Systems Analysis of Political Life.* New York: Wiley.

Edelman, Murray [J.] 1964. *The Symbolic Uses of Politics.* Urbana: University of Illinois Press.

Edelman, Murray [S.] 1991. "The gay vote, 1990." Paper presented at the annual meeting of the American Political Science Association, Washington, D.C.

———. 1993. "Understanding the gay and lesbian vote in '92." *Public Perspective* 4 (3): 32–33.

Editors of the Harvard Law Review. 1990. *Sexual Orientation and the Law.* Cambridge: Harvard University Press.

Elazar, Daniel J. 1965. *American Federalism: A View from the States.* New York: Crowell.

Epstein, Robert. 1986. *The Times of Harvey Milk.* San Francisco: Pacific Arts Group. Videorecording of feature film.

Fay, Robert E., Charles F. Turner, Albert D. Klassen, and John H. Gagnon. 1989. "Prevalence and patterns of same-gender sexual contact among men." *Science,* n.s., 243:338–48.

Fenno, Richard F. 1978. *Home Style: House Members in Their Districts.* Boston: Little, Brown.

Fiorina, Morris P. 1981. *Retrospective Voting in American National Elections.* New Haven: Yale University Press.

Gallagher, John. 1992. "A new attitude." *Advocate,* no. 617 (1 December): 20–23.

Galst, Liz. 1992. "Throwaway kids: Abandoned by their families, lesbian and gay homeless youth are desperate for help." *Advocate,* no. 619 (29 December): 54–57.

Gamson, William A. 1968. *Power and Discontent.* Homewood, Ill.: Dorsey Press.

Gibson, Gifford Gay, with Mary Jo Risher. 1977. *By Her Own Admission: A Lesbian Mother's Fight to Keep Her Son.* Garden City, N.Y.: Doubleday.

Gilens, Martin. 1988. "Gender and support for Reagan: A comprehensive model of presidential approval." *American Journal of Political Science* 32:19–49.

Goldstein, Anne B. 1988. "History, homosexuality, and political values: Searching for the hidden determinants of *Bowers v. Hardwick.*" *Yale Law Review* 97:1073–110.

Gottsfield, Robert L. 1985. "Child custody law and sexual lifestyle." *Conciliation Courts Review* 23 (June): 43–46.

Gross, Larry. 1993. *Contested Closets: The Politics and Ethics of Outing.* Minneapolis: University of Minnesota Press.

Harry, Joseph. 1986. "Sampling gay men." *Journal of Sex Research* 22 (1): 21–34.

———. 1990. "A probability sample of gay males." *Journal of Homosexuality* 19 (1): 89–104.

Herek, Gregory M. 1984. "Attitudes toward lesbians and gay men: a factor-analytic study." *Journal of Homosexuality* 10 (1–2): 39–52.

Hertzog, Mark W. 1992. "Is there a sexuality gap? A comparative analysis of gay men, lesbians and heterosexuals in the 1990 national and state exit polls." Paper presented at the annual meeting of the American Political Science Association, Chicago.

Humphrey, Mary Ann. 1990. *My Country, My Right to Serve: Experiences of Gay Men and Women in the Military, World War II to the Present.* New York: Harper and Row.

Institute for Sex Research [Kinsey, Alfred C., et al.]. 1953. *Sexual Behavior in the Human Female.* Philadelphia: Saunders.

Jacobson, Gary C. 1983. *The Politics of Congressional Elections.* Boston: Little, Brown.

Janus, Samuel S., and Cynthia L. Janus. 1993. *The Janus Report on Sexual Behavior.* New York: Wiley.

Jay, Karla, and Allen Young. 1979. *The Gay Report.* New York: Summit Books.

———, eds. 1977. *Out of the Closets: Voices of Gay Liberation.* 2d ed. New York: Jove Publications.

Jenkins, Adelbert H. 1982. *The Psychology of the Afro-American: A Humanistic Approach.* New York: Pergamon Press.

Kardiner, Abram, and Lionel Ovesey. 1962. *The Mark of Oppression: Explorations in the Personality of the American Negro.* Meridian ed. Cleveland: Meridian Books.

Key, V. O., Jr. 1949. *Southern Politics in State and Nation.* New York: Alfred A. Knopf.

King, Michael, and Elizabeth McDonald. 1992. "Homosexuals who are twins: A study of 46 probands." *British Journal of Psychiatry* 160:407–9.

Kingdon, John W. 1989. *Congressmen's Voting Decisions.* 3d ed. Ann Arbor: University of Michigan Press.

Kinsey, Alfred C., Wardell B. Pomeroy, and Clyde E. Martin. 1948. *Sexual Behavior in the Human Male.* Philadelphia: Saunders.

Kirk, Marshall, and Hunter Madsen. 1989. *After the Ball: How America Will Conquer Its Fear and Hatred of Gays in the '90s.* New York: Doubleday.

Kramer, Staci. 1993. " 'Coming out': Many say it isn't a funnies matter." *Washington Post,* 13 April, B5.

Kristiansen, Connie M. 1990. "The symbolic/value-expressive function of outgroup attitudes among homosexuals." *Journal of Social Psychology* 130 (1): 61–69.

Laumann, Edward O., Robert Michael, John Gagnon, and Gina Kolata. 1994. *The Social*

Organization of Sexuality: Sexual Practices in the United States. Chicago: University of Chicago Press.

LeVay, Simon. 1991. "A difference in hypothalamus structure between heterosexual and homosexual men." *Science,* n.s., 253:1034–37.

Levine, Martin P. 1979. "Gay ghetto." *Journal of Homosexuality* 4:363–77.

Maguen, Shira. 1991. "Teen suicide: The government's cover-up and America's lost children." *Advocate,* no. 586 (24 September): 40–47.

Marcus, Eric. 1992. *Making History: The Struggle for Gay and Lesbian Equal Rights, 1945–1990.* New York: HarperCollins.

Marotta, Toby. 1981. *The Politics of Homosexuality.* Boston: Houghton Mifflin.

Martin, Del, and Phyllis Lyon. 1972. *Lesbian/Woman.* San Francisco: Glide Publications.

Mayhew, David R. 1974. *Congress: The Electoral Connection.* New Haven: Yale University Press.

McAllister, Bill. 1992. "Gay rights groups applaud Clinton's win: Arkansas governor said to get 72 percent support of homosexual voters." *Washington Post,* 5 November, A30.

Messina, Anthony M. 1985. "Ethnic minority representation and party competition in Britain: The case of Ealing Borough." *Political Studies* 35:224–38.

Miller, Arthur H., Patricia Gurin, Gerald Gurin, and Oksana Malanchuk. 1981. "Group consciousness and political participation." *American Journal of Political Science* 25:494–511.

Miller, Mike W., and Kathy Bukolt. 1990. "Student government report to the Board of Trustees: Homosexuality." With miscellaneous supporting documents. Student Government, University of Notre Dame du Lac, 26 April.

Mohr, Richard D. 1992. *Gay Ideas: Outing and Other Controversies.* Boston: Beacon Press.

Morin, Richard. 1989. "The real secret of '88: Why negative political ads didn't much matter." *Washington Post,* 12 February, C1–2.

Murdoch, Joyce. 1993. "Laws against sodomy survive in 24 states: As District attempts repeal, Maryland and Virginia statutes remain on the books." *Washington Post,* 11 April, A20.

Nie, Norman H., Sidney Verba, and John R. Petrocik. 1976. *The Changing American Voter.* Cambridge: Harvard University Press.

Ornstein, Norman J., Andrew Kohu, and Larry McCarthy. 1988. *The People, the Press and Politics: The Times Mirror Study of the American Electorate.* Reading, Mass.: Addison-Wesley.

Patterson, Charlotte J. 1992. "Children of lesbian and gay parents." *Child Development* 63:1025–42.

Phelan, Shane. 1989. *Identity Politics: Lesbian-Feminism and the Limits of Community.* Philadelphia: Temple University Press.

Polikoff, Nancy D. 1990. "This child does have two mothers: Redefining parenthood to meet the needs of children in lesbian-mother and other nontraditional families." *Georgetown Law Review* 78:459–575.

Powell, Jenifer L., and Quinn Mitrovich. 1992. "Experiences of discrimination and harassment of gay men, lesbians and bisexuals in Charlottesville." Unpublished term paper, Sexual Minorities course, Department of Psychology, University of Virginia, spring term.

Pressman, Steven. 1983. "The gay community struggles to fashion an effective lobby." *Congressional Quarterly Weekly Report* 41:2543–47.

Pugh, Clifford. 1992. "Despite platform, gays say they'll figure in future GOP." *Houston Post,* 18 August, C11.

Reinisch, June M., with Ruth Beasley. 1990. *The Kinsey Institute New Report on Sex: What You Must Know to Be Sexually Literate.* Comp. and ed. Debra Kent. New York: St. Martin's Press.

Rensberger, Boyce. 1993. "Sex survey: What men want and think they might get." *Washington Post,* 15 April, A1.

Revson, James A. 1978. "Will they overcome? The struggle for gay rights in America." *Columbia University School of Journalism, Major Papers 1978,* vol. 11, entry 8.

Richmond, Len, and Gary Noguera, eds. 1979. *The New Gay Liberation Book: Writings and Photographs about Gay (Men's) Liberation.* Palo Alto, Calif.: Ramparts Press.

Rosenthal, Andrew. 1992. "Bush tries to recoup from harsh tone on 'values.' " *New York Times,* 21 September, A1.

Rotello, Gabriel. 1994. "The battle for marriage: What we have to lose." *Out* (October): 106–7.

Samar, Vincent J. 1991. *The Right to Privacy: Gays, Lesbians, and the Constitution.* Philadelphia: Temple University Press.

Schiller, Greta, and Robert Rosenberg. 1985. *Before Stonewall: The Making of a Gay and Lesbian Community.* New York: Cinema Guild. Videorecording of television film.

Schmalz, Jeffrey. 1992a. "Gay rights and AIDS emerging as divisive issues in campaign." *New York Times,* 20 August, A1.

———. 1992b. "Gay politics goes mainstream." *New York Times Magazine,* 11 October, 18–21.

———. 1993. "Poll finds an even split on homosexuality's cause." *New York Times,* 5 March, A14.

Schwartz, Maralee. 1992. "Gay groups are told GOP has no time for their testimony." *Washington Post,* 20 May, A14.

Shapiro, Eric. 1990. *Gay Bashing.* New York: Ambrose Video Publishing. Videorecording of a segment of the CBS News program *48 Hrs.*

Sherrill, Kenneth S. 1991. "Half empty: Gay power and gay powerlessness in American politics." Paper presented at the annual meeting of the American Political Science Association, Washington, D.C.

Sherrill, Kenneth S., Scott H. Sawyer, and Stanley J. Segal. 1990. "Coming out and political attitudes: The experiences of lesbians and gay men." Paper presented at the annual meeting of the American Political Science Association, San Francisco.

Shilts, Randy. 1982. *The Mayor of Castro Street: The Life and Times of Harvey Milk.* New York: St. Martin's Press.

———. 1987. *And the Band Played On: Politics, People, and the AIDS Epidemic.* New York: St. Martin's Press.

———. 1993. *Conduct Unbecoming: Gays and Lesbians in the U.S. Military.* New York: St. Martin's Press.

Shingles, Richard D. 1981. "Black consciousness and political participation: The missing link." *American Political Science Review* 75:76–90.

Signorile, Michelangelo. 1993. *Queer in America: Sex, the Media, and the Closets of Power.* New York: Random House.

Steffan, Joseph, III. 1992. *Honor Bound.* New York: Villard Books.

Stoddard, Thomas J., et al. 1983. *The Rights of Gay People: The Revised Edition of the Basic ACLU Guide to a Gay Person's Rights.* New York: Bantam Books.

Suseoff, Steve. 1985. "Assessing children's best interests when a parent is gay or lesbian: Toward a rational custody standard." *UCLA Law Review* 32:852–903.

Tate, Katherine. 1991. "Black political participation in the 1984 and 1988 presidential elections." *American Political Science Review* 85:1159–76.

Timmons, Stuart. 1990. *The Trouble with Harry Hay: Founder of the Modern Gay Movement.* Boston: Alyson Publications.

Tobin, Kay, and Randy Wicker. 1975. *The Gay Crusaders.* New York: Arno Press.

Tripp, C. A. 1975. *The Homosexual Matrix.* New York: McGraw-Hill.

Turque, Bill, et al. 1992. "Gays under fire." *Newsweek,* 14 September, 34–40.

Verba, Sidney, and Norman Nie. 1972. *Participation in America: Political Democracy and Social Equality.* New York: Harper and Row.

Vieira, Norman. 1988. "*Hardwick* and the right of privacy." *University of Chicago Law Review* 55:1181–92.

Weekes, Richard V. 1989. "Gay dollars: Houston's Montrose district is an affluent, overlooked market — gay men and women." *American Demographics* 11 (10): 45–48.

White, Joseph L. 1984. *The Psychology of Blacks: An Afro-American Perspective.* Englewood Cliffs, N.J.: Prentice-Hall.

Wolfinger, Raymond E., and Steven J. Rosenstone. 1980. *Who Votes?* New Haven: Yale University Press.

Young, Iris Marion. 1990. *Justice and the Politics of Difference.* Princeton: Princeton University Press.

Zonana, Victor F. 1978. "California is roiled by a new initiative, over homosexuals: state voters to decide Nov. 7 whether school boards may fire 'gay' teachers." *Wall Street Journal,* 10 October, 1.

Additional Works Consulted

Abbott, Sidney, and Barbara Love. 1985. *Sappho Was a Right-On Woman: A Liberated View of Lesbianism.* 2d paperback ed. New York: Stein and Day.

Adam, Barry D. 1978. *The Survival of Dominance: Inferiorization and Everyday Life.* New York: Elsevier North-Holland.

————. 1985. "Structural foundations of the gay world." *Comparative Studies in Society and History* 27:658–71.

Aguero, Joseph E., Laura Bloch, and Donn Byrne. 1984. "The relationship among beliefs, attitudes, experience, and homophobia." *Journal of Homosexuality* 10 (1–2): 95–107.

Allen, Vernon L., and David A. Wilder. 1979. "Group categorization and attribution of belief similarity." *Small Group Behavior* 10:73–80.

Asher, Herbert B. 1992. *Polling and the Public: What Every Citizen Should Know.* 2d ed. Washington, D.C.: CQ Press.

Bayer, Ronald. 1985. "AIDS and the gay community: Between the specter and the promise of medicine." *Social Research* 52:581–606.

Bayes, Jane H. 1982. *Minority Politics and Ideologies in the United States.* Novato, Calif.: Chandler and Sharp.

Benenson, Robert. 1984. "Gay politics." *Editorial Research Reports,* 29 June, 471–88.

Berelson, Bernard R., Paul F. Lazarsfeld, and William N. McPhee. 1954. *Voting: A Study of Opinion Formation in a Presidential Campaign.* Chicago: University of Chicago Press.

Biren, Joan E. 1989. *For Love and for Life: The 1987 March on Washington for Lesbian and Gay Rights.* Washington: Moonforce Media. Videorecording.

Bock, Gisela, and Susan James, eds. 1992. *Beyond Equality and Difference: Citizenship, Feminist Politics and Female Subjectivity.* New York: Routledge.

Britton, Dana. 1990. "Homophobia and homosociality: An analysis of boundary maintenance." *Sociological Quarterly* 31:423–40.

Brown, Howard. 1976. *Familiar Faces, Hidden Lives: The Story of Homosexual Men in America Today.* New York: Harcourt Brace Jovanovich.

Browning, Frank. 1993. *The Culture of Desire: Paradox and Perversity in Gay Lives Today.* New York: Crown Publishers.

Bullert, Gary. 1987. "The homosexual rights movement: Its ideology, goals, and tactics." *Journal of Social, Political and Economic Studies* 12:3–27.

Burgoyne, Elizabeth, ed. 1985. *Race and Politics.* New York: H. W. Wilson.

Cass, Vivienne C. 1990. "The implications of homosexual identity formation for the Kinsey model and scale of sexual preference." In *Homosexuality/Homosexualities: Concepts of Sexual Orientation,* ed. David P. McWhirter, Stephanie A. Sanders, and June Machover Reinisch, 239–66. New York: Oxford University Press.

Cheseboro, James W., ed. 1981. *Gayspeak: Gay Male and Lesbian Communication.* New York: Pilgrim Press.

Cohan, A. S. 1982. "Obstacles to equality: Government responses to the gay rights movement in the United States." *Political Studies* 30:59–76.

Coleman, Eli. 1982. "Developmental stages of the coming-out process." *American Behavioral Scientist* 25:469–82.

Copely, Ursula Enters, ed. 1975. *Directory of Homosexual Organizations and Publications: Annotated.* Hollywood, Calif.: Tangent Group.

Crew, Louie, ed. 1978. *The Gay Academic.* Palm Springs, Calif.: ETC Publications.

Davidson, Chandler. 1972. *Biracial Politics: Conflict and Coalition in the Metropolitan South.* Baton Rouge: Louisiana State University Press.

Davison, Gerald C. 1982. "Politics, ethics, and therapy for homosexuals." *American Behavioral Scientist* 25:423–34.

Deckard, Barbara Sinclair. 1979. *The Women's Movement: Political, Socioeconomic and Psychological Issues.* 2d ed. New York: Harper and Row.

Dorencamp, Monica, and Richard Henke, eds. 1995. *Negotiating Lesbian and Gay Subjects.* New York: Routledge.

Dressler, Joshua. 1979. "Judicial homophobia: Gay rights' biggest roadblock." *Civil Liberties Review* 5:19–27.

DuBay, William H. 1987. *Gay Identity: The Self under Ban.* Jefferson, N.C.: McFarland and Co.

Duberman, Martin B., Martha Vicinus, and George Chauncey Jr., eds. 1989. *Hidden from History: Reclaiming the Gay and Lesbian Past.* New York: NAL Books.

Duckitt, John H., and Laetitia du Toit. 1989. "Personality profiles of homosexual men and women." *Journal of Psychology* 123:497–505.

Dworkin, Anthony Gary, and Rosalind J. Dworkin. 1982. *The Minority Report: An Introduction to Racial, Ethnic, and Gender Relations.* 2d ed. New York: Holt, Rinehart and Winston.

Dynes, Wayne R., and Stephen Donaldson, eds. 1992. *History of Homosexuality in Europe and America.* New York: Garland.

Edwards, Tim. 1994. *Erotics and Politics: Gay Male Sexuality, Masculinity and Feminism.* London: Routledge.

Elazar, Daniel J. 1989. *People and Polity: The Organizational Dynamics of World Jewry.* Detroit: Wayne State University Press.

Eulau, Heinz. 1963. *The Behavioral Persuasion in Politics.* New York: Random House.

Fanon, Frantz. 1963. *The Wretched of the Earth.* Trans. Constance Farrington. New York: Grove Press.

Franke, R., and M. R. Leary. 1991. "Disclosure of sexual orientation by lesbians and gay men: A comparison of private and public processes." *Journal of Social and Clinical Psychology* 10:262–69.

Friedman, Joel W. 1979. "Constitutional and statutory challenges to discrimination in employment based on sexual orientation." *Iowa Law Review* 64:527–72.

Gallup Organization. 1982. "Homosexuality: Little change in Americans' attitudes toward gays; unfavorable stereotypes persist, belying broad acceptance of gay lifestyle; but majority favors equal job opportunities." *Gallup Report* (October): 3–19.

———. 1987. "Homosexuality: Backlash against gays appears to be levelling off." *Gallup Report* (March): 12–18.

Gay Left Collective, eds. 1980. *Homosexuality, Power and Politics.* New York: Allison and Busby.

Geis, Gilbert, Richard Wright, Thomas Garrett, and Paul R. Wilson. 1976. "Reported consequences of decriminalization of consensual adult homosexuality in seven American states." *Journal of Homosexuality* 1:419–26.

Gibson, James L. 1987. "Homosexuals and the Ku Klux Klan: A contextual analysis of political tolerance." *Western Political Quarterly* 40:427–48.

Gibson, James L., and Kent L. Tedin. 1988. "The etiology of intolerance of homosexual politics." *Social Sciences Quarterly* 69:587–604.

Godfrey, Brian J. 1988. *Neighborhoods in Transition: The Making of San Francisco's Ethnic and Nonconformist Communities.* Berkeley: University of California Press.

Goldberg, Steven. 1982. "Is homosexuality normal?" *Policy Review,* no. 21:119–38.

Gonsoriek, John C. 1982a. "Results of psychological testing on homosexual populations." *American Behavioral Scientist* 25:385–96.

———. 1982b. "Social psychological concepts in the understanding of homosexuality." *American Behavioral Scientist* 25:483.

Goodman, Gerre, George Lakey, Judy Lashof, and Erika Thorne. 1983. *No Turning Back: Lesbian and Gay Liberation for the '80s.* Philadelphia: New Society Publishers.

Gopoian, David, Derek J. Hackett, Daniel Parelman, and Leo Perotta. 1987. "The Democratic Party coalition in the eighties: A reassessment of Ladd's Old Class/New Class explanation of intra-party conflict." *Western Political Quarterly* 40:247–64.

Gottlieb, Rhonda. 1984. "The political economy of sexuality." *Review of Radical Political Economy* 16:143–65.

Gough, Jamie, and Mike Macnair. 1985. *Gay Liberation in the Eighties.* London: Pluto Press.

Grahn, Judy. 1984. *Another Mother Tongue: Gay Words, Gay Worlds.* Boston: Beacon Press.

Greenberg, David F., and Marcia H. Byrstryn. 1984. "Capitalism, bureaucracy, and male homosexuality." *Contemporary Crises* 8 (1): 33–56.

Grönfors, Martii, and Olli Stålström. 1987. "Power, prestige, profit: AIDS and the oppression of homosexual people." *Acta Sociologica* 30:53–66.

Gurin, Patricia. 1982. "Group consciousness." *Institute for Social Research Newsletter* 10 (1–2): 4–5.

Gurwitt, Rob. 1985. "Democrats' link with gays comes under fire." *Congressional Quarterly Weekly Report* 43:1823–27.

Haas, Michael. 1987. "Comparing paradigms of ethnic politics in the United States: The case of Hawaii." *Western Political Quarterly* 40:647–72.

Hamilton, Wallace. 1973. *Christopher and Gay: A Partisan's View of the Greenwich Village Homosexual Scene.* New York: Saturday Review Press.

Harry, Joseph, and William B. DeVall. 1978. *The Social Organization of Gay Males.* New York: Praeger.

Herek, Gregory M. 1986. "The social psychology of homophobia: Toward a practical theory." *New York University Review of Law and Social Change* 14:923–34.

Horowitz, David, Michael Lerner, and Craig Pyes. 1972. *Counterculture and Revolution.* New York: Random House.

Hudson, Walter W., and Wendell A. Ricketts. 1980. "A strategy for the measurement of homophobia." *Journal of Homosexuality* 5:357–72.

Humm, Andrew. 1980. "The personal politics of lesbian and gay liberation." *Social Policy* 11 (2): 40–45.

Humphreys, Laud. 1972. *Out of the Closets: The Sociology of Homosexual Liberation.* Englewood Cliffs, N.J.: Prentice-Hall.

Hyman, Herbert H. 1969. *Political Socialization: A Study in the Psychology of Political Behavior.* New ed. New York: Free Press.

International Lesbian and Gay Association. 1988. *Second ILGA Pink Book: A Global View of Lesbian and Gay Liberation and Oppression.* Utrecht Series on Gay and Lesbian Studies, no. 12. Utrecht, The Netherlands: Rijksuniversiteit Utrecht.

Jennings, M. Kent, and Harmon Ziegler. 1966. "Class, party and race in four types of elections: The case of Atlanta." *Journal of Politics* 28:391–407.

Katz, Jonathan. 1976. *Gay American History: Lesbians and Gay Men in the U.S.A.* New York: Thomas Y. Crowell.

Kelly, George A. 1975. *The Political Struggle of Active Homosexuals to Gain Social Acceptance.* Chicago: Franciscan Herald Press.

Kennard, Jean E. 1984. "Ourself behind ourself: A theory for lesbian readers." *Signs* 9:647–62.

Klein, Ethel. 1984. *Gender Politics: From Consciousness to Mass Politics.* Cambridge: Harvard University Press.

Koertge, Noretta. 1990. "Constructing concepts of sexuality: A philosophical commentary." In *Homosexuality/Homosexualities: Concepts of Sexual Orientation,* ed. David P. McWhirter, Stephanie A. Sanders, and June Machover Reinisch, 387–97. New York: Oxford University Press.

Krieger, Susan. 1982. "Lesbian identity and community: Recent social science literature." *Signs* 8:91–108.

Larsen, Knud S., Michael Reed, and Susan Hoffman. 1980. "Attitudes of heterosexuals toward homosexuality: A Likert-type scale and construct validity." *Journal of Sex Research* 16:245–57.

Lee, John Alan. 1977. "Going public: A study in the sociology of gay liberation." *Journal of Homosexuality* 3:49–78.

LeMay, Michael C. 1985. *The Struggle for Influence: The Impact of Minority Groups on Politics and Public Policy in the United States.* Lanham, Md.: University Press of America.

Licata, Salvatore J. 1980–81. "The homosexual rights movement in the United States: A traditionally overlooked area of American history." *Journal of Homosexuality* 6 (1–2): 161–89.

Maloney, Stephen R. 1976. "The lavender menace: Though many homosexuals are harmless and even goodly, the 'gay liberation' movement is tawdry, libertine, and barbaric." *Alternative* 10 (December): 12–15.

Marshall, Eliot. 1991. "Sullivan overrules NIH on sex survey." *Science,* n.s., 253:502.

Martin, John L., and Laura Dean. 1990. "Developing a community sample of gay men for an epidemiological study of AIDS." *American Behavioral Scientist* 33:546–61.

Matlack, Carol. 1989. "Gay clout: Galvanized by the AIDS crisis, gay and lesbian activists are lobbying for civil rights along with government action to fight the epidemic; politicians are ill at ease." *National Journal* 22 (6 January): 16–19.

McKenzie, Nancy F., ed. 1991. *The AIDS Reader: Social, Political, Ethical Issues.* Silver Spring, Md.: Meridian.

Mohr, Richard D. 1982. "Gay rights." *Social Theory and Practice* 8:31–42.

———. 1988. *Gays/Justice: A Study of Ethics, Society and Law.* New York: Columbia University Press.

Newman, Bernie S. 1989. "The relative importance of gender role attitudes to male and female attitudes toward lesbians." *Sex Roles* 21:451–65.

Nordic Association of Migrant and Minority Researchers. 1986. *New Ways for the Research on Migrants and Minorities: Report from the Seminar at the University of Örebro, 17–18 October 1983.* Stockholm, Sweden: Vig Tryck AB.

Phelan, Shane. 1994. *Getting Specific: Postmodern Lesbian Politics.* Minneapolis: University of Minnesota Press.

Poirier, Richard. 1988. "AIDS and traditions of homophobia." *Social Research* 55:461–75.

"Research on the violations of civil liberties of homosexual men and women." 1977. Symposium. *Journal of Homosexuality* 2:313–42.

Rich, Adrienne. 1980. "Compulsory heterosexuality and lesbian existence." *Signs* 5:631–60.

Richards, David A. J. 1988. "Human rights, public health, and the idea of moral plague." *Social Research* 55:491–528.

Ricklefs, Roger. 1976. "A new constituency: Political candidates seek out gay votes: In cities where homosexuals are well-organized, risks of such campaigns fade." *Wall Street Journal,* 20 October, 1.

Roberts, Joan I. 1985. "Alternatives to the patriarchy: The choices, costs, and consequences." *Women and Politics* 5:23–50.

Rosenfeld, Jeffrey P. 1986. "Demographics of vacation: Gray travel, gay travel, and touring teens are just some of the lucrative markets for the vacation industry." *American Demographics* 8 (January): 38–41.

Rutledge, Leigh W. 1992. *The Gay Decades: From Stonewall to the Present: The People and Events that Shaped Gay Lives.* New York: Plume.

Sandel, Michael. 1989. "Moral argument and liberal toleration: Abortion and homosexuality." *California Law Review* 77:521–38.

Schneider, William. 1987. "Homosexuals: Is AIDS changing attitudes?" *Public Opinion* 10 (2): 6–8.

Schneider, William, and I. A. Lewis. 1984. "The straight story on homosexuality and gay rights." *Public Opinion* 7 (2): 16–20.

Shafer, Byron E. 1985. "The new cultural politics." *P.S.* 18:221–31.

Shively, Michael G., Christopher Jones, and John P. De Cecco. 1984. "Research on sexual orientation: Definitions and methods." *Journal of Homosexuality* 9 (2–3): 127–36.

Snyder, William P., and Kenneth L. Nyberg. 1980. "Gays and the military: An emerging policy issue." *Journal of Political and Military Sociology* 8:71–84.

Stember, Charles Herbert. 1976. *Sexual Racism: The Emotional Barrier to an Integrated Society.* New York: Elsevier.

Sullivan, Gerald. 1984. "A bibliographic guide to government hearings and reports, legislative action, and speeches made in the House and Senate of the United States Congress on the subject of homosexuality." *Journal of Homosexuality* 10 (1–2): 135–89.

Sunstein, Cass R. 1988. "Sexual orientation and the Constitution: A note on the relationship between due process and equal protection." *University of Chicago Law Review* 55:1161–80.

Tajfel, Henri, and J. C. Turner. 1986. "The social identity theory of intergroup behavior." In *Social Psychology of Intergroup Relations,* ed. Stephen Worchel and William G. Austin. 2d ed., 7–24. Chicago: Nelson-Hall.

Teal, Donn. 1971. *The Gay Militants.* New York: Stein and Day.

Thompson, Karen, and Julie Andrzejewski. 1988. *Why Can't Sharon Kowalski Come Home?* San Francisco: Spinsters/Aunt Lute.

Tilly, Louise A., and Patricia Gurin, eds. 1990. *Women, Politics, and Change.* New York: Russell Sage Foundation.

Turner, John C., with M. A. Hogg, P. J. Oakes, S. Reicher, and M. S. Wetherell. 1987. *Rediscovering the Social Group: A Self-Categorization Theory.* Oxford, England: Blackwell.

Turner, Jonathan H., Royce Singleton Jr., and David Musick. 1984. *Oppression: A Socio-History of Black-White Relations.* Chicago: Nelson-Hall.

U.S. National Commission on the Observance of International Women's Year. 1977. *Workshop Guideline on Sexual Preference.* Washington, D.C.: U.S. Government Printing Office.

Vander Zanden, James W. 1983. *American Minority Relations.* 4th ed. New York: Alfred A. Knopf.

Vida, Ginny, ed. 1978. *Our Right to Love: A Lesbian Resource Book.* Produced in cooperation with the National Gay Task Force. Englewood Cliffs, N.J.: Prentice-Hall.

Warren, Carol A. B. 1974. *Identity and Community in the Gay World.* New York: John Wiley and Sons.

Weinberg, George. 1972. *Society and the Healthy Homosexual.* New York: St. Martin's Press.

Weinberg, M. S. 1970. "Homosexual samples: Differences and similarities." *Journal of Sex Research* 6:312–25.

West, D. J. 1988. "Homosexuality and public policy: The case for a more informed approach." *Law and Contemporary Problems* 51:181–200.

Weston, Kathleen M., and Lisa B. Rofel. 1984. "Sexuality, class, and conflict in a lesbian workplace." *Signs* 9:623–82.

Wise, Donna L. 1980. "Challenging sexual preference discrimination in private employment." *Ohio State Law Journal* 41:501–31.

INDEX

ACT UP (AIDS Coalition To Unleash Power), 44–46, 166, 250, 257

Adam, Barry: establishes hypothesis of LGB movement as neoleftist, 9, 222–23

Age: as factor in LGB self-identification, 54, 178–79, 210–11, 251; as factor in other differences among LGB voters, 55, 74–76, 88–89, 192–94, 197–98, 206–7

AIDS (acquired immune deficiency syndrome): as area of political issue, 43–46, 151. *See also* ACT UP (AIDS Coalition to Unleash Power); Clinton, Bill; Kramer, Larry

American Voter, The (Campbell et al.), 17–19

Anti-gay ballot initiatives, 5–6, 43, 249

Anti-gay violence, 7, 24

Bailey, Robert W., 11, 13, 145, 235, 259

Bawer, Bruce, 47

Belotti, Francis, 104, 108–9, 127

"Big Green" California environmental ballot initiative, 107–8, 254

Bisexuality, 150, 209–11, 246, 250–51; among lesbians, 152, 223; factor in 1992 demographic, attitudinal figures, 175–76, 179, 195–96

Buchanan, Patrick, 3, 4, 227

Bush, George: anti-gay tone of 1992 campaign, 3–4, 230; as factor in 1990 mid-term elections, 61–62, 65–67, 86; and LGB Republicans, 3, 4, 188, 190, 195–96, 201, 219, 230. *See also* Buchanan, Patrick; Quayle, Dan; Religious Right movement

California: 1990 elections in, 102–3, 107–8; political culture of, 101. *See also* "Big Green" California environmental ballot initiative; Feinstein, Dianne; Wilson, Pete

Cass, Vivienne: stages of LGB identity development, 19, 28–31

Christian conservatism. *See* Religious Right movement

Civic Culture, The (Almond and Verba), 32–34

Clinton, Bill: and AIDS, 4, 226; and 1992 election, 1, 4, 175, 187–89, 190, 192–94, 195–96, 200–202, 205, 207–8; and military ban, 4–5, 6, 226; support for, among LGBs, 12–13, 226–27

Clinton, Hillary Rodham, 176

Dannemyer, William: attacks HHS report on LGB teen suicide, 23–24, 45

Democratic Party: and LGB voters, 4, 9, 71–76, 228–29

"Diffuse support" for political system, 32–33

Dole, Robert: attitudes toward homosexuality, 228, 230, 259; contribution to, by Log Cabin Federation, 227, 259

Dukakis, Michael, 104, 108, 118

Edelman, Murray J., 32, 34–35

Edelman, Murray S., 11, 97–98, 145, 177, 235, 258

Education: correlation of levels among LGB voters with group consciousness, 55, 99, 124, 134, 179, 197, 212

Elazar, Daniel: typology of state political cultures, 97, 100–102, 253

Exit polls: in 1988 elections, 11, 13, 247; in 1990 national general elections, 11, 13, 51–95, 234–36; in 1990 state-level general elections, 11, 13, 96–140, 235–36; in 1992 general elections, 11, 14, 175–208, 236; in 1993 mayoral elections, 14, 259; Glick poll (1990), 14, 141–74; methodology of, 52, 146–47, 233–34, 237

Falwell, Jerry, 3, 44

"Family values" issues in 1992 election, 184–85, 199–200, 216

275

DATE DUE

MAY 1 9 1998			
NOV 1 4 '00			
DEC 0 1 2004			
GAYLORD			PRINTED IN U.S.A.